CLOSE READING

—— *of* ——

COMPLEX TEXTS

Diane Lapp

Barbara Moss

Maria Grant

Kelly Johnson

D1072843

Sadlier School

William H. Sadlier, Inc.
9 Pine Street
New York, NY 10005-4700

Printed in the United States of America.
ISBN: 978-1-4217-1423-3
1 2 3 4 5 6 7 8 9 10 WEBC 22 21 20 19 18

CONTENTS

Teaching Students to Read Closely and Critically

Close reading is a powerful instructional strategy designed to help students develop the reading, writing, speaking, listening, and viewing skills crucial to success in college and the workplace. During close reading, students have a close, deep encounter with a complex text, whether a traditional written text or a visual text. Close reading engages students in the analysis of the language of texts, moving them beyond superficial understanding. They read and reread challenging texts, digging more deeply into the text with each subsequent reading.

Students participate in a broad range of scaffolded literacy activities during close reading. They annotate the text as they look for key information. They answer text-dependent questions at increasingly challenging levels of difficulty. They talk about the text, working collaboratively with their peers to grapple with the deeper meanings within it. They write in response to the text by articulating opinions, arguments, and explanations based on the text itself. Through these and other scaffolded experiences, students develop the critical analytic reading skills they need to succeed in every content area, whether science, social studies, mathematics, or English language arts.

Close Reading of Complex Texts addresses multiple aspects of content-area literacy in a single program. With the support of their teachers, students develop improved comprehension of all text types in a variety of disciplines, through deliberate, ongoing, and scaffolded literacy instruction.

Research into essential aspects of close reading confirms its efficacy.

- Reading complex texts, when coupled with teacher scaffolding, can accelerate reading achievement (Shanahan, 2014).

- The multiple readings required during close reading contribute to improved fluency, which has a strong link to reading comprehension (Paige, 2011).

- Close reading provides deliberate practice with complex texts over time, which contributes to reading performance (Ericcson, Krampe, & Tesch-Romer, 1993).

- The careful attention to vocabulary and syntax required by close reading is strongly correlated to improved reading comprehension (Goff, Pratt & Ong, 2005).

The ability to negotiate challenging texts in science, social studies, mathematics, and English language arts is essential to student success throughout the grades as well as in a college or career setting. Think, for example, of your content-based textbooks during your freshman year of college and the challenges they posed even for good readers. Think, too, about your local mechanic reading from an auto repair manual as he fixes your car's air conditioning. Both of these disciplinary texts contain challenging content-specific vocabulary terms, heavy concept loads, and visual features, including maps, graphs, charts, and time-lines. They pose unique challenges for readers, regardless of topic.

Students who have learned to read successfully in the primary grades often struggle in the elementary grades when faced with the demands of reading rigorous texts across the subject areas. These students may not have been exposed to the informational texts that are central to learning in these disciplines. ***Close Reading of Complex Texts*** provides students with many opportunities to read texts from a variety of genres, including informational texts, thereby broadening their knowledge about how these texts work, and what they mean.

Developing Students' Critical Comprehension

Each of the book's eight units contains three thematically related texts, including a Visual Text, that students closely read and analyze. Each engaging text set represents a range of genres. Text sets encourage students to dig deeply into a specific content-related theme by building rich connections across texts.

Research indicates that using a range of genres can improve students' reading comprehension and conceptual understanding of a topic (Hoffman, Sailors, Duffy, & Berettas, 2004; Corvette, Wright, & Hwang, 2016). In addition, reading a range of texts about a topic helps to build students' background knowledge. When students increase their knowledge base through encounters with multiple text genres, they are better prepared to learn from texts they will experience in the future (Duke, Pearson, Strachan, & Billman, 2011). Exposure to a broad range of text types also prepares students for the multiplicity of text genres they will encounter on high-stakes assessment.

A key feature of *Close Reading of Complex Texts* is the inclusion of Visual Texts, which are gaining increasing importance in the lives of students. Their engage-ment potential and their prominence in recent state standards make them important inclusions in close reading. According to Stone (2007), we can "no longer treat reading as being solely about print or about the understanding of individual texts. Rather, we need to address a full range of modalities being used by young people" (p. 60).

A Focus Question unifies the text sets. Students accumulate evidence to support their answers to the Focus Question as they work through the unit. At the end of the unit, students synthesize their learnings from the different texts and write an extended response to the Focus Question. In this way, each unit builds students' knowledge of the authors' purposes, the characteristics of different genres, and the similarities and differences between the presentation of information.

Engaging in Multiple Readings of Complex Texts

First, Second, and Third Reads, focused by independent annotation and collaborative conversations about Text-Dependent Questions from the Teacher's Edition, invite analysis of what the text means at deeper levels.

During each First Read, students gain general understanding of the text, or what the text says. They annotate, make notes, and respond to broad Text Dependent Questions, such as, *What is this text about?*

During the Second Read, students deepen their understanding of how the text works. These Text-Dependent Questions require them to analyze language and the organizational structures used to convey information and describe experiences.

Students synthesize the insights uncovered in earlier readings during their Third Read. They make inferences about author's positioning, or what the text means. Students also make connections across topically related texts.

It is not necessary that students reread the entire text during each Read. The goal of a reread is to deepen understanding, and sometimes an additional Text-Dependent Question that pushes students to consider just one sentence is all that is needed for students to accomplish this understanding. Teachers may choose to use particular questions based on their ongoing in-class assessment of student understanding. In this way, the close reading task is personalized to meet the needs of a particular classroom of students. The goal, however, is always for the teacher to guide students to access complex, high-level content in meaningful ways.

Students should accomplish all three Reads of a text in one day so that their developing understanding of the information is uninterrupted. The text can always be revisited the next day, especially if it is being compared to another topically related text.

Features of the Student Worktext

Together with the instruction and questions in this Teacher's Edition, the Student Worktext of *Close Reading of Complex Texts* provides the framework that students need to gain a deeper understanding of the complex texts they read. The **Getting Started** unit takes students through the elements that they will apply during close readings of the program texts. Units 1–8 reinforce the application of each of those elements.

In addition to Focus Questions and the visual and traditional texts themselves, Units 1–8 of the Student Worktext include the following recurring features:

Self-Monitoring Strategies
The **Self-Monitoring Strategies** chart that appears before Text 1 in each unit engages students in metacognitive thinking and reminds them of the strategies that will help them better understand each of the unit texts.

Multiple Reads
First, Second, and Third Reads help students gain the deepest insights about the text they are reading. Students read and reread a text or part of a text, developing greater understanding with each Read.

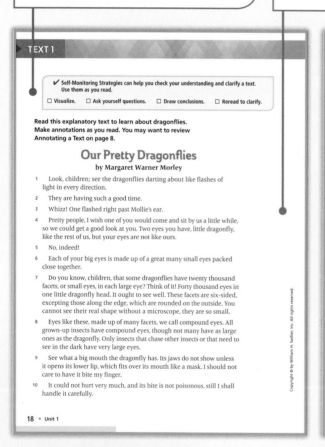

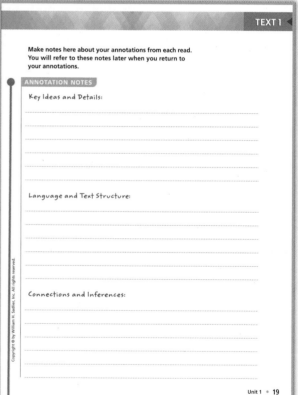

Annotations and Annotation Notes
By using specific annotation symbols to mark directly on the text, students identify questions, confusing language or sections, and important ideas or words that support their deepened understanding. The Annotation Notes page allows them to expand on or clarify their thinking.

Return to the Text

Respond to Reading, which appears after Texts 1 and 2, asks students to demonstrate their understanding of the text with a graphic organizer, summary, and other text-related questions. Comprehension Check gives teachers the opportunity to assess students' inferential understanding.

Analyze and Synthesize Across Texts

After students have read all the texts in a unit, they use the Focus Question to synthesize their learning and draw conclusions across the texts. A graphic organizer helps students organize text evidence and their Annotation Notes.

Return to the TEXT

Respond to Reading: Our Pretty Dragonflies

Review the annotations and notes you made while reading "Our Pretty Dragonflies." Think about how they can help you understand the text.

1. Use this Summary Chart to help you summarize the text.

Summary Chart		
Informational Text		
Who?	the people or subjects	
What?	the topic or problem	
Where?	the location or region where the events occur	
When?	the date, year, or time	
How?	the events, steps, or process	

2. Use the completed graphic organizer from Item 1 to help you write a summary of "Our Pretty Dragonflies."

_____
_____
_____
_____

REFLECT What word or phrase did you find confusing? What Self-Monitoring Strategy did you use to gain a better understanding of it?

_____
_____

ANALYZE and SYNTHESIZE ACROSS TEXTS

Return to the Focus Question: How do some characteristics help animals survive?

Review your answers to questions about the texts as well as your annotations and Annotation Notes. Think about the discussions you've had about the texts. How does that information help you answer the Focus Question?

Use the graphic organizer to organize information about the texts.

1. In the boxes, record the details from each text that help you answer the Focus Question.

2. Make connections between those details to help you answer the Focus Question. Write your answer in the box provided.

```
Giraffes on Samburu        Our Pretty Dragonflies        Alaskan Animal
Reserve (Visual Text)                                     Adaptations

           How do some characteristics help animals survive?
```

REFLECT How did making connections between the three texts help you to answer the Focus Question?

_____
_____
_____

WRITE

Writing About the Focus Question

Now that you have answered the Focus Question using all three texts, develop your ideas into a longer piece of writing.

USE EVIDENCE

• Explain how different some characteristics help animals survive. Use at least one piece of evidence from each text to support your answer.

• If you need more room, use additional paper.

MONITOR

• Use the Writing Checklist as you work to make sure your writing has all of the important pieces of information.

• Use the rubric on page 30 when you have completed your first draft to help you evaluate, revise, and edit your work.

WRITING CHECKLIST ✔

Does my writing . . .

☐ answer the Focus Question?

☐ provide text evidence to support my ideas?

☐ have a clear beginning, middle, and end?

☐ use correct language, spelling, and conventions?

Write

The unit culminates in a writing activity that requires students to demonstrate critical thinking, cite textual evidence, and engage in intertextual analysis in their responses.

Reflect

These metacognitive elements ask students to explain their thinking.

Features of the Teacher's Edition

The Teacher's Edition supports busy teachers as they implement *Close Reading of Complex Texts*. Scaffolded supports streamline the instructional process, providing Text-Dependent Questions, modeling of strategic thinking, discussion prompts, writing prompts, and more.

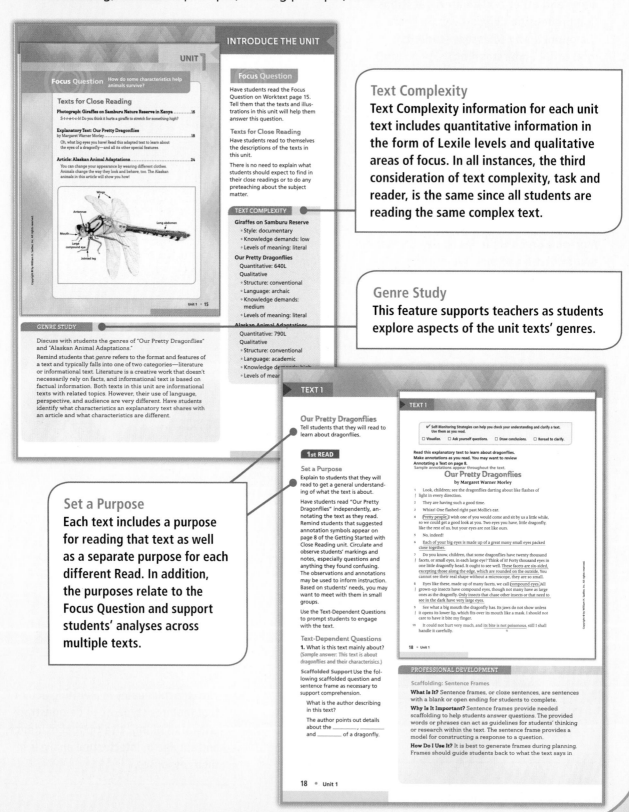

Text Complexity

Text Complexity information for each unit text includes quantitative information in the form of Lexile levels and qualitative areas of focus. In all instances, the third consideration of text complexity, task and reader, is the same since all students are reading the same complex text.

Genre Study

This feature supports teachers as students explore aspects of the unit texts' genres.

Set a Purpose

Each text includes a purpose for reading that text as well as a separate purpose for each different Read. In addition, the purposes relate to the Focus Question and support students' analyses across multiple texts.

Text-Dependent Questions

Teachers guide student understanding during each Read by asking Text-Dependent Questions, or TDQ's. TDQ's are derived from the information presented in the text and require students to return to the text for the answers.

Vocabulary

Carefully crafted TDQ's help students unlock word meaning through context, connections, and evidence from the text in ways that are most effective in supporting academic language development.

Our Pretty Dragonflies

2nd READ

Set a Purpose

Students will return to "Our Pretty Dragonflies" to understand the text structure and the effects of the author's choice of words.

Text-Dependent Questions

1. Who is the narrator in the text talking to? How do you know? (Sample answer: The narrator is talking to a group of children. She says, "Look, children" in paragraph 1 and "Do you know, children," in paragraph 7.)

2. What is the effect of the dialogue in the text? (Sample answer: The dialogue draws in the reader and makes him or her interested to learn information about dragonflies.)

3. Vocabulary: Figurative Language Discuss contextual meanings of familiar words and phrases.

Paragraph 17: What image does the figurative language "look like glass" create of a dragonfly's wings? (Sample answer: I visualize wings that are very delicate and almost clear, like glass is.)

Partner Talk Have students discuss how the author's choice of words helps them to understand the text and the point of view from which the text is told.

---

11 Some call the dragonfly a darning needle, and say it sews up people's ears when they lie on the grass. This is not true. It does not sew up anything. It has nothing to sew with. Why should it want to sew up people's ears, anyway? It does nothing unpleasant but bite fingers, and it never goes out of its way to do that.

12 If we let it alone, it always lets us alone.

13 The French have given it a pretty name, *demoiselle*, or damselfly, and that is quite deserved, for the dragonfly is a graceful little creature, as pretty as pretty can be.

14 See, sticking out of the front of its head are two little feelers, antennae, as we must call them. They are very short, but it does not need long ones. Insects smell with their feelers, you know, but our dragonflies see as well they do not need to smell very well, I suppose.

15 See how it can turn its head around. That is because it has a little short neck between its head and its body. Its eyes, its mouth, and its antennae belong to its head.

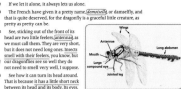

This illustration shows the parts of a dragonfly's body.

16 Of course our demoiselle can fly well; one need only look at those wings to know that. To fly well is quite as necessary to one of its habits as to see well. What would be the use of seeing an insect if it could not fly fast enough to catch it?

17 We all like your pretty wings, little dragonfly; they look like glass and they shine in the sun. How fast the wings can move! See that dragonfly skimming over the pond; its wings make a whizzing sound as it darts about.

18 Why does it zigzag so? Why doesn't it fly in a straight line?

19 Yes, Mollie, you are right, it goes zigzagging along after insects. It sees one it wants off at one side—whizz! around it turns after it. Shouldn't you like to fly like that, children?

20 And yet we would not be willing to exchange our arms and hands for wings. We could not whittle a stick nor write a letter if we had only wings. In fact we could not do most of the things we now do.

21 I am glad I have my hands.

22 We are glad, too, that the dragonflies have their pretty, swift wings.

20 • Unit 1

PROFESSIONAL DEVELOPMENT

Self-Monitoring Strategy: Visualize

What Is It? Visualization is a **Self-Monitoring Strategy** that encourages students to imagine a scene using mental images.

Why Is It Important? Visualization can help students understand lengthy or difficult descriptions or complex action sequences. It can also enhance reading enjoyment and motivation for reluctant readers. Visualization helps good readers create pictures in their minds as they read.

Make notes here about your annotations from each read. You will refer to these notes later when you return to your annotations. Sample notes appear below.

ANNOTATION NOTES

Key Ideas and Details:

Some people think the dragonfly sews up people's ears.

Dragonflies have antennae or feelers.

Insects smell with their feelers.

Dragonflies see well.

Language and Text Structure:

Demoiselle is in italics—it is a French word.

repeats the word "See" in paragraphs 9, 14, and 15 = look closely

Paragraphs 9–17 describe a dragonfly.

unfamiliar words: "darning needle" and "whittle"

Paragraph 17 compares dragonfly wings to glass.

Connections and Inferences:

Dragonflies don't need to smell well because they see so well. Do people use one sense more than another sense?

All parts of a dragonfly have a task or purpose. People use their hands for different tasks or purposes.

Unit 1 • 21

Our Pretty Dragonflies

3rd READ

Set a Purpose

Students will read to make inferences.

Text-Dependent Questions

1. What is the author's opinion of dragonflies? (Sample answer: I can infer that the author thinks dragonflies are interesting and attractive. In paragraph 7, she says that dragonfly eyes have as many as twenty thousand facets and follows that with "Think of it!" That shows that she thinks dragonflies are amazing. In paragraph 13, she describes dragonflies as "graceful" and "pretty as pretty can be," so we know she thinks they're nice to look at.)

2. What connection does the author make between human arms and hands and dragonfly wings? (Sample answer: The author thinks you can have one or the other, but not both. People may want to "fly like that," but then they would have to "exchange your arms and hands for wings." If we did that, we could not "whittle a stick or write a letter.")

Think Aloud The diagram makes it look as though the dragonfly has two sets of wings. The text doesn't mention this. I asked myself, what would be the use of two sets of wings? The text says the dragonfly "darts about" so the two sets of wings must help it fly really fast.

Partner Talk Have students discuss the inferences they made and how that helped them understand the text.

Unit 1 • 21

How Do I Use It? Use visualization with texts that have rich descriptions and vivid scenes. Informational texts, like "Our Pretty Dragonflies," often include visual details. Model the strategy using a Think Aloud: *When I read paragraph 17, phrases like "your pretty wings," "they look like glass," "they shine so in the sun" really help me picture a dragonfly's wings. I also can imagine the narrator and the audience of children all looking at a dragonfly and studying its wings. Visualizing the scene helps make me a part of the audience, too.* Make difficult words more accessible by providing images from the Internet, your own sketches, or realia, and encourage students to make sketches of their own to help them understand words and ideas.

Think Aloud

Optional Think Alouds throughout the unit support teachers in modeling their strategic reading processes as they demonstrate Self-Monitoring Strategies. Think Alouds offer students opportunities to look inside the mind of an expert reader and then apply these strategies as they read challenging texts independently.

Alaskan Animal Adaptations

Students will read the article to learn about animal adaptations in Alaska.

1st READ

Set a Purpose

Explain to students that they will read to find out what "Alaskan Animal Adaptations" is about.

Have students read "Alaskan Animal Adaptations" independently, annotating the text as they read. Remind students that suggested annotation symbols appear on page 8 of the Getting Started with Close Reading unit. Circulate and observe students' markings and notes, especially questions and anything they found confusing. The observations and annotations may be used to inform instruction. Based on students' needs, you may want to meet with them in small groups.

Text-Dependent Questions

1. What is this text about? (Sample answer: It is about the characteristics animals in Alaska have developed in order to survive.)

Scaffolded Support Use the following scaffolded question and sentence frame as necessary to support comprehension.

What are some animals mentioned in the text?

All species have _____ that help them _____.

● **Partner Talk** Have students discuss behavioral adaptations mentioned in the text and how they help the animals survive in their habitat.

24 ● Unit 1

TEXT 2

Read this article to learn about animal adaptations in Alaska. Make annotations as you read. You may make different annotations each time you read.
Sample annotations and notes appear throughout the text.

Alaskan Animal Adaptations

1 An adaptation is a mutation that helps a plant or animal survive in its environment. These mutations are passed down through generations. Slowly, more organisms inherit the mutation. Then the mutation becomes a typical part of the species. The mutation has become an adaptation.

2 All species have adaptations. There are physical adaptations that change the way an animal looks. There are behavioral adaptations that change the way an animal behaves. Adaptations help an animal survive the weather and find food. Adaptations can help an animal use tools and hide from predators.

3 **Arctic Foxes** have many adaptations. Their fur turns white in winter to match the snow. Their big fluffy tails wrap around their bodies for warmth. Sharp teeth and claws help them catch and eat their prey.

4 **Caribou** have adaptations like fur, antlers, and hooves. Their fur keeps them warm in Alaska's cold climate. They use their antlers to fight off predators. Their large hooves support the animal in snow and soft tundra.

5 **Grizzly Bears** have large muscles that make the bears' hump on their shoulders. This adaptation is useful for digging. It also helps grizzly bears run fast enough to capture moose or caribou for food. Grizzly bears also hibernate in winter as an adaptation. Hibernating is a state of inactivity. It lowers grizzly bears' body temperatures and heart rates. Hibernating allows the grizzly bears to use less energy during the winter, when food is scarce.

6 **Musk Oxen** have a thick fur coat to keep them warm in the winter. Underneath the long, shaggy coat there is a layer of short, dense hair that provides extra warmth. Musk oxen also change their behavior to protect themselves from predators. When danger approaches, musk oxen run together. If only one predator is nearby, the musk oxen form a line. Sometimes several predators surround the group. Then the oxen form a circle and face outward.

7 **Walruses** have developed big tusks for defending their territory and pulling themselves out of the water. Walruses also have thick blubber. This blubber helps keep them warm in cold water. Walruses' mouths and tongues are narrow to help them suck clams out of their shells.

24 ● Unit 1

PROFESSIONAL DEVELOPMENT

Academic Language: ELL

What Is It? Academic language falls into two categories: general academic and domain-specific language. Academic language is formal language, vocabulary, and sentence structure used in books and formal discussions, including classroom discussions. Domain-specific language is vocabulary and idioms from a specific field of knowledge.

Why Is It Important? Academic language is necessary for school and professional success. Knowledge of domain-specific language may be necessary to understand unfamiliar but essential topics, such as the science topics covered in this unit.

Professional Development

Select spreads of the Teacher's Edition feature Professional Development boxes that include point-of-use application to provide context for instruction.

Stop and Assess

In conjunction with the Student Worktext's Comprehension Check, rubrics support teachers' assessment of students' understanding of the text purpose for Texts 1 and 2.

Partner Talk and Collaborate

The Teacher's Edition identifies strategic points at which students collaborate with their peers to answer TDQ's, respond to the text, and pose new questions. The questions and prompts engage students in using the language of the text as teachers assess peer performance.

---

*R*eturn to the TEXT

Comprehension Check: Alaskan Animal Adaptations
Answer the questions to demonstrate an understanding of what the text means.

1. What was the author's purpose for writing "Alaskan Animal Adaptations"? Use text evidence in your answer.

Sample answer: The author's purpose was to explain animal mutations and adaptations. The author uses different examples to show how some animals in Alaska have adapted to food and weather conditions there. For example, Arctic foxes have fur that "turns white in winter" to match the snow to help them hide from predators.

2. What do the descriptions of the animals' adaptations tell you about surviving winter in Alaska? Provide text evidence to support your answer.

Sample answer: The animals all have adaptations that help them survive cold weather: "big, fluffy tails," "thick fur coats," "dense hair," and "thick blubber" are some of the things that help animals in Alaska keep warm in the winter.

3. What makes grizzly bears' adaptation different from the adaptations described for the other animals? Provide text evidence to support your answer.

Sample answer: Most of the animals have adaptations that keep them warm, but grizzly bears instead lower their "body temperatures and heart rates" as part of hibernation. Lower body temperatures and heart rates allow grizzly bears "to use less energy during winter, when food is scarce."

Unit 1 ● 27

---

*R*eturn TO THE TEXT

Stop and Assess
Use the following rubrics to assess your students' understanding of the text.

Item 1 answers indicate:

2	that the author's purpose was to inform readers about animal adaptations, with strong text support.
1	an informational purpose, with some text support.
0	no understanding of purpose, with no text support.

Item 2 answers indicate:

2	that many of the adaptations are for surviving cold weather, with specific supporting details.
1	that the animals have adapted to cold weather, with some text support.
0	no understanding of the weather in Alaska, with no support.

Item 3 answers indicate:

2	that hibernating lowers the bear's body temperature and heart rate, while other animals have adaptations to keep them warm, with specific text support.
1	that the grizzly bear hibernates, with some text support.
0	no understanding of the grizzly bear's adaptation, with no support.

How Do I Use It? An appropriate amount of wait time varies by topic. Encourage students to watch other students' facial expressions and body language to better understand what an appropriate wait time is for the current conversation. As students review and discuss their summaries in the Collaborate activity, have them be mindful of wait time during their discussions. If pauses become disruptive to the flow of conversation, the wait time is too long. If the conversation stops after the first guess or at surface-level analysis, wait time may be too short to allow deeper thinking.

Unit 1 ● 27

Building Vocabulary

Designed to help students develop independence in strategically identifying and unlocking new terms, *Close Reading of Complex Texts* provides students with rich vocabulary experiences. In addition, it builds on students' existing language abilities by emphasizing focused collaborative conversations designed to increase students' metacognitive awareness and discussion skills.

For example, Text-Dependent Questions in which students are directed to determine word meanings through context clues are provided for each lesson in the Teacher's Edition. In addition, the Teacher's Edition's Collaborate activities provide discussion prompts designed to develop student's oral language abilities.

The Teacher's Edition focuses students on key terms central to the text's meaning by exploring topics including: multiple-meaning words, denotation and connotation, idioms, foreign words, and figurative language. Teachers may choose to create additional Text-Dependent Questions that require students to explore text meaning through vocabulary.

Collaborating with Peers

Every unit in *Close Reading of Complex Texts* involves students in collaborative conversations that promote authentic student participation. Talking with peers is an essential feature of close reading and one that supports the deepening of thinking. During each Read, students discuss Text-Dependent Questions with their peers. Partner Talk prompts in the Teacher's Edition provide pairs with opportunities to delve deeper into texts after each Read. The Connect Text feature on the **Analyze and Synthesize Across Texts** page of the Teacher's Edition encourages small groups to use academic language to discuss how each of the four texts they've read answers the Focus Question.

When collaborating, students hear the ideas of others and compare them to their own. Best of all, they learn to value and to communicate with others. The teacher is not driving these conversations; they are occurring between peers. Students are free to ask questions, challenge one another, and identify multiple perspectives regarding the same text or question, using the academic vocabulary they have recently learned and previously knew.

In addition, as students hear the thoughts of their peers and compare them to their own, they evaluate the depth of their thinking. They become aware of their own processing of the textual information, defined as metacognitive awareness. As metacognition develops so, too, does students' ability to understand, analyze, and control all of their cognitive processes that support learning.

Assessing Understanding and Differentiating Learning

Teachers assess student understanding and responses at multiple strategic points during the close reading process. Formative assessments can include teacher assessment of student text annotations and student responses to Text-Dependent Questions and prompts during Partner Talk and small and whole group discussions. Students' completion of graphic organizers and uses of Self-Monitoring Strategies also provide opportunities for assessment. In addition, the **Return to the Text** pages that follow Texts 1 and 2 provide an opportunity for formative assessment of students' understanding of each text, especially as it relates to the Focus Question.

Writing prompts at the end of each unit provide teachers with a summative assessment. The writing responses focus students on demonstrating their ability to analyze and synthesize across texts. A rubric that allows both student self-assessment and teacher summative assessment appears at the end of every unit. Teachers can differentiate end-of-unit projects with the Differentiate and Extend activity on the **Write** page of each unit.

For students who struggle with doing a close reading of a text on their own, a close reading of a paragraph situated within a larger text that is being presented as a shared reading is very appropriate. By situating a close reading within a shared reading, teachers support students with an appropriate sized and complex text within a context they understand. The teacher may begin by reading the first paragraph or section orally as students read silently. Then the teacher can pose a question related to the material that was read. After collaboration that addresses the question, the teacher, continuing the shared reading, may continue reading a second section of the text, and when finished, again engage students in a discussion focused on the language or structures the author uses. After student collaboration, the teacher may say, *Now I want you to closely read the next section and identify the author's intent.*

As **Close Reading of Complex Texts** authors Diane Lapp, Barbara Moss, Maria Grant, and Kelly Johnson note in their book *Turning the Page on Complex Texts: Differentiated Scaffolds for Close Reading*, if it becomes obvious during close reading that students are not deeply comprehending the text, additional questions may need to be asked. If initial questions do not support students' developing this deep understanding, teachers may use the Scaffolded Support that accompanies many of the Text-Dependent Questions or create their own layered questions that serve as scaffolds to understanding. The questions should be asked about the areas of the text that seem to be holding the students back from comprehending. For example, if students are not able to infer a character's traits in a narrative text or identify reasons for the timeline of a historical event in an informational text, additional questions should push them to look at specific words, phrases, sentences, or patterns in the text.

At the conclusion of the text, teachers may offer an extension activity that promotes in-depth thinking about the topic. For example, students might do additional reading from texts related to the unit theme or research a topic connected to the theme. In addition, teachers can also work with smaller groups of students who may need additional scaffolded supports.

Using the Interactive Student Edition

The Interactive Edition of *Close Reading of Complex Texts* enhances the learning experience for students by allowing them to work independently on readings after classroom instruction and to make use of a personalized digital notebook.

The Notebook captures and saves student's annotations for each Read of the texts. In addition, the Interactive Edition allows students to work independently by providing instructional guidance throughout the texts through features such as Text-Dependent Questions and Think Alouds that model metacognitive thinking.

Through use of their Notebooks and saved annotations, students are able to review and revisit their thinking across multiple readings. They can reference their notes and make connections while crafting responses for their assignments. Interactive graphic organizers help students organize their written responses and develop their ability to read critically. When prompted to provide written responses, students are able to toggle between the texts and the Notebook. These responses serve as formative assessment in real time.

The Notebook allows teachers to interact with students and respond instantly—a virtual teacher-student conference. Teachers can easily view students' personalized notes and comment on student work without having to gather and redistribute materials. With the Interactive Edition, teachers gain immediate insight into students' understanding by reading, reviewing, and commenting on students' annotations, notes, and responses to assignments and can intervene with students as necessary.

The Interactive Edition is an optional purchase to be used along with the print edition as part of a blended solution. The Interactive Edition is accessed via Sadlier Connect, Sadlier's learning platform, at **SadlierConnect.com.**

Implementing the Program

Close Reading of Complex Texts can be used to supplement a core reading program or be integrated into a literature-based curriculum. Below is one example of how teachers may choose to pace the instruction. These ten days need not be successive and may alternate with other classwork, independent reading and writing, and instruction.

Suggested 10-Day Implementation Model Pacing Guide

Day 1	Day 2	Day 3	Day 4	Day 5
• Introduce the Unit Focus Question and three texts. • Introduce the Visual Text. • Have students "read" the Visual Text and annotate. • Have students answer Student Worktext questions independently. • Support partner, small group, or whole group discussion of Student Worktext questions.	• Introduce Text 1. • Have students conduct a First Read of Text 1, or parts of Text 1, and annotate. • Have students do a Second and Third Read of Text 1, or parts of Text 1, and annotate. • Ask Text-Dependent Questions with each Read. • Have students discuss Partner Talk prompts.	• Have students revisit Text 1 as necessary. • Have students review Text 1 annotations. • Have students work independently to answer Respond to Reading questions.	• Assessment: Have students complete Comprehension Check. • Work with small groups or individual students for re-teaching and support as necessary.	• Introduce Text 2. • Have students conduct a First Read of Text 2, or parts of Text 2, and annotate. • Have students do a Second and Third Read of Text 2, or parts of Text 2, and annotate. • Ask Text-Dependent Questions with each Read. • Have students discuss Partner Talk prompts.

Day 6	Day 7	Day 8	Day 9	Day 10
• Have students revisit Text 2 as necessary. • Have students review Text 2 annotations. • Have students work independently to answer Respond to Reading questions.	• Assessment: Have students complete Comprehension Check. • Work with small groups or individual students for re-teaching and support as necessary.	• Have students discuss the three texts collaboratively then complete Analyze and Synthesize Across Texts independently. • Work with small groups or individual students for re-teaching and support as necessary.	• Have students write first drafts of Writing About the Focus Question. • Work with small groups or individual students for re-teaching and support as necessary.	• Have students revise their writing. • Have students complete Self-Assess and Reflect. • Work with small groups or individual students for re-teaching and support as necessary.

Sources

Cervetti, G. N., Wright, T. S., Hwang, H. J. (2016). "Conceptual Coherence, Comprehension, and Vocabulary Acquisition: A knowledge effect?" *Reading and Writing: An Interdisciplinary Journal*, 29 (4), p. 761–779.

Duke, N. K., Pearson, P. D., Strachan, S. L., and Billman, A. K. (2011). "Essential elements of fostering and teaching reading comprehension." In A. E. Farstrup and S. J. Samuels (Eds.), *What research has to say about reading instruction* (4th ed., pp. 51–93). Newark, DE: International Reading Association.

Ericcson, K. A., Krampe, R. T., and Tesch-Romer, C. (1991). "The role of deliberate practice in the acquisition of expert performance." *Psychological Review* 100(3), 363–406.

Goff, D. A., Pratt, C., and Ong, B. (2005). "The relations between children's reading comprehension, working memory, language skills, and components of reading decoding in a normal sample." *Reading and Writing*, 18 (7–9), 583–616.

Hoffman, J. V., Sailors, M., Duffy, G. G., and Beretvas, S. N. (2004). "The effective elementary classroom literacy environment: Examining the validity of the TEX-IN3 observation system." *Journal of Literacy Research*, 36 (3), 303–334.

Lapp, D., Moss, B., Grant, M., Johnson, K. (2015). *A Close Look at Close Reading* Alexandria, VA: ASCD. *Turning the Page on Complex Texts* Bloomington, IN: Solution Tree Press.

Paige, D. D. (2011). "Engaging struggling adolescent readers through situational interest: A model proposing the relationships among extrinsic motivation, oral reading, fluency, comprehension, and academic achievement." *Reading Psychology*, 32(5), 395–425.

Shanahan, T. (2014). "Should we teach students at their reading level?" *Literacy Leadership*, 14–15.

Stone, J. C. (2007). "Popular websites in adolescents' out-of-school lives: Critical lessons on literacy." In M. Knobel and C. Lankshear (Eds.), *A new literacies sampler* (pp. 49–65). New York, NY: Peter Lang.

——————————— ❖ ———————————

CONTENTS

Getting Started with Close Reading

Unit 1

Unit 2

Unit 3

Unit 4

Getting Started with Close Reading

USING THIS UNIT

Getting Started with Close Reading introduces the essential elements of close reading that students need to learn and to practice in order to become successful critical readers of complex texts.

Before you teach units 1–8, have students complete this introductory unit. The activities included here provide focused instruction and practice with very brief texts. By learning and practicing each element individually first, students will be better able to practice and apply those elements simultaneously as they move through the units.

After students complete this unit, encourage them to refer back to it to support their work throughout units 1–8.

READING CLOSELY

Each unit of *Close Reading of Complex Texts* includes three texts—a Visual Text, Text 1, and Text 2. The Visual Text is an image that begins each unit, and the two other texts are written texts. All texts in a unit relate to the unit Focus Question. Reading all three texts provides students with the opportunity to synthesize information from all the texts in order to answer the Focus Question, but if time is an issue, it is possible for them to closely read only the Visual Text and Text 1 to answer the Focus Question.

Students will be conducting multiple reads of the texts in order to gain a deeper understanding of them. Tell students that they will read an entire text during a First Read but may read or concentrate on only part of the text during subsequent reads.

1st READ

Tell students that in the First Read, they will try to understand what the text is about or what is happening.

Have students independently read the bulleted list of questions and then discuss them as a class. Ask students to suggest other questions they might ask the first time they read a text.

After students have had a chance to independently complete the activity on page 6 of the Student Worktext, ask them to discuss their responses with their partners or as a whole class.

READING CLOSELY

Close reading is reading a text more than once. Reading the text again and again helps you understand its deeper meaning. You see meaning that you might not have noticed when you read it the first time. You draw connections between the ideas and details in the texts. You understand how the text relates to the bigger topics.

You will read the texts in *Close Reading of Complex Texts* three times, with a different purpose each time.

1st READ Key Ideas and Details

Determine what the text is about. Look for key ideas and details. Read to find out:

- Who or what is this text telling me about?
- Where does the action take place?
- What happens?

Read this adapted excerpt from the novel *Just—William*.

Just—William
by Richmal Crompton

It was Sunday, and William went to the shed to continue the teaching of Rufus, the dancing rat. Rufus was to be taught to dance; the other, now named Cromwell, was to be taught to be friends with William's dog, Jumble. So far this training had only reached the point of Cromwell's sitting motionless in the cage, while in front of it William restrained the enraged Jumble from murder. Still, William thought, if they looked at each other long enough, friendship would grow. So they looked at each other each day till William's arm ached. As yet friendship had not grown. He was sure that with another half-hour's practice Rufus would dance and Cromwell would be friends with Jumble. He was a boy not to be daunted by circumstance.

Who or what is *Just—William* telling the reader about?

a boy who has two pet rats he is trying to train, and a dog

PROFESSIONAL DEVELOPMENT

Text Complexity

What Is It? The term *complexity* refers to a text's level of difficulty. Qualitative measurement of text complexity takes into account elements such as text structure, the author's style and use of language, tone, theme, the relationship of ideas within the text, the use of visual supports, and readers' prior knowledge and levels of reading comprehension and cognition.

Why Is It Important? Advancement in education depends on a student's ability to read complex texts independently. Therefore, teachers should be giving students increasingly complex texts to read and interpret.

2nd READ Language and Text Structure

Focus on the language the author uses and how the text is structured. As you read, make a note of answers to these questions:

- How is the text organized? In time order? In a problem and solution structure? As cause and effect?
- What words or phrases are repeated?
- What figurative language does the author use?
- What is the author's purpose?
- What message is the author communicating?

Reread *Just—William* on page 6. How does the author's language help set the tone of the scene?

The word "friendship" is repeated to describe the relationship between

the dog and the rat, who are clearly enemies. The tone is humorous

because William is taking so seriously a task that seems silly.

3rd READ Connections and Inferences

Look for meaning by making connections and inferences. Think about whether the text answers these questions:

- What inferences can I make from the text?
- How can I connect any of the ideas in the text to another text I've read or something I've learned?
- What is the theme of the text?
- What larger point or message do the author's ideas add up to?

Reread *Just—William* again. What inference can you make about William?

Sample answer: I can infer that William is eager and hard-working but not

very realistic. He is willing to work hard, but he is not making any progress.

He is "not to be daunted by circumstance."

How Do I Use It? Challenge students constantly to read beyond their current reading level. Before you introduce a given text, read it and note vocabulary that will be new to students and passages they might find confusing. Formulate scaffolded questions and prompts to use when students need extra support, taking care to ask questions that can be answered from the text. In discussions following Second and Third Reads, refrain as much as possible from giving students information or answers; instead, have them make inferences from the text, share prior knowledge, or otherwise discover answers for themselves. Your questions should serve as scaffolds that push comprehension.

2nd READ

Tell students that in the Second Read they will be paying attention to how the author communicates ideas and builds the text.

Have students independently read the bulleted list of questions and then discuss them as a class. Ask students to identify which questions relate to the authors' use of language and which questions relate to text structure. Have students identify other questions they might ask when they read a text for language and structure.

After students have had a chance to independently complete the Second Read activity on page 7 of the Student Worktext, ask them to discuss their responses with their partners or as a whole class.

3rd READ

Tell students that they will make inferences and connections during a Third Read. Explain that when a reader makes an inference, he or she uses the information that the author states in the text to understand what the author isn't saying directly.

Have students independently read the bulleted list of questions and then discuss the list with the class. Have students explain how making connections with other texts and identifying the theme of a text help readers understand texts better.

After students have had a chance to independently complete the Third Read activity on page 7 of the Student Worktext, ask them to discuss their responses with their partners or as a whole class.

ANNOTATING A TEXT

Explain to students that the annotations of skillful readers identify what they don't understand and point out major points they want to remember and use in discussions and writing. Caution students that over-annotating will be confusing rather than helpful.

Review the bulleted list of annotations on Student Worktext page 8 with students. Encourage them to suggest other symbols to use when annotating text.

Read the excerpt from *Just— William* with the class. Point out the circle around the word *Sunday*. Discuss why the reader may have made this annotation during the First Read. (Sample answer: During a First Read, the reader wanted to identify some basic things about the story to understand what it is about. *Sunday* tells when the story is taking place.)

Have the class conduct a Second Read of *Just—William* and ask volunteers to identify which annotations and notes the reader likely made during the Second Read and explain why. (Sample answer: During the Second Read, the reader probably placed a question mark next to the line with *enraged* because it is an unfamiliar word.)

Have students read *Just—William* a final time and ask them to suggest what annotations and notes the reader made during the Third Read. (Sample answer: The reader probably wrote the note "final sentence means he will keep trying." The reader inferred that William will not give up "training" even though it is not changing the relationship between Jumble and Cromwell or teaching Rufus to dance.)

ANNOTATING A TEXT

Skillful readers annotate as they read. When you annotate a text, you mark the text and write notes or questions about it. Annotating will help you keep track of your ideas and questions.

Just as you read with a purpose, you should annotate with a purpose. You can use the following symbols to help you organize your annotations:

- <u>Underline</u> key ideas and major points.
- Write a *?* next to anything that is confusing, such as unfamiliar words or unclear information.
- (Circle) key words or phrases or anything the author says in an interesting way.
- Put an *!* next to surprising or important information or information that helps you make a connection.

Read the adapted excerpt from *Just—William* three times. Think about which annotations and notes the reader made during each read.

Just—William
by Richmal Crompton

It was (Sunday,) and (William) went to the shed to continue the teaching of (Rufus,) the dancing rat. <u>Rufus was to be taught to dance; the other, now named (Cromwell,) was to be taught to be friends with William's dog, (Jumble.)</u> So far this training had only reached the point of Cromwell's sitting motionless in the cage, while in front of it William restrained the enraged Jumble from murder. Still, William thought, if they looked at each other long enough, friendship would grow. So they looked at each other each day till William's arm ached. As yet friendship had not grown. <u>He was sure that with another half-hour's practice Rufus would dance and Cromwell would be friends with Jumble. He was a boy not to be daunted by circumstance.</u>

?

!

ANNOTATION NOTES

boy is teaching a rat to dance

William's "arm ached" because he has to restrain Jumble.

final sentence means he will keep trying

PROFESSIONAL DEVELOPMENT

Annotations

What Is It? Annotations are text markings that record a reader's thoughts, ideas, and understandings while reading. Annotations include underlining, circling text to identify key words and ideas, recording important or surprising information, and placing a question mark next to anything confusing and an exclamation mark next to anything interesting or any place the reader makes a connection.

Why Is It Important? Annotations allow readers to record their initial thoughts and questions about a text and anything they learned. They are a metacognitive strategy for self-monitoring comprehension. Annotations also provide the teacher with valuable information regarding what students

Now it's your turn. Read this adapted excerpt from the article "What is Aerodynamics?" three times. Make annotations and write your notes on the lines each time you read.
Sample annotations are indicated.

What Is Aerodynamics?

What Is Aerodynamics?

Aerodynamics is the way air moves around things. Anything that moves through air reacts to aerodynamics. A rocket blasting off the launch pad and a kite in the sky react to aerodynamics. Aerodynamics even acts on cars.

What Are the Four Forces of Flight?

The four forces of flight are lift, weight, thrust, and drag. These forces make an object move up and down and faster or slower. How much there is of each force changes how the object moves through the air.

What Is Weight?

Weight comes from the force of gravity pulling down on objects. To fly, a plane needs something to push it in the opposite direction from gravity. The weight of an object controls how strong the push has to be.

ANNOTATION NOTES

aerodynamics: how air moves around things like planes, rockets, kites, or cars

Weight is one force of flight described in the text—weight comes from gravity.

Heavier objects need more force to push away from gravity.

Tell students to read the "What is Aerodynamics?" excerpt three times, making appropriate annotations and notes for each read. Remind them of the purpose of each read.

1st READ

Determine what the excerpt is about or what happens. Note the key ideas and details.

2nd READ

Focus on the words and phrases used by the author. Look at the way the author structures the text. Note the author's language and the text's structure.

3rd READ

Make inferences. Connect the text to another text. Note inferences and connections.

Refer students to pages 6 and 7 for questions they might ask during each read. Circulate through the class as students read and annotate the text, making note of any difficulties students have.

Throughout the units, students will return to their annotations to answer Text-Dependent Questions, respond to readings, participate in class discussions, and collaborate. Tell them to review their annotations and notes and make sure they are clear so that when they return to them, they will be useful.

Ask volunteers to explain the annotations and notes they made.

do and do not understand and can pinpoint areas of confusion to address during a scaffolded close reading of the text and any subsequent instruction. Annotations also can be used for informal assessment.

How Do I Use It? Have students mark up each text during their first independent read. Prompt them to mark key ideas, key vocabulary, and anything they find confusing. Encourage them to note Self-Monitoring Strategies they used to make meaning from the text when confronted with challenges. Students can also record their initial reactions to the text and write a brief summary of 2 or 3 sentences to check their overall comprehension.

SELF-MONITORING STRATEGIES

Texts that are worthy of a close reading are often challenging. Throughout the year, as students become more adept at reading texts closely, the texts can become even more complex. However, for students to gain a deeper understanding of a text, they must have a basic understanding of it. Self-Monitoring Strategies allow students to work independently to gain that basic understanding.

Review the Self-Monitoring Strategies on Student Worktext page 10 with students. Model using a Self-Monitoring Strategy for *Just—William* on page 8.

Think Aloud (Read the title and the first paragraph of the excerpt.) *I'm trying to figure out who the boy is, what he is doing, and why. The title is* Just—William *so William is the main character. Rufus the rat is "to be taught to dance" and Cromwell is another rat. William wants Cromwell to be friends with his dog, Jumble. But how is he going to get a dog and a rat to be friends? I reread and see that William thinks "if they looked at each other long enough, friendship would grow." I visualized the rat "sitting motionless in the cage" while William "restrained the enraged Jumble from murder." The visualization helped me realize that William's plan is not very realistic and is probably not going to work.*

SELF-MONITORING STRATEGIES

As you read, you can keep track of what you do and do not understand to help you better comprehend what you're reading. The process is called "self-monitoring." This checklist contains suggestions for ways you can self-monitor your reading.

> ## ✔ Self-Monitoring Strategies
>
> ☐ **Visualize.**
> Picture in your mind the people or other characters, places, and events in the text.
>
> ☐ **Ask yourself questions.**
> Clarify what you read by asking questions such as:
> *Does what I just read make sense?*
> *Are there words I don't know?*
> *What happened?*
>
> ☐ **Draw conclusions.**
> Based on details in the text, draw conclusions about the topic or what the characters or subjects do or say.
>
> ☐ **Reread to clarify.**
> Go back to certain confusing parts of the text to see if reading slower or more carefully helps you understand the text.

PROFESSIONAL DEVELOPMENT

Self-Monitoring Strategies

What Is It? As students read independently, they pause at intervals to check comprehension. **Self-Monitoring Strategies** include visualizing, asking questions, drawing conclusions, and rereading to clarify.

Why Is It Important? The strategies allow students to work independently and to better understand what they are reading. Visualizing helps students focus on details in the text. Asking questions provides invaluable preparation for tests and writing assignments. Drawing conclusions builds confidence for participation in class discussions. Rereading to clarify

Read this adapted excerpt from the novel _Little House in the Big Woods_. In the Self-Monitoring Strategies box on page 10, put a checkmark next to the strategies you use as you read.

Little House in the Big Woods
by Laura Ingalls Wilder

Once upon a time, sixty years ago, a little girl lived in the Big Woods of Wisconsin, in a little gray house made of logs. The great, dark trees of the Big Woods stood all around the house, and beyond them were other trees and beyond them were more trees. As far as a man could go to the north in a day, or a week, or a whole month, there was nothing but woods. There were no houses. There were no roads. There were no people. There were only trees and the wild animals who had their homes among them.

So far as the little girl could see, there was only the one little house where she lived with her Father and Mother, her sister Mary and baby sister Carrie. A wagon track ran before the house, turning and twisting out of sight in the woods where the wild animals lived, but the little girl did not know where it went, nor what might be at the end of it.

Choose one self-monitoring strategy that you used. Explain which one you chose and how it helped you to better understand _Little House in the Big Woods_.

Sample answer: From the author's description, I can visualize one house

surrounded by woods with nothing else around, so that even if I

traveled for a month I wouldn't find anything else. I can see how tiny

the house is with big trees all around it.

Have students read _Little House in the Big Woods_ and complete page 11 of the Student Worktext.

Ask volunteers to explain what Self-Monitoring Strategies they used and how using the strategies improved their understanding of the text.

increases comprehension and focuses attention. All these strategies build good study habits.

How Do I Use It? Introduce the strategies by discussing the value of independence in reading. Model each strategy by reading a text out loud and then applying the strategy. For English learners or less fluent readers, introduce, practice, and apply only one strategy at a time. For example, explain to students how to visualize the settings, characters, or actions in a text and then have them read and visualize independently. Repeat the process with the other strategies, using a different text for each strategy.

SUMMARIZING

Summarizing requires students to use text evidence to support their ideas. It also provides them with a means to demonstrate that they understand the major points and key details of a text and to self-assess their comprehension.

Ask students to think about a book they recently read or a movie or TV show they recently saw. Then have them share the most important idea about that book, movie, or TV show. For students who are having difficulty identifying one important idea, use one of these sentence frames:

> The main idea of the book/movie/TV show is _____.
>
> The big problem in the book/movie/TV show is _____.

SUMMARIZING

By summarizing a text, you show that you understand what you have read. A strong summary answers the question "What is the text about?"

A summary of any text should include only important information. It should leave out unimportant details. Sometimes details are interesting or fun to read, but they should not be included in a summary if they are not important to understanding the author's big ideas.

In general, a summary answers the questions asked in this Summary Chart.

Summary Chart		
	Literature	
Who?	the characters	a little girl, her father and mother, and her sisters, Mary and Carrie
What?	the conflict or problem	The family lives in the woods without roads, other people, or other houses near them.
Where?	the place characters are in	Wisconsin
When?	the era, year, or time	"sixty years ago"
How?	the plot or major events	The woods are so big that the little girl doesn't know that there is anything else in the world.

PROFESSIONAL DEVELOPMENT

Graphic Organizers

What Is It? Graphic organizers are visual organizational tools that help students record ideas and information from the texts. Graphic organizers include main idea and details charts, Venn diagrams to compare and contrast information, word webs, thought maps, and many other visual resources.

Why Is It Important? Graphic organizers help students organize their ideas about what they read. Graphic organizers can aid students with comprehension, text structure, and text-based writing. Graphic organizers are not an end product. Rather, they support students as they write and speak about texts.

The Summary Chart works well for summaries of both literary and informational texts. A Story Map can also help you focus on the important pieces of information for your summary of literature.

Characters (Who)	Setting (Where and When)
a little girl, her father and mother, and sisters, Mary and Carrie	Wisconsin, "sixty years ago"

Conflict (What)	Main Events (How)
The family lives in the woods without roads, other people, or other houses near them.	The woods are so big that the little girl doesn't know that there is anything else in the world.

Write a 2–3 sentence summary of *Little House in the Big Woods*. Use the Summary Chart or the Story Map to organize your thoughts. You may use the annotations and notes you created when you read to help you find the key information in a text. Leave out the details you don't need.

Sample answer: "Sixty years ago" in Wisconsin, a little girl lived with her

family in a house in the woods. Her family members were her father and

mother, and her sisters, Mary and Carrie. The woods are so big that you

could travel for "a whole month" and not find anything else. There are no

other houses or families anywhere near the little girl's family.

Have students complete the Summary Chart or Story Map on Student Worktext pages 12–13. Then tell them to write their summary on page 13.

Ask volunteers to explain whether they used the Summary Chart or the Story Map to help them write their summaries, why they chose one over the other, and whether their choices were helpful in writing their summaries.

As a class, discuss which details make the text enjoyable to read but don't belong in a summary.

Ask volunteers to read their summaries out loud.

How Do I Use It? Graphic organizers help students analyze and synthesize information from one or more texts before they write or speak about their conclusions. Graphic organizers are temporary scaffolds—that is, they should be used when introducing or initially practicing a skill or strategy but removed as students become more familiar with the skill or strategy. Have students use the target skill or strategy without the graphic organizer to determine if they have mastered it. If not, continue using the graphic organizer for additional support.

READING A VISUAL TEXT

Discuss with the class the different types of images they see regularly. Point to different images and symbols in the classroom. Have students explain the meaning of the images. Then ask students to name other images they see throughout their days and tell what the images mean.

Before students complete the exercises on Student Worktext page 14, direct their attention to the Visual Text, *Central Park*. Provide support before they begin analyzing the image independently. Use such prompts as:

- Start by looking at the entire image. Think about what might be happening.

- Next, examine the details. Look for clues that might help you understand what the image means.

- Then, look at the entire image again. How did the details add to your comprehension of the Visual Text?

Have students make annotations on the image and complete the activity on Student Worktext page 14. Suggest they use arrows, labels, circles, margin notes, and other markings to highlight details that will help them gain a better understanding of the meaning of the image. Discuss their annotations and answers.

READING A VISUAL TEXT

Like written texts, images—paintings, drawings, and photographs—can communicate information in ways that words cannot. They can provide viewers with a scene in a single instant. In this way, an image is a "visual text." Like written texts, visual texts often deserve more than one close look.

Look at the Visual Text. What do you see? Make annotations on the image.

Central Park

Now answer the following questions about the Visual Text. Review the image or parts of the image as many times as necessary.

1. What is your first impression of what is going on in this painting?

   People are walking, riding horses, and driving carriages in a park.

2. What details in the image make you think that?

   People are walking down a path with grass and trees. People are riding horses on another path, and there are horse-drawn carriages.

3. When you look again, what do you think about what is happening?

   These people are out in the park for fun. They do not seem to be traveling quickly and some have stopped to chat.

VISUAL LITERACY

Close Reading of Visual Texts

Visual literacy is important when reading graphic novels, drawing connections between texts and their graphics, appreciating art, and understanding signs and symbols everywhere. As with written texts, sometimes an image requires only a quick glance—as soon as we see a red octagon on a street corner we know we are supposed to stop—and sometimes multiple viewings can deepen a viewer's understanding and enrich an experience. In these instances, looking more closely at the details is crucial to comprehension.

UNIT 1

Focus Question How do some characteristics help animals survive?

Texts for Close Reading

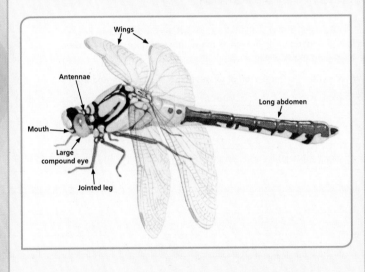

Wings · Antennae · Mouth · Large compound eye · Jointed leg · Long abdomen

Unit 1 • 15

GENRE STUDY

Discuss with students the genres of "Our Pretty Dragonflies" and "Alaskan Animal Adaptations."

Remind students that *genre* refers to the format and features of a text and typically falls into one of two categories—literature or informational text. Literature is a creative work that doesn't necessarily rely on facts, and informational text is based on factual information. Both texts in this unit are informational texts with related topics. However, their use of language, perspective, and audience are very different. Have students identify what characteristics an explanatory text shares with an article and what characteristics are different.

Focus Question

Have students read the Focus Question on Worktext page 15. Tell them that the texts and illustrations in this unit will help them answer this question.

Texts for Close Reading

Have students read to themselves the descriptions of the texts in this unit.

There is no need to explain what students should expect to find in their close readings or to do any preteaching about the subject matter.

TEXT COMPLEXITY

Giraffes on Samburu Reserve
- Style: documentary
- Knowledge demands: low
- Levels of meaning: literal

Our Pretty Dragonflies
Quantitative: 640L
Qualitative
- Structure: conventional
- Language: archaic
- Knowledge demands: medium
- Levels of meaning: literal

Alaskan Animal Adaptations
Quantitative: 790L
Qualitative
- Structure: conventional
- Language: academic
- Knowledge demands: high
- Levels of meaning: literal

Unit 1 • 15

Giraffes on Samburu Reserve

Set a Purpose

Explain to students that they will look at the image on page 16 to begin to gain a deeper understanding of how some characteristics help animals survive.

Visual Text Analysis

Remind students that an image can be analyzed as a text by looking at its details and making inferences. Direct students' attention to the image on Student Worktext page 16.

Encourage students to annotate the Visual Text. Suggest they use arrows, labels, circles, margin notes, and other markings to highlight details that will help them gain a better understanding of the meaning of the image.

1. Have students record their first impressions about the image. Lead them to discuss as a whole class, in small groups, or with a partner what they think is happening in the photograph.

2. Encourage students to make note of the details that support their observations in question 1. Have them identify not only the animals in the photo but also their characteristics and the characteristics of their environment. Have them explain as a whole class, in small groups, or with a partner what details they noted and what those details might tell them about how some characteristics help animals survive.

3. Guide students to synthesize all the details they see in the photograph to draw a conclusion about the photographer's message.

Giraffes on Samburu Nature Reserve in Kenya

Look at this Visual Text, and make annotations on the image. Review the image or parts of the image as many times as necessary to answer the following questions.

1. What is your first impression of what's going on in this photograph?

Sample answer: A family of giraffes is eating leaves from the top of a tree in a big park.

PROFESSIONAL DEVELOPMENT

Text Complexity: How to Manage Challenges

What Is It? Occasionally, complex texts may be inaccessible to students because of high knowledge demands and lack of background information. Students without sufficient background information will have difficulty comprehending a text, no matter how deeply they analyze it.

Why Is It Important? Building background information allows all students an equal opportunity to comprehend the complex texts you assign them to read.

2. What do you see that makes you think that?

Sample answer: I see three giraffes on the right whose faces are close to a tree. It looks like they're eating it. Two giraffes on the left have their faces in the leaves of a tree, so they are eating from it as well. One more giraffe is almost hidden in the trees on the left of the photograph. In the background is a tall, brown hill. There are big giraffes and little giraffes that might be babies. They are all together like a family would be.

3. What do you conclude is the photographer's message?

Sample answer: I conclude that the photographer is showing us that the giraffes' long necks help them eat from tall trees.

Unit 1 • **17**

Text-Dependent Questions

As necessary, encourage discussion with such prompts as:

1. What characteristic or characteristics of the giraffes strike you first? (Sample answer: The giraffes are very tall, with very long necks, and they have interesting markings that look like check or tile patterns.)

2. What are these giraffes doing? (Sample answer: They are eating the leaves off a tree. They are standing and stretching their necks up to get the leaves.)

3. How would you describe the behavior of the giraffes you see in this photograph? (Sample answer: They look very focused on what they're doing. They all seem to be sharing and getting along.)

4. What conclusion can you draw about giraffes' characteristics from the photograph? (Sample answer: I can conclude that the giraffes' long necks help them reach high leaves. Also, they all eat together in a friendly way, which makes me think they like to stay together.)

How Do I Use It? Encourage student-led investigation about background knowledge, and have students conduct their own research with provided materials so they can practice using visual text features. Use group and partner work if peers have additional background knowledge. Peer explanations help both the learner and the more knowledgeable student connect the knowledge to the text. "Giraffes on Samburu Reserve" show animals and behavior that may be unfamiliar to some students and so impede understanding. Encourage students to share their background knowledge.

Unit 1 • **17**

Our Pretty Dragonflies

Tell students that they will read to learn about dragonflies.

1st READ

Set a Purpose

Explain to students that they will read to get a general understanding of what the text is about.

Have students read "Our Pretty Dragonflies" independently, annotating the text as they read. Remind students that suggested annotation symbols appear on page 8 of the Getting Started with Close Reading unit. Circulate and observe students' markings and notes, especially questions and anything they found confusing. The observations and annotations may be used to inform instruction. Based on students' needs, you may want to meet with them in small groups.

Use the Text-Dependent Questions to prompt students to engage with the text.

Text-Dependent Questions

1. What is this text mainly about? (Sample answer: This text is about dragonflies and their characterisics.)

Scaffolded Support Use the following scaffolded question and sentence frame as necessary to support comprehension.

> What is the author describing in this text?

> The author points out details about the _____, _____ and _____ of a dragonfly.

> ✔ **Self-Monitoring Strategies can help you check your understanding and clarify a text. Use them as you read.**
>
> ☐ Visualize. ☐ Ask yourself questions. ☐ Draw conclusions. ☐ Reread to clarify.

Read this explanatory text to learn about dragonflies. Make annotations as you read. You may want to review Annotating a Text on page 8.
Sample annotations appear throughout the text.

Our Pretty Dragonflies
by Margaret Warner Morley

1   Look, children; see the dragonflies darting about like flashes of
!   light in every direction.

2   They are having such a good time.

3   Whizz! One flashed right past Mollie's ear.

4   (Pretty people,) I wish one of you would come and sit by us a little while, so we could get a good look at you. Two eyes you have, little dragonfly, like the rest of us, but your eyes are not like ours.

5   No, indeed!

6   Each of your big eyes is made up of a great many small eyes packed close together.

7   Do you know, children, that some dragonflies have twenty thousand
!   facets, or small eyes, in each large eye? Think of it! Forty thousand eyes in one little dragonfly head. It ought to see well. These facets are six-sided, excepting those along the edge, which are rounded on the outside. You cannot see their real shape without a microscope, they are so small.

8   Eyes like these, made up of many facets, we call (compound eyes.) All
!   grown-up insects have compound eyes, though not many have as large ones as the dragonfly. Only insects that chase other insects or that need to see in the dark have very large eyes.

9   See what a big mouth the dragonfly has. Its jaws do not show unless
!   it opens its lower lip, which fits over its mouth like a mask. I should not care to have it bite my finger.

10 It could not hurt very much, and its bite is not poisonous, still I shall handle it carefully.

PROFESSIONAL DEVELOPMENT

Scaffolding: Sentence Frames

What Is It? Sentence frames, or cloze sentences, are sentences with a blank or open ending for students to complete.

Why Is It Important? Sentence frames provide needed scaffolding to help students answer questions. The provided words or phrases can act as guidelines for students' thinking or research within the text. The sentence frame provides a model for constructing a response to a question.

How Do I Use It? It is best to generate frames during planning. Frames should guide students back to what the text says in

Make notes here about your annotations from each read.
You will refer to these notes later when you return to
your annotations. Sample notes appear below.

ANNOTATION NOTES

Key Ideas and Details:

A dragonfly's eyes have lots of little eyes inside big eyes.

Little eyes are called facets.

Facets have six sides.

Eyes made of facets are called compound eyes.

Not all insects have large eyes.

A dragonfly bite is not poisonous.

Language and Text Structure:

Paragraph 1 compares dragonflies to flashes of light.

"Whizz!" in paragraph 3 = the sound a dragonfly makes with its wings

"Look, children"—author talks directly to an audience of children.

Paragraph 9 compares a dragonfly's lower lip to a mask.

Connections and Inferences:

Paragraph 8 says all grown-up insects have compound eyes, but not as

large as a dragonfly's. I wonder how large other insects' eyes are?

2. Why do dragonflies need to fly well? (Sample answer: Paragraph 16 says dragronflies must fly well to catch other flying insects.)

3. What dragonfly body parts can you see in the diagram? (Sample answer: large compound eye, mouth, antennae, jointed leg, long abdomen, and wings)

Think Aloud *The author of this text gives a very detailed description of a dragonfly's eyes. I can visualize the eyes as I read. She says that each of the two big eyes is made up of thousands of small eyes that are six-sided. In other words, the small eyes are hexagons. I can visualize them connected on their sides to form a dome with a circular base—the small eyes along the bottom edge are "rounded on the outside."*

Partner Talk Have students work together to discuss what they learned about dragonflies.

order to build greater meaning. A thoughtful frame has two components: a "hint" within the provided part of the sentence and a blank that is somewhat open-ended but elicits an answer that is a step in formulating an answer to a Text-Dependent Question. In the sentence frame *A dragonfly's eyes help it* _____, the word *eyes* is a hint that guides students to a specific part of the text. Students can use this hint to locate several possible answers: *to see, to hunt, to find insects.* Multiple answers can guide students to understand that compound eyes are a characteristic that helps dragonflies survive by helping them to hunt for food.

Our Pretty Dragonflies

2nd READ

Set a Purpose

Students will return to "Our Pretty Dragonflies" to understand the text structure and the effects of the author's choice of words.

Text-Dependent Questions

1. To whom is the narrator in the text talking? How do you know? (Sample answer: The narrator is talking to a group of children. She says, "Look, children" in paragraph 1 and "Do you know, children," in paragraph 7.)

2. What is the effect of the dialogue in the text? (Sample answer: The dialogue draws in the reader and makes him or her interested to learn information about dragonflies.)

3. Vocabulary: Figurative Language Discuss contextual meanings of familiar words and phrases.

Paragraph 17: What image does the figurative language "look like glass" create of a dragonfly's wings? (Sample answer: I visualize wings that are very delicate and almost clear, like glass is.)

Partner Talk Have students discuss how the author's choice of words helps them to understand the text and the point of view from which the text is told.

11 Some call the dragonfly a darning needle, and say it sews up people's
? ears when they lie on the grass. This is not true. It does not sew up anything. It has nothing to sew with. Why should it want to sew up people's ears, anyway? It does nothing unpleasant but bite fingers, and it never goes out of its way to do that.

12 If we let it alone, it always lets us alone.

13 The French have given it a pretty name, demoiselle, or damselfly, and that is quite deserved, for the dragonfly is a graceful little creature, as pretty as pretty can be.

14 See, sticking out of the front of its head are two little feelers, antennae, as we must call them. They are very short, but it does not need long ones. Insects smell with their feelers, you know, but
! our dragonflies see so well they do not need to smell very well, I suppose.

15 See how it can turn its head around. That is because it has a little short neck between its head and its body. Its eyes, its mouth, and its antennae belong to its head.

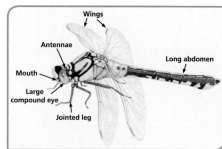

This illustration shows the parts of a dragonfly's body.

16 Of course our demoiselle can fly well; one need only look at those wings to know that. To fly well is quite as necessary to one of its habits as to see well. What would be the use of seeing an insect if it could not fly fast enough to catch it?

17 We all like your pretty wings, little dragonfly; they look like glass and
! they shine so in the sun. How fast the wings can move! See that dragonfly skimming over the pond; its wings make a whizzing sound as it darts about.

18 Why does it zigzag so? Why doesn't it fly in a straight line?

19 Yes, Mollie, you are right, it goes zigzagging along after insects. It sees one it wants off at one side—whizz! around it turns after it. Shouldn't you like to fly like that, children?

20 And yet we would not be willing to exchange our arms and hands for
? wings. We could not whittle a stick nor write a letter if we had only wings. In fact we could not do most of the things we now do.

21 I am glad I have my hands.

22 We are glad, too, that the dragonflies have their pretty, swift wings.

20 • Unit 1

PROFESSIONAL DEVELOPMENT

Self-Monitoring Strategy: Visualize

What Is It? Visualization is a **Self-Monitoring Strategy** that encourages students to imagine a scene using mental images.

Why Is It Important? Visualization can help students understand lengthy or difficult descriptions or complex action sequences. It can also enhance reading enjoyment and motivation for reluctant readers. Visualization helps good readers create pictures in their minds as they read.

Make notes here about your annotations from each read. You will refer to these notes later when you return to your annotations. **Sample notes appear below.**

ANNOTATION NOTES

Key Ideas and Details:

Some people think the dragonfly sews up people's ears.

Dragonflies have antennae or feelers.

Insects smell with their feelers.

Dragonflies see well.

Language and Text Structure:

Demoiselle is in italics—it is a French word.

repeats the word "See" in paragraphs 9, 14, and 15 = look closely

Paragraphs 9–17 describe a dragonfly.

unfamiliar words: "darning needle" and "whittle"

Paragraph 17 compares dragonfly wings to glass.

Connections and Inferences:

Dragonflies don't need to smell well because they see so well. Do people

use one sense more than another sense?

All parts of a dragonfly have a task or purpose. People use their hands for

different tasks or purposes.

How Do I Use It? Use visualization with texts that have rich descriptions and vivid scenes. Informational texts, like "Our Pretty Dragonflies," often include visual details. Model the strategy using a Think Aloud: *When I read paragraph 17, phrases like "your pretty wings," "they look like glass," "they shine so in the sun" really help me picture a dragonfly's wings. I also can imagine the narrator and the audience of children all looking at a dragonfly and studying its wings. Visualizing the scene helps make me a part of the audience, too.* Make difficult words more accessible by providing images from the Internet, your own sketches, or realia, and encourage students to make sketches of their own to help them understand words and ideas.

Our Pretty Dragonflies

3rd READ

Set a Purpose
Students will read to make inferences.

Text-Dependent Questions

1. What is the author's opinion of dragonflies? (Sample answer: I can infer that the author thinks dragonflies are interesting and attractive. In paragraph 7, she says that dragonfly eyes have as many as twenty thousand facets and follows that with "Think of it!" That shows that she thinks dragonflies are amazing. In paragraph 13, she describes dragonflies as "graceful" and "pretty as pretty can be," so we know she thinks they're nice to look at.)

2. What connection does the author make between human arms and hands and dragonfly wings? (Sample answer: The author thinks you can have one or the other, but not both. People may want to "fly like that," but then they would have to "exchange your arms and hands for wings." If we did that, we could not "whittle a stick or write a letter.")

Think Aloud *The diagram makes it look as though the dragonfly has two sets of wings. The text doesn't mention this. I asked myself, what would be the use of two sets of wings? The text says the dragonfly "darts about" so the two sets of wings must help it fly really fast.*

Partner Talk Have students discuss the inferences they made and how that helped them understand the text.

Respond to Reading

You may want to check students' understanding by having them complete page 22 in the Student Worktext.

1. Remind students that a summary should only include the key ideas and details essential to understanding what the text is about. Point out that they can use the graphic organizer on Student Worktext page 22 to capture and organize those key ideas and details. The graphic organizer should then guide them in writing their summaries.

2. Refer students to pages 12 and 13 in Getting Started to help them write their individual summaries.

Have students work independently to answer the questions on page 22 of their Worktexts.

COLLABORATE Have students exchange their final summaries with their partners and review each other's summaries. Remind pairs that when they review and discuss their partners' summaries, they should consider whether or not the summary has the following elements:

- contains only important information
- answers as many of the following as possible: Who? What? When? Where? and How?

REFLECT Have students identify the **Self-Monitoring Strategies** they used to clear up confusions as they read. Reviewing their annotations may help them recall the confusions that arose.

Return to the TEXT

Respond to Reading: Our Pretty Dragonflies

Review the annotations and notes you made while reading "Our Pretty Dragonflies." Think about how they can help you understand the text.

1. Use this Summary Chart to help you summarize the text.

Summary Chart		
	Informational Text	
Who?	the people or subjects	dragonflies, the narrator, the children
What?	the topic or problem	dragonflies have special abilities and a unique appearance
Where?	the location or region where the events occur	in nature where dragonflies live
When?	the date, year, or time	?
How?	the events, steps, or process	big eyes to chase insects, small feelers to smell, fast wings to fly well and catch food

2. Use the completed graphic organizer from Item 1 to help you write a summary of "Our Pretty Dragonflies."

Sample answer: Dragonflies live in nature. They have special abilities like being able to see well and fly well. They have a unique appearance, with big compound eyes, big mouths, antennae, and short necks. Dragonflies are pretty to look at and are good at catching other insects.

REFLECT What word or phrase did you find confusing? What Self-Monitoring Strategy did you use to gain a better understanding of it?

Sample answer: I didn't know what a "darning needle" is. When I reread paragraph 11, I figured out that a real darning needle is used for sewing. I visualized a needle like the one you can sew clothes with.

PROFESSIONAL DEVELOPMENT

Classroom Management: Discussions

What Is It? Discussions are conversations that take place among the entire class, small groups, partners, or between teachers and individual students. Discussions can take place at any stage of text analysis but are often most productive to deepen students' understanding after an initial read and before writing.

Why Is It Important? Discussions expose students to different perspectives, challenge early conclusions or assumptions, deepen understanding, and encourage social skills and participation. Discussions also allow you to monitor student engagement and understanding in an unobtrusive way.

Comprehension Check: Our Pretty Dragonflies

Answer the questions to demonstrate an understanding of what the text means.

1. How does the tone of the passage support the author's purpose and the audience she is addressing? Give two pieces of evidence from the text to support your answer.

   Sample answer: The text has an informal and informative tone. The text is in first person. The phrases "Look, children" and "Do you know, children" make it seem as if a teacher is talking to students. Details like dragonflies have as many as "twenty thousand facets" in their eyes and "insects smell with their feelers" support the author's purpose to teach the audience about dragonflies.

2. What claim does the author make in the last three paragraphs of the explanatory text? Provide evidence from the text to support your answer.

   Sample answer: In the last three paragraphs, the author claims that even though dragonflies are beautiful, people would not want to trade places with them. In paragraph 20, it says, "And yet we would not be willing to exchange our arms and hands for wings." Paragraph 21 says, "I am glad I have my hands."

3. How does the diagram support the author's purpose in the text? Use evidence from the text to support your answer.

   Sample answer: The diagram provides a visual to go with the author's description of a dragonfly. The diagram shows the "compound eyes," "big mouth," "little short neck," and "pretty wings" of the dragonfly described in the text.

Stop and Assess

Use the following rubrics to assess your students' understanding of the text.

Item 1 answers indicate:	
2	that the tone is informal and informative to teach children about dragonflies, with strong supporting text evidence.
1	that the tone is informal and informative, with some text evidence.
0	no recognition of the tone or author's purpose, and no text support.

Item 2 answers indicate:	
2	humans and dragonflies each have characteristics that help them, with strong text support.
1	humans and dragonflies are different, with little text support.
0	no understanding of the author's claim, and no text support.

Item 3 answers indicate:	
2	that the diagram supports the descriptive details from the passage, with text examples.
1	that the diagram supports the descriptive details, with no text support.
0	no connection between the diagram and the text, with no details and no text examples.

How Do I Use It? In order for discussions to be fruitful, plan group sizes. Broader topics covering main ideas are well suited for whole-class discussion. Topics that require more reflection or connection are best suited for smaller groups. Pairs are most effective when students are asked to review each other's writing, as in the Collaborate activity on page 22, or otherwise respond to each other's work. Before class begins, preview the day's questions. Envision how each would be best discussed— whole class, small group, or pairs. Set a time limit for each discussion, and remind students to stay on topic. Don't overlook nonverbal expression.

Alaskan Animal Adaptations

Students will read the article to learn about animal adaptations in Alaska.

1st READ

Set a Purpose

Explain to students that they will read to find out what "Alaskan Animal Adaptations" is about.

Have students read "Alaskan Animal Adaptations" independently, annotating the text as they read. Remind students that suggested annotation symbols appear on page 8 of the Getting Started with Close Reading unit. Circulate and observe students' markings and notes, especially questions and anything they found confusing. The observations and annotations may be used to inform instruction. Based on students' needs, you may want to meet with them in small groups.

Text-Dependent Questions

1. What is this text about? (Sample answer: It is about the characteristics animals in Alaska have developed in order to survive.)

Scaffolded Support Use the following scaffolded question and sentence frame as necessary to support comprehension.

What are some animals mentioned in the text?

All species have _____ that help them _____.

Partner Talk Have students discuss behavioral adaptations mentioned in the text and how they help the animals survive in their habitat.

Read this article to learn about animal adaptations in Alaska. Make annotations as you read. You may make different annotations each time you read.
Sample annotations and notes appear throughout the text.

Alaskan Animal Adaptations

1   An adaptation is a mutation that helps a plant or animal survive in its environment. These mutations are passed down through generations. Slowly, more organisms inherit the mutation. Then the mutation becomes a typical part of the species. The mutation has become an adaptation.

2   All species have adaptations. There are physical adaptations that change the way an animal looks. There are also behavioral adaptations that change the way an animal behaves. Adaptations help an animal survive the weather and find food. Adaptations can help an animal use tools and
?   hide from predators.

3   **Arctic Foxes** have many adaptations. Their fur turns white in winter to match the snow. Their big fluffy tails wrap around their bodies for
?   warmth. Sharp teeth and claws help them catch and eat their prey.

4   **Caribou** have adaptations like fur, antlers, and hooves. Their fur keeps them warm in Alaska's cold climate. They use their antlers to fight off predators. Their large hooves support the animal in snow and soft tundra.

5   **Grizzly Bears** have large muscles that make the bears' hump on their
?   shoulders. This adaptation is useful for digging. It also helps grizzly bears run fast enough to capture moose or caribou for food. Grizzly bears also hibernate in winter as an adaptation. Hibernating is a state of inactivity. It lowers grizzly bears' body temperatures and heart rates. Hibernating allows the grizzly bears to use less energy during the winter, when food is scarce.

6   **Musk Oxen** have a thick fur coat to keep them warm in the winter. Underneath the long, shaggy coat there is a layer of short, dense hair that provides extra warmth. Musk oxen also change their behavior to protect themselves from predators. When danger approaches, musk oxen run together. If only one predator is nearby, the musk oxen form a line. Sometimes several predators surround the group. Then the oxen form
!   a circle and face outward.

7   **Walruses** have developed big tusks for defending their territory and
?   pulling themselves out of the water. Walruses also have thick blubber. This blubber helps keep them warm in cold water. Walruses' mouths and tongues are narrow to help them suck clams out of their shells.

24 • Unit 1

PROFESSIONAL DEVELOPMENT

Academic Language: ELL

What Is It? Academic language falls into two categories: general academic and domain-specific language. Academic language is formal language, vocabulary, and sentence structure used in books and formal discussions, including classroom discussions. Domain-specific language is vocabulary and idioms from a specific field of knowledge.

Why Is It Important? Academic language is necessary for school and professional success. Knowledge of domain-specific language may be necessary to understand unfamiliar but essential topics, such as the science topics covered in this unit.

Make notes here about your annotations from each read. You will refer to these notes later when you return to your annotations. **Sample notes appear below.**

ANNOTATION NOTES

Key Ideas and Details:

Adaptations are mutations passed down over generations.

Mutations that help animals survive become adaptations.

There are physical and behavioral adaptations.

Physical adaptation: Arctic foxes turn white in winter to match the snow.

Behavioral adaptation: musk oxen run together or form a line or circle for protection.

Language and Text Structure:

unfamiliar words: "adaptation," "predator," "prey," and "blubber"

"mutation" repeated in paragraph 1 = must be important to adaptations

Most paragraphs start with a boldface term that names the animal that the paragraph is about.

Connections and Inferences:

Adaptations help animals survive the weather and find food.

Adaptations help animals escape predators and use tools—I wonder what adaptations humans have?

I wonder if other animals make a circle to fight a group of predators?

Unit 1 • **25**

How Do I Use It? Some ELL students may have advantages and disadvantages when encountering Academic language. Many Romance languages (Spanish, Portuguese, and French/Haitian Creole, for example) are based in Latin, and share many roots and word parts with Latin-based English academic vocabulary, specifically scientific vocabulary. Point out cognates that may be familiar to Romance-language speakers. For example, *The English word* mutation, *introduced in paragraph 1 on page 24, is a lot like the Spanish* mutación, *the Portuguese* mutação, *the French* mutation, *and Haitian* mitasyon. *What other cognates do you recognize?*

Alaskan Animal Adaptations

2nd READ

Set a Purpose

Students will examine how the ideas in the text are organized.

Text-Dependent Questions

1. What is the purpose of the bold-face words? (They identify the animal the paragraph describes.)

2. Vocabulary: Meaning from Context Discuss how context clues can help define unfamiliar words.

Paragraph 5: What does *hibernating* tell you about a grizzly bear adaptation? (The word *hibernating* is defined in the text as "a state of inactivity." That helps me understand how they use less energy in winter.)

Partner Talk Have students identify and define academic terms from the text.

3rd READ

Set a Purpose

Students will read to make inferences about Alaska.

Text-Dependent Questions

1. What can you infer about weather conditions in Alaska? (Sample answer: The conditions in Alaska are very cold and very harsh.)

2. What details tell you this? (Sample answer: Many animals have extra fur and some have body parts adapted to keep them warm, and to help them live in snow and find food.)

Partner Talk Have students summarize the adaptations that many Alaskan animals have in common.

Unit 1 • **25**

Respond to Reading

You may want to check students' understanding by having them complete page 26 in the Student Worktext.

1. Remind students that the text under each heading included both physical and behavioral adaptations. Students can look for one of each for each animal to fill out the graphic organizer.

2. Have students use the information they recorded on their graphic organizers to explain how Alaskan animals use both behavior and physical traits to survive.

3. Refer students to pages 12 and 13 of Getting Started to help them write their individual summaries.

Have students work independently to answer the questions on page 26 of their Worktexts.

COLLABORATE When finished, have students exchange summaries with their partners and review each other's summaries. Remind pairs that when they review and discuss their partners' summaries, they should consider whether or not the summary has the following elements:

- contains only important information
- answers as many of the following as possible: Who? What? When? Where? and How?

REFLECT Remind students to use their annotations, especially question marks and confusions, to help focus their rereading.

Respond to Reading: Alaskan Animal Adaptations

Review the annotations and notes you made while reading "Alaskan Animal Adaptations." Think about how your annotations can help you answer the questions.

1. Use information from the text to complete the graphic organizer.

Animals' Physical Adaptations	Animals' Behavioral Adaptations
Arctic foxes turn white. Caribou have fur and antlers. Grizzly bears have muscular humps. Musk oxen have a thick fur coat. Walruses have tusks and blubber.	Grizzly bears hibernate. Musk oxen run together when danger is near. With one predator, musk oxen form a line. With many predators, musk oxen form a circle.

2. Use your graphic organizer to explain how the author compares and contrasts physical and behavioral adaptations of animals in Alaska.

Sample answer: The author explains that physical adaptations change the way animals look. Arctic foxes' fur "turns white" and walruses have "big tusks," "thick blubber," and narrow mouths. Behavioral adaptations change animals' behavior. The ways grizzly bears hibernate and musk oxen escape predators are behavioral adaptations. All adaptations help animals survive.

3. Write a brief summary of "Alaskan Animal Adaptations."

Sample answer: Animals have adaptations to survive where they live. In Alaska, Arctic foxes, caribou, grizzly bears, musk oxen, and walruses have physical adaptations. Grizzly bears and musk oxen have behavioral adaptations.

REFLECT What words, phrases, or sections did you have to reread to make sure that you understood?

Sample answer: I reread paragraphs 1 and 2. Rereading helped me understand the difference between physical and behavioral adaptations.

PROFESSIONAL DEVELOPMENT

Productive Conversation: Providing Appropriate Wait Time

What Is It? Wait time is the silence between comments or following a question during a group discussion. Providing an appropriate amount of wait time is an important part of managing productive conversations.

Why Is It Important? It is during wait time that students are pushed to consider new perspectives, make connections between ideas, and/or come up with their own answers to questions. If wait time is too short, students won't have time to process information independently. Encourage students to provide wait time and to be better listeners in group discussion.

Comprehension Check: Alaskan Animal Adaptations

Answer the questions to demonstrate an understanding of what the text means.

1. What was the author's purpose for writing "Alaskan Animal Adaptations"? Use text evidence in your answer.

Sample answer: The author's purpose was to explain animal mutations and adaptations. The author uses different examples to show how some animals in Alaska have adapted to food and weather conditions there. For example, Arctic foxes have fur that "turns white in winter" to match the snow to help them hide from predators.

2. What do the descriptions of the animals' adaptations tell you about surviving winter in Alaska? Provide text evidence to support your answer.

Sample answer: The animals all have adaptations that help them survive cold weather: "big, fluffy tails," "thick fur coats," "dense hair," and "thick blubber" are some of the things that help animals in Alaska keep warm in the winter.

3. What makes grizzly bears' adaptation different from the adaptations described for the other animals? Provide text evidence to support your answer.

Sample answer: Most of the animals have adaptations that keep them warm, but grizzly bears instead lower their "body temperatures and heart rates" as part of hibernation. Lower body temperatures and heart rates allow grizzly bears "to use less energy during winter, when food is scarce."

Unit 1 • 27

Stop and Assess

Use the following rubrics to assess your students' understanding of the text.

Item 1 answers indicate:	
2	that the author's purpose was to inform readers about animal adaptations, with strong text support.
1	an informational purpose, with some text support.
0	no understanding of purpose, with no text support.

Item 2 answers indicate:	
2	that many of the adaptations are for surviving cold weather, with specific supporting details.
1	that the animals have adapted to cold weather, with some text support.
0	no understanding of the weather in Alaska, with no support.

Item 3 answers indicate:	
2	that hibernating lowers the bear's body temperature and heart rate, while other animals have adaptations to keep them warm, with specific text support.
1	that the grizzly bear hibernates, with some text support.
0	no understanding of the grizzly bear's adaptation, with no text support.

How Do I Use It? An appropriate amount of wait time varies by topic. Encourage students to watch other students' facial expressions and body language to better understand what an appropriate wait time is for the current conversation. As students review and discuss their summaries in the Collaborate activity on page 26 of this guide, have them be mindful of wait time during their discussions. If pauses become disruptive to the flow of conversation, the wait time is too long. If the conversation stops after the first guess or at surface-level analysis, wait time may be too short to allow deeper thinking.

Unit 1 • 27

ANALYZE and SYNTHESIZE ACROSS TEXTS

Return to the Focus Question

Explain to students that they will fill out a graphic organizer that will help them answer the Focus Question: How do some characteristics help animals survive?

CONNECT TEXTS Have small groups of students discuss how each text they read helps them answer the Focus Question. Have small groups share and compare their discussion notes with another small group.

Scaffolded Support You may provide the following sentence frames to support students in their use of academic language:

> In the text _____, the author/photographer makes the point that _____. He/she does this by _____.

Remind students to use their annotations and summaries to support their answers. They can also reread portions of the texts, if necessary.

Have students complete their graphic organizers individually and then answer the Focus Question.

REFLECT Remind students that each text discusses specific characteristics of individual animals. Ask, *How did reading the texts give you a greater understanding of how some characteristics help animals survive?*

Return to the Focus Question: How do some characteristics help animals survive?

Review your answers to questions about the texts as well as your annotations and Annotation Notes. Think about the discussions you've had about the texts. How does that information help you answer the Focus Question?

Use the graphic organizer to organize information about the texts.

1. In the boxes, record the details from each text that help you answer the Focus Question.

2. Make connections between those details to help you answer the Focus Question. Write your answer in the box provided.

Our Pretty Dragonflies
Sample answer: Dragonflies have body parts with different tasks and purposes.

Giraffes on Samburu Reserve (Visual Text)
Sample answer: Long necks help giraffes get food.

Alaskan Animal Adaptations
Sample answer: Physical and behavioral adaptations help against weather and predators.

How do some characteristics help animals survive?
Sample answer: Adaptations help animals survive by helping them to cope with the food and weather conditions in their habitats. Some adaptations also help animals protect themselves from predators.

REFLECT How did making connections between the three texts help you to answer the Focus Question?

Sample answer: Giraffes have long necks, dragonflies have compound eyes and other parts, and Alaskan animals have behavioral and physical adaptations. By putting the information together, I saw how different characteristics help animals survive.

PROFESSIONAL DEVELOPMENT

Intertextual Analysis: Compare and Contrast Authors' Use of Language and Text Structure

What Is It? When students compare texts on similar topics, they compare not only events and ideas, but how different authors present those events and ideas.

Why Is It Important? Language and text structure reveal different authors' purposes and points of view. Students analyze authors' use of language and text structure to draw larger inferences, connections, and conclusions.

Writing About the Focus Question

Now that you have answered the Focus Question using all three texts, develop your ideas into a longer piece of writing.

USE EVIDENCE

- Explain how different some characteristics help animals survive. Use at least one piece of evidence from each text to support your answer.
- If you need more room, use additional paper.

MONITOR

- Use the Writing Checklist as you work to make sure your writing has all of the important pieces of information.
- Use the rubric on page 30 when you have completed your first draft to help you evaluate, revise, and edit your work.

WRITING CHECKLIST ✔

Does my writing . . .

- ☐ answer the Focus Question?
- ☐ provide text evidence to support my ideas?
- ☐ have a clear beginning, middle, and end?
- ☐ use correct language, spelling, and conventions?

Writing About the Focus Question

USE EVIDENCE Remind students that they should use their graphic organizers as well as their annotations in the texts to write their responses.

Allow students to revisit the texts as frequently as they need to in order to support comprehension and to respond to the Focus Question.

MONITOR After students have completed their responses, have them review the Writing Checklist and revise their writing responses.

DIFFERENTIATE AND EXTEND

In addition to or instead of the writing response, consider having students complete one of the following assignments:

Write Beyond Have students assume the role of biologists in Alaska and write brief blog posts to an audience of other animal scientists describing animals they encounter and explaining the animals' adaptations to their environment.

Research Have students research the adaptation of camouflage and how animals hide from prey or predators.

Create a Visual Text Have students create infographics or captioned image slideshows that compare different animal adaptations in Alaska an how each one helps the animals survive.

Interview an Expert Have students develop questions for an interview with a biologist or geneticist about how animal adaptations occur over time.

How Do I Use It? Help students compare purposes by examining "Our Pretty Dragonflies" and "Alaskan Animal Adaptations" for tone and intended audience. Have students identify elements of the familiar, almost literary language of "Our Pretty Dragonflies" and compare this with the academic language of "Alaskan Animal Adaptations." Though both texts intend to inform, the language gives clues to differences in the author's purposes: "Our Pretty Dragonflies" conveys a sense of wonder, while "Alaskan Animal Adaptations" stays firmly grounded in scientific facts.

SELF-ASSESS and REFLECT

SELF-ASSESS Have students use the Writing Rubric on page 30 to self-assess their writing response. Tell them to assign themselves a score from 1–4 (with "4" being the highest) for each category in the first column.

REFLECT Use the Writing Rubric on Student Worktext page 30 to assess each student's writing. Record points for each category in the first column of the rubric. Have students remove the page from their Student Worktexts and place it in their writing portfolios, along with the drafts and final versions of their responses.

SELF-ASSESS and REFLECT

Focus Question How do some characteristics help animals survive?

This is the rubric that your teacher will use to assess your writing. Refer to it as you revise your work. After you have finished your final version, review your writing and record your points for each category on the "Student" line in the first column.

	Accomplished (4 points)	Competent (3 points)	Developing (2 points)	Beginning (1 point)
RESPONSE Score: Student _____ Teacher _____	The response answers the question effectively and with insight.	The response answers the question effectively.	The response partially responds to the question but does not adequately address it.	The response addresses the texts but does not address the question.
ORGANIZATION Score: Student _____ Teacher _____	The main idea is convincingly stated. Ideas are organized in cohesive paragraphs that support the main idea.	The main idea is clearly stated. Ideas are organized in logical paragraphs.	The main idea is weak. Ideas are organized in a somewhat logical and cohesive way.	The main idea is missing. The organization of the paragraphs is not logical.
TEXT EVIDENCE Score: Student _____ Teacher _____	Response includes more than one piece of appropriate text evidence from each text. Evidence supports the main idea in a thorough way.	Response includes one piece of text evidence from each text. Evidence supports the main idea clearly.	Response does not include at least one piece of text evidence from each text. Text evidence does not adequately support the main idea.	Response does not contain relevant evidence.
LANGUAGE Score: Student _____ Teacher _____	Writing includes precise and sophisticated vocabulary related to the topic.	Writing includes appropriate vocabulary related to the topic.	Writing includes imprecise and inaccurate vocabulary.	Writing does not include vocabulary that appropriately reflects the topic of the response.
SPELLING AND CONVENTIONS Score: Student _____ Teacher _____	Response includes correct spelling, grammar, and punctuation consistently.	Response includes mostly correct spelling, grammar, and punctuation.	Response has many errors in spelling, grammar, and punctuation.	Response's errors in spelling, grammar, and punctuation make it extremely difficult to understand the response.

UNIT 2

Focus Question
What are the different ways people care for animals?

Texts for Close Reading

Unit 2 • 31

GENRE STUDY

Discuss with students the genres of *Black Beauty* and "Save Our Big Cats!"

Remind students that *genre* refers to the format and features of a text and typically falls into one of two categories— literature or informational text. Literature is a creative work that doesn't necessarily rely on facts, and informational text is based on factual information. *Black Beauty* is a literary novel, a long form of creative fiction. "Save Our Big Cats!" is an explanatory text used to inform. The novel uses narrative and literary devices such as figurative language, imagery, and foreshadowing, while an explanatory text is more direct. Have students identify characteristics shared by a novel and an explanatory text and characteristics unique to each genre.

Focus Question

Have students read the Focus Question on Worktext page 31. Tell them that the texts and illustrations in this unit will help them answer this question.

Texts for Close Reading

Have students read to themselves the descriptions of the texts in this unit.

There is no need to explain what students should expect to find in their close readings or to do any preteaching about the subject matter.

TEXT COMPLEXITY

Girl Feeding Lambs in a Barn
- Style: documentary
- Knowledge demands: low
- Levels of meaning: literal/ inferential

Black Beauty
Quantitative: 790L
Qualitative
- Structure: conventional
- Language: archaic
- Knowledge demands: high
- Levels of meaning: literal/ inferential

Save Our Big Cats!
Quantitative: 720L
Qualitative
- Structure: conventional
- Language: academic
- Knowledge demands: medium
- Levels of meaning: literal

Girl Feeding Lambs

Set a Purpose

Explain to students that they will look at the image on page 32 to begin to gain a deeper understanding of how people care for animals.

Visual Text Analysis

Remind students that an image can be analyzed as a text by looking at its details and making inferences. Direct students' attention to the image on Student Worktext page 32.

Encourage students to annotate the Visual Text. Suggest they use arrows, labels, circles, margin notes, and other markings to highlight details that will help them gain a better understanding of the meaning of the image.

1. Have students record their first impressions about the image. Lead them to discuss as a whole class, in small groups, or with a partner what they think is happening in the photograph.

2. Encourage students to make note of the details that support their observations in question 1. Have students study the girl and each of the lambs, identifying body language and expressions. Have them explain as a whole class, in small groups, or with a partner what details they noted and what those details might tell them about how people care for animals.

3. Guide students to synthesize all the details they see in the photograph to draw conclusions about the photographer's message.

VISUAL TEXT

Girl Feeding Lambs in a Barn

Look at this Visual Text, and make annotations on the image. Review the image or parts of the image as many times as necessary to answer the following questions.

1. What is your first impression of what's going on in this photograph?

   Sample answer: A young girl is feeding a lamb in a barn. They seem happy to

   be together.

PROFESSIONAL DEVELOPMENT

Visual Text: Visual Learners

What Is It? Visual learners prefer pictorial information such as maps, diagrams, and images. Some visual learners process written instructions better than verbal instructions.

Why Is It Important? Visual learners benefit from visual support in many contexts, including when background knowledge is limited or when a text includes unfamiliar or difficult vocabulary. When you include a variety of visual supports as differentiated scaffolding prior to, during, and after a text reading, you provide visual learners with the tools they need to best comprehend the text.

2. What details in the photograph help give you that impression?

Sample answer: One lamb stands close to the girl. The girl is sitting on straw. She

has one hand on the lamb's neck and the other hand is holding food close to the

lamb's mouth. The girl is smiling. She looks happy. The lamb seems to know her and

accepts food from her hand.

_____

_____

_____

_____

_____

_____

_____

3. What do you conclude is the message of the photograph?

Sample answer: The message is that caring for animals makes people and animals

happy. The photograph shows how the girl cares for the lambs and likes to be with

them, and the lambs like to be with the girl.

_____

_____

_____

_____

_____

_____

_____

_____

Text-Dependent Questions

As necessary, encourage discussion with such prompts as:

1. What attitude does the girl in the photograph show? (Sample answer: She is happy and confident. She looks as though she is used to being around animals and likes to feed them.)

2. How do you know? (Sample answer: She is smiling. She is sitting in a relaxed way and doesn't look tense or afraid of the lambs.)

3. What attitude do the lambs in the photograph show, and how do you know? (Sample answer: The lambs are relaxed. One is lying down. Another comes close to eat food from the girl's hand.)

4. What can you infer from the setting about how people care for animals? (Sample answer: I can infer that giving animals food and shelter and companionship is a way to care for them. The floor is covered with soft straw, and there is a basket stuffed with hay for eating. This is where the lambs stay when it is too hot or too cold to be outside.)

How Do I Use It? Preview texts, including Visual Texts, to anticipate where visual learners will need support or where they may offer support to their peers. Provide background information as necessary to help them access content in images. Make use of visual learners' skills to pull meaning from images for the class. In the case of "Girl Feeding Lambs in a Barn," visually oriented students might be helpful in identifying elements of the setting and details that convey the girl's relationship to the lambs.

Black Beauty

Tell students that they will read to find out some of the ways that people care for animals.

1st READ

Set a Purpose

Explain to students that they will read to get a general understanding of what the text is about.

Have students read *Black Beauty* independently, annotating the text as they read. Remind students that suggested annotation symbols appear on page 8 of the Getting Started with Close Reading unit. Circulate and observe students' markings and notes, especially questions and anything they found confusing. The observations and annotations may be used to inform instruction. Based on students' needs, you may want to meet with them in small groups.

Use the Text-Dependent Questions to prompt students to engage with the text.

Text-Dependent Questions

1. What is this text about? (Sample answer: It is about a horse being bought at a horse fair and brought to his new home.)

Think Aloud *I had a lot of trouble figuring out who was telling the story. I figured that it must be a person, until I got to paragraph 3. To find out what was going on, I reread the first five paragraphs and circled every time I saw the words* my, me, *and* I. *I looked at what happened to the narrator and what the narrator did. Then, it was clear that the narrator was one of the horses for sale.*

> ✔ **Self-Monitoring Strategies** can help you check your understanding and clarify a text. Use them as you read.
>
> ☐ Visualize. ☐ Ask yourself questions. ☐ Draw conclusions. ☐ Reread to clarify.

Read this adapted novel excerpt to find out some of the ways that people care for animals. Make annotations as you read. You may want to review Annotating a text on page 8.
Sample annotations appear throughout the text.

Black Beauty
by Anna Sewell

A Horse Fair

1   No doubt a (horse fair) is a very amusing place to those who have nothing to lose. At any rate, there is plenty to see at a horse fair. Long strings of young horses out of the country, fresh from the marshes.

?   Droves of shaggy little Welsh ponies and hundreds of cart horses of all sorts. There were some splendid animals quite in their prime and fit for anything. But there were also a

!   number of poor things, sadly broken down with hard work, with their

?   knees knuckling over. And there were some very dejected looking old horses, with the under lip hanging down. They looked as if there were no more pleasure in life, and no more hope. There were some so thin you could see their ribs, and some with old sores on their backs and hips. These were sad sights for a horse to look upon. This was especially true

!   for a horse who knows not but he may come to the same state.

2   There was a great deal of bargaining here. I should say there were more lies told and more trickery than a clever man could give an account of. I was put with two or three other strong horses, and a good many people came to look at us. The gentlemen always turned from me when they saw my skinned knees, though the man who owned me swore it was only a slip in the stall.

PROFESSIONAL DEVELOPMENT

Annotations: Important or Surprising Information

What Is It? Readers use exclamation points to mark words and passages they consider surprising or important. These items are usually—but not always—important or surprising pieces of information in the passage. The teacher uses students' annotations as the basis for a discussion of content and for building comprehension.

Why Is It Important? When students annotate, they are focusing on the text. Observing students as they annotate enables you to identify which parts of the text grab students' attention.

Make notes here about your annotations from each read. You will refer to these notes later when you return to your annotations. Sample notes appear below.

Key Ideas and Details:

A horse fair is a busy and confusing scene.

Some horses are "splendid"; some are broken down with hard work;

some are old, thin, and sad.

lots of bargaining, lies, and trickery

Language and Text Structure:

"Droves" must mean something like "hundreds" or "crowds."

"Dejected" must mean "sad" or "hopeless."

The story is told from a horse's point of view. Black Beauty?

paragraphs 2 and 3: narrator is for sale at fair

Picture shows scene described in the text.

Connections and Inferences:

Narrator can tell which people are nice and which are mean—he must have

experience with both types of people.

---

2. Who comes to look at the narrator at the fair? (Sample answer: In paragraph 2 the narrator says a "good many people" come to look at him, and paragraph 4 says one especially kind man and one "very hard-looking, loud-voiced man" handled him.)

Scaffolded Support Use the following scaffolded question and sentence frame as necessary to support comprehension.

Who is at the horse fair?

Some people handle the narrator _____, while others handle him _____.

3. What happens to the narrator at the end of the story? (Sample answer: Paragraphs 7 through 14 describe how a kind man buys the narrator and brings him home to London.)

Partner Talk Have students take turns describing the narrator and the people the narrator interacts with in the excerpt.

How Do I Use It? As you circulate among readers, note the items they mark. If you see several students marking the same passages, prompt class discussion of those passages, providing support as needed. Exclamation points that mark surprising facts present good opportunities to motivate students and to practice listening and speaking skills. Ask readers to explain what surprised them or why they think those words are important. In literature, exclamation point annotations can mark important plot or character developments that often hint at themes and signal higher student motivation to keep reading.

Black Beauty

2nd READ

Set a Purpose

Students will return to *Black Beauty* to understand the effects of the author's choice of words.

Text-Dependent Questions

1. What impression does the narrator's description of his new owner give the reader? (Sample answer: Paragraph 4 describes the man as "well made, and quick." He speaks "gently" and has a "kindly, cheery look." The description makes the man seem like a nice and good person.)

2. How do the narrator's feelings described in paragraphs 1 and 4 compare to his feelings in paragraphs 13 and 14? (Sample answer: The narrator starts off feeling afraid and ends up feeling happy. He describes "sad sights" in paragraph 1 and being "dreadfully afraid" of the loud-voiced man in paragraph 4. Later he had a "good feed," and in paragraphs 13 and 14 he enjoyed "how good it felt" to be petted by the girl. He felt he "was going to be happy.")

3. Vocabulary: Multiple-Meaning Words Help students access the meaning of words in context.

Paragraph 4: What is a *pound* in this context, and what context clues help you know? (Sample answer: The kind man offers 23 pounds in exchange for the horse, and then increases the offer to "the salesman" to 24 pounds and "the money was paid on the spot." Pounds must refer to money.)

Partner Talk Have students discuss how the author's use of language helped them identify the time and place in which it is set.

3   The first thing they would do was pull my mouth open and look at my eyes. Then they'd feel all the way down my legs. What a difference there was in the way these things were done. Some did it in a rough, offhand way, as if I were only a piece of wood. Others would take their hands gently over my body, with a pat now and then.

4   There was one man, I thought, if he would buy me, I should be happy. He was rather a small man, but well made, and quick in all his motions. I knew in a moment by the way he handled me, that he was used to horses. He spoke gently, and his gray eyes had a kindly, cheery look. He offered twenty-three pounds for me, but that was refused, and he walked away. I looked after him, but he was gone, and a very hard-looking, loud-voiced man came. I was dreadfully afraid he would have me; but he walked off. But just then the gray-eyed man came back again. I could not help reaching out my head toward him. He stroked my face kindly.

5   ?   "Well, old chap," he said, "I think we should suit each other. I'll give twenty-four for him."

6   "Done," said the salesman; "and you may depend upon the quality in that horse."

7   The money was paid on the spot, and my new master took my halter, and led me out of the fair. He gave me a good feed of oats and stood by while I ate it, talking to himself and talking to me. Half an hour later we were on our way to London. We traveled steadily, till in the twilight we reached the great city.

8   We soon turned up one of the side streets, and then a very narrow street. My owner pulled up at one of the houses and whistled. The door flew open, and a young woman, followed by a little girl and boy, ran out. There was a very lively greeting as my rider dismounted.

9   "Now, then, Harry, my boy, open the gates, and mother will bring us the lantern."

10   The next minute they were all standing round me in a small stable-yard.

11   "Is he gentle, father?"

12   "Yes, Dolly, as gentle as your own kitten; come and pat him."

13   At once the little hand was patting about all over my shoulder without fear. How good it felt!

14   Then, I was led into a comfortable, clean-smelling stall, with plenty of dry
?   straw. After a capital supper I lay down, thinking I was going to be happy.

PROFESSIONAL DEVELOPMENT

Self-Monitoring Strategies: Ask Yourself Questions

What Is It? In self-monitoring, students keep track of their own progress as they read. The purpose of self-monitoring is to encourage and help students read independently outside the classroom.

Why Is It Important? Asking themselves questions and formulating answers keeps students' attention on the text while removing the stress of direct quizzing by the teacher. Self-monitoring builds confidence because it increases comprehension. Asking and answering self-formulated questions also help students prepare for class discussions, writing assignments, and assessments.

Make notes here about your annotations from each read.
You will refer to these notes later when you return to
your annotations. Sample notes appear below.

ANNOTATION NOTES

Key Ideas and Details:

The horse for sale sees one kind man. The man's offer to buy the horse is

refused, but then he comes back. The salesman and the buyer agree on a

higher price. The horse's new owner takes him to London, where the

owner's family welcomes him with kindness.

Some people are rough to the horse, but others are kind.

Language and Text Structure:

look up "pounds," "old chap," and "capital"

Horse says he "could not help reaching out my head toward him"—shows

horse is communicating with the kind man.

Connections and Inferences:

When he tells the story, the horse mentions kindness and gentleness

several times. Kindness and human care for animals are important in the

overall message of the story.

Unit 2 • **37**

How Do I Use It? Remind students of the strategy if they find
parts of the text confusing. For example, model asking and
answering questions about the two men who consider buying
the horse. *How does the horse know the man is kind? The man
speaks gently, and his eyes have a kindly, cheery look. Why is
the horse afraid of the other man? The text says that he is hard-
looking and loud-voiced.*

Black Beauty

3rd READ

Set a Purpose
Students will read to draw inferences and make connections.

Text-Dependent Questions
1. What inference can you make
about how the narrator feels
based on his descriptions of the
fair in paragraph 1? (Sample answer:
He feels sorry for horses that have
been treated roughly and is nervous
about what will happen to him.)

Scaffolded Support Use the following scaffolded question and
sentence frame as necessary to
support comprehension.

> What does the narrator say
> about the other horses he sees?

> The narrator feels _____
> when the hard-looking
> man approaches.

2. What can you infer about the
narrator from his descriptions of
people at the fair in paragraphs 2
and 3? (Sample answer: The horse has
a lot of experience with people and
can tell when people are lying, who
knows horses well, who is kind, and
who might be mean.)

3. Why does the narrator think he
will be happy at the end of the
text? (Sample answer: He has come to
live with gentle people, and he has a
clean stall and plenty to eat.)

Partner Talk Have students discuss connections between Text 1
and the Visual Text on caring for
animals.

Unit 2 • **37**

Respond to Reading

You may want to check students' understanding by having them complete page 38 in the Student Worktext.

1. Remind students that a summary should only include the key ideas and details essential to understanding what the text is about. Point out that they can use the graphic organizer on Student Worktext page 38 to capture and organize those key ideas and details. The graphic organizer should then guide them in writing their summaries.

2. Refer students to pages 12 and 13 in Getting Started to help them write their individual summaries.

Have students work independently to answer the questions on page 38 of their Worktexts.

COLLABORATE Have students exchange their final summaries with their partners and review each other's summaries. Remind pairs that when they review and discuss their partners' summaries, they should consider whether or not the summary has the following elements:

- contains only important information
- answers as many of the following as possible: Who? What? When? Where? and How?

REFLECT Have students review their annotations to identify unfamiliar words and phrases they encountered while reading and then reflect on the strategies they used to clear up their confusions.

Respond to Reading: Black Beauty

Review the annotations and notes you made while reading *Black Beauty*. Think about how they can help you understand the text.

1. Use this Story Map to help you summarize the text.

Characters (Who)	Setting (Where and When)
narrator (horse), owner/seller, kind man, Harry, Dolly, mother	a horse fair far away from London a small stable-yard in London

Conflict (What)	Main Events (How)
Narrator has skinned knees, so maybe no one will buy him, or maybe an unkind person will buy him.	The horse fair is crowded and confusing and has a lot of bargaining. Buyers and sellers try to trick each other. A kind man buys narrator. His family is kind. The horse is happy.

2. Use the completed graphic organizer from Item 1 to help you write a summary of the excerpt from *Black Beauty*.

Sample answer: At the horse fair in London, the narrator, a horse for sale, hopes a kind man will buy him. The kind man makes an offer, but it is refused. Then he offers more money and buys the narrator. The narrator and the kind man travel to London. The narrator feels he will be happy.

REFLECT What word or phrase did you find confusing? What Self-Monitoring Strategy did you use to gain a better understanding of it?

Sample answer: I wasn't sure what "old chap" meant. The kind man and horse seem to like each other. I concluded that "old chap" is a friendly term, like "pal" or "buddy."

PROFESSIONAL DEVELOPMENT

Differentiation: Scaffolding with Graphic Organizers

What Is It? Graphic organizers are visual organizational tools that assist students in recording their understandings of texts they are reading. They include main idea charts, Venn diagrams to compare and contrast information, word webs, thinking maps, and many other visual resources. You can present graphic organizers as scaffolding during whole-class and small-group discussion or have students make and complete simple graphic organizers of their own.

Comprehension Check: Black Beauty

Answer the questions to demonstrate an understanding of what the text means.

1. Why does the author tell the story from the horse's point of view? Give evidence from the text to support your answer.

   Sample answer: By making the narrator a horse, the author lets the reader

   learn more about the life of horses and how they are treated by people. In

   paragraph 4, the horse is "dreadfully afraid" that he will be sold to an unkind

   person. In paragraph 1, the horse says the "poor things" at the fair are "sad...to

   look upon" especially if, like him, "he may come to the same state."

2. What inference can you make based on the kind man's decision to return to buy the horse? Cite at least two examples of text evidence that support your answer.

   Sample answer: I can infer that the kind man really wanted to own the horse.

   When he comes back, he "stroked" the horse "kindly." He says, "I think we

   should suit each other," so he likes the horse and thinks they will get along

   well. He thinks the horse is worth the money.

3. What does the author want us to understand about the ways in which people can care for animals? Give at least two pieces of text evidence to support your answer.

   Sample answer: Kindness and good food are ways that people show they

   care for animals. For example, the kind man gives the horse "a good feed

   of oats" after he buys him. He talks to the horse as the horse eats. The man's

   daughter pats the horse on the shoulder and they give him a "comfortable,

   clean-smelling stall, with plenty of dry straw" and a "capital" dinner. He is happy.

Unit 2 • **39**

Stop and Assess

Use the following rubrics to assess your students' understanding of the text.

Item 1 answers indicate:	
2	that having the horse tell the story gives readers a different perspective, with specific text examples.
1	that having the horse tell the story gives readers a different perspective, with few text examples.
0	no understanding of the effect of having the horse tell the story, and no text support.

Item 2 answers indicate:	
2	that the kind man really wanted the horse, with specific text citations.
1	that the kind man wanted the horse, but insufficient text examples.
0	no understanding that the kind man wanted the horse, and no text examples.

Item 3 answers indicate:	
2	animals should be handled with kindness, with text support.
1	animals should be handled kindly, with some text support.
0	no understanding of the author's message, and no text support.

Why Is It Important? Graphic organizers represent a shortened, visual, preformatted guide to analyzing ideas and relationships. They can provide a significant scaffold for students who are having difficulty, especially with abstract ideas.

How Do I Use It? For students who need help annotating, allow them to fill in a graphic organizer while they read or study an image. Model how to note connections (web diagram), comparisons (T-chart or Venn diagram), or main ideas or events (flow charts). Emphasize that they are not a final product. They are a thinking aid, like annotations, that students can use as a step toward finding meaning.

Save Our Big Cats!

Students will read the text to learn about some ways people care for animals.

1st READ

Set a Purpose

Explain to students that they will read to find out what "Save Our Big Cats!" is about.

Have students read "Save Our Big Cats!" independently, annotating the text as they read. Remind students that suggested annotation symbols appear on page 8 of the Getting Started with Close Reading unit. Circulate and observe students' markings, especially questions and anything they found confusing. The observations and annotations may be used to inform instruction. Based on students' needs, you may want to meet with them in small groups.

Text-Dependent Questions

1. What is this text telling the reader about? (The text tells the reader about sanctuaries where people care for big cats that need help.)

Scaffolded Support Use the following scaffolded sentence frame as necessary to support comprehension.

In a sanctuary, animals

_____ .

Think Aloud *I was surprised that the sanctuary does not let visitors touch the animals. But when I reread, I understood that the sanctuary does not want big cats treated like pets.*

Partner Talk Have students discuss the things people do for animals in a sanctuary.

Read this explanatory text to learn about some ways people care for animals. Make annotations as you read. You may make different annotations each time you read.
Sample annotations and notes appear throughout the text.

Save Our Big Cats!

1   People care for animals in many different ways. Sometimes, for example, people form rescue groups. Rescue groups build and maintain animal sanctuaries. A sanctuary is a safe place. In a sanctuary, animals receive the food and shelter they need. If they are sick or injured, animal doctors called veterinarians, or vets, care for them.

2   Some sanctuaries focus on special types of animals. Big cats, for example, often need rescue groups. Big cats include lions, tigers, leopards, jaguars, and cougars. Cougars are also called mountain lions.

3   Big cats need sanctuaries for many reasons. Some of them are abandoned pets. Their owners have deserted them. Big cats almost never make good pets. Big cat owners in today's world are usually not doing their oversized pets any favors.

4   ? Some rescued animals have been orphaned in the wild. Their mothers have died or have been killed. Still others have been in circuses or zoos and are no longer wanted. Finally, some animals need to be rescued from sanctuaries that have failed or been shut down by the government for bad treatment.

5   Sanctuaries often ask people to give money to support the animals there. This money is called a donation. How do you know if you should give?

6   If at all possible, you should make a personal visit and judge for yourself. Are the animals well cared for? Do they have enough space? Do they look healthy? Do they have a good diet?

7   One big cat sanctuary in Florida has 74 animals. The public can come see the cats, but they cannot touch them. The sanctuary wants visitors to realize that big cats are not pets. It provides a safe home and open space for big cats. Veterinarians donate their time to care for ill and injured animals. There is even has a dentist to look after those big teeth!

8   Another way sanctuaries care for big cats is by supporting action on international trade in endangered species. They fight against poaching— the illegal capture of animals in the wild and the outlawed trade in animal products. This trade contributes to the problem of abandoned and abused big cats and furthers the need for the sanctuaries.

PROFESSIONAL DEVELOPMENT

Productive Conversation: Adding On

What Is It? Productive Conversation is partner talk or small-group discussion that centers on a specific topic and is designed to develop certain skills. Adding on elicits related ideas or connecting ideas already discussed.

Why Is It Important? Adding on occurs often in natural conversation and gives students practice contributing their own ideas to a discussion. It may also encourage reluctant speakers to join without the pressure of starting the discussion.

Make notes here about your annotations from each read.
You will refer to these notes later when you return to
your annotations. **Sample notes appear below.**

Key Ideas and Details:

Animal sanctuaries are safe places with shelter, food, and medical care.

Big cats often need sanctuaries. The cats may be abandoned or orphaned.

Good sanctuaries also try to help save endangered species.

Language and Text Structure:

important words = "sanctuary," "orphaned," and "donation"

List of questions in paragraph 6: If answer to all is "yes," that shows the

sanctuary is doing a good job.

Connections and Inferences:

Some sanctuaries have failed or been shut down because they treat the

animals badly, so sanctuaries need to be monitored.

I can conclude that it takes a lot of money to care for these animals.

Unit 2 • 41

Copyright © by William H. Sadlier, Inc. All rights reserved.

How Do I Use It? Use adding on during a first read or brainstorming portion of the lesson to draw out students' ideas. To formalize the discussion and keep it on topic, call on individuals (whole class/small group) or assign turns (small group/partner). Help students build on ideas already discussed with questions such as, *What is your response to what Kira said? Do you have an idea that is different from Dennis's? Did you have a similar or different response to the same statement?*

Save Our Big Cats!

2nd READ

Set a Purpose

Students will examine the author's use of language.

Text-Dependent Questions

1. What is the effect of the repetition of *care* in the text? (It emphasizes the goal of sanctuaries.)

2. How does the author describe the sanctuaries and the animals in them? (*Safe, care,* and *support* describe the sanctuaries and *sick, injured,* and *abandoned* show why cats need the sanctuaries.)

Partner Talk Have students discuss examples of academic vocabulary in the text.

3rd READ

Set a Purpose

Students will read to determine the main message of the text.

Text-Dependent Questions

1. How is the care provided by sanctuaries similar or different to the care people provide for pets? (Sanctuaries treat animals kindly by giving them food, shelter, and care, like pet owners do. Paragraph 7 says one big cat sanctuary does not allow visitors to pet the big cats because they are not pets.)

2. Why don't big cats make good pets? (I can infer that because they have "big teeth" and are "oversized" they are too large and possibly dangerous to have as pets.)

Partner Talk Have students explain the things a big cat might need that a pet might not.

Unit 2 • 41

Respond to Reading

You may want to check students' understanding by having them complete page 42 in the Student Worktext.

1. Have students refer to the first few paragraphs and review the explanation of what sanctuaries are and why they are needed to fill out the graphic organizer.

2. Have students use the information they recorded on their graphic organizers to explain how people care for big cats.

3. Refer students to pages 12 and 13 of Getting Started to help them write their individual summaries.

Have students work independently to answer the questions on page 42 of their Worktexts.

COLLABORATE When finished, have students exchange summaries with their partners and review each other's summaries. Remind pairs that when they review and discuss their partners' summaries, they should consider whether or not the summary has the following elements:

- contains only important information

- answers as many of the following as possible: Who? What? When? Where? and How?

REFLECT Have students use their own descriptive words to explain their visualization.

Return to the TEXT

Respond to Reading: Save Our Big Cats!

Review the annotations and notes you made while reading "Save Our Big Cats!" Think about how your annotations can help you answer the questions.

1. Use information from the text to complete the graphic organizer.

Why Big Cats Need Sanctuaries	How Sanctuaries Care for Big Cats
Sample answer: abandoned by pet owners orphaned in the wild sent away by circuses or zoos	Sample answer: provide a safe home, food, and open space give medical and dental care fight poaching and illegal trade

2. Use your graphic organizer to explain what problems big cats have and how sanctuaries help them.

Sample answer: Big cats need homes when they are abandoned by owners, orphaned in the wild, or are no longer used in circuses and zoos. Good sanctuaries give big cats a home, enough open space, a healthy diet, and medical care. The sanctuaries fight for species conservation and against poaching.

3. Write a short summary of "Save Our Big Cats!"

Sample answer: Animal sanctuaries are safe places where people can care for animals that are abandoned or orphaned. Good sanctuaries feed their animals well, give them enough space, and support protecting endangered species.

REFLECT What words, phrases, or sections did you visualize to understand the text better?

Sample answer: After reading "If they are sick or injured, animal doctors called veterinarians, or vets, care for them," I visualized the way doctors care for patients to understand how a veterinarian might care for an animal.

PROFESSIONAL DEVELOPMENT

Intertextual Analysis: Compare and Contrast Authors' Perspectives

What Is It? An effective way to analyze more than one text is to focus on the authors' perspectives. A perspective, or point of view, is the author's way of looking at the world. We compare authors' perspectives by considering their life experiences and the times in which they lived, and by analyzing language for the attitudes it reveals.

Why Is It Important? An author's perspective determines many aspects of a text, such as purpose, word choice, and arguments. Asking questions such as *What is the author's attitude? How does he or she feel about _____?* may help

Comprehension Check: Save Our Big Cats!

Answer the questions to demonstrate an understanding of what the text means.

1. What is the author's purpose for writing this text? Provide text evidence to support your answer.

   Sample answer: The author wants readers to know that not all animals have

   nice lives, and they "often need rescue groups." In paragraph 1, the author

   describes an animal sanctuary as a "safe place" for animals. In a sanctuary,

   animals receive shelter, food, and medicine if they need it.

2. What does the author want you to understand about why people create and maintain animal sanctuaries? What information from the text supports your answer?

   Sample answer: The author wants us to understand that people create the

   sanctuaries to solve the problem of how to care for animals that need care, but

   do not get it. Paragraphs 3 and 4 say animals may need safe places for many

   different reasons. For example, rescued animals may be "abandoned pets,"

   "orphaned in the wild," or are "no longer wanted."

3. What inference can you make about the people who work at animal sanctuaries? Provide text evidence to support your answer.

   Sample answer: I can infer that the people who work at sanctuaries love the

   animals. They work to stop the things that cause animals to need sanctuaries,

   like capturing wild animals and "the outlawed trade in animal products." Also,

   these veterinarians take care of the animals for free so they must care about

   the animals.

Stop and Assess

Use the following rubrics to assess your students' understanding of the text.

Item 1 answers indicate:	
2	a purpose of explaining the benefits of sanctuaries, with adequate text support.
1	a purpose of describing sanctuaries, with some text support.
0	no understanding of purpose, with no text support.

Item 2 answers indicate:	
2	why some animals lack care, creating a need for sanctuaries, with specific text support.
1	why some animals need sanctuaries, with some text support.
0	no understanding of why people create sanctuaries, with no text support.

Item 3 answers indicate:	
2	an inference that people are kind, generous, and understand animal needs, with text evidence.
1	an inference that people are kind, with some text evidence.
0	no inference about the people at sanctuaries, and no text evidence.

readers draw inferences from the author's statements to better understand the text.

How Do I Use It? *Black Beauty* and "Save Our Big Cats!" describe ways people treat animals with kindness. However, the two texts approach the topic using very different techniques and perspectives. Use graphic organizers, such as Venn diagrams, to help students isolate and compare details in order to make larger comparisons. Have students compare word choice (such as adjectives), details the authors chose to include, intended audiences, and tone. Students can draw conclusions about authors' perspectives from these details.

Return to the Focus Question

Explain to students that they will fill out a graphic organizer that will help them answer the Focus Question: What are the different ways people care for animals?

CONNECT TEXTS Have small groups of students discuss how each text they read helps them answer the Focus Question. Have small groups share and compare their discussion notes with another small group.

Scaffolded Support You may provide the following sentence frames to support students in their use of academic language:

> In the text _____, the author/photographer makes the point that _____. He/she does this by _____.

Remind students to use their annotations and summaries to support their answers. They can also reread portions of the texts, if necessary.

Have students complete their graphic organizers individually and then answer the Focus Question.

REFLECT Remind students that each text is about relationships between people and animals. Ask, *How did reading the texts give you a greater understanding of the different ways people care for animals?*

ANALYZE and SYNTHESIZE ACROSS TEXTS

Return to the Focus Question: What are the different ways people care for animals?

Review your answers to questions about the texts as well as your annotations and Annotation Notes. Think about the discussions you've had about the texts. How does that information help you answer the Focus Question?

Use the graphic organizer to organize information about the texts.

1. In the boxes, record the details from each text that help you answer the Focus Question.

2. Make connections between those details to help you answer the Focus Question. Write your answer in the box provided.

Black Beauty
Sample answer: by being kind and gentle and providing food and shelter

Girl Feeding Lambs in a Barn (Visual Text)
Sample answer: by feeding and petting them and by liking them

Save Our Big Cats!
Sample answer: by creating safe places for animals needing shelter, medical care, and food

What are the different ways people care for animals?
Sample answer: People care for animals by showing kindness and gentleness. They can give animals shelter and food and medical care if they need it. They also create sanctuaries and take action to save endangered species.

REFLECT How did making connections between the three texts help you to answer the Focus Question?

Sample answer: There are many ways people can care for animals. The Visual Text

and Text 1 show how people can treat animals kindly with gentleness and respect.

Text 2 showed how sanctuaries help animals that need food, shelter, and care.

PROFESSIONAL DEVELOPMENT

Intertextual Analysis: Citing Evidence from Multiple Texts

What Is It? When analyzing across texts, students must cite text evidence from each text in order to adequately support conclusions.

Why Is It Important? Continually citing text evidence gives students practice returning to the text and providing support for claims and arguments. Citing every text ensures that students do not draw conclusions that are only supported by one or a few texts. Additional text evidence can also introduce nuances and variations of conclusions or ideas.

Writing About the Focus Question

Now that you have answered the Focus Question using all three texts, develop your ideas into a longer piece of writing.

USE EVIDENCE

- Explain the different ways people care for animals. Use at least one piece of evidence from each text to support your answer.
- If you need more room, use additional paper.

MONITOR

- Use the Writing Checklist as you work to make sure your writing has all of the important pieces of information.
- Use the rubric on page 46 when you have completed your first draft to help you evaluate, revise, and edit your work.

Unit 2 • 45

WRITING CHECKLIST ✔

Does my writing . . .

☐ answer the Focus Question?

☐ provide text evidence to support my ideas?

☐ have a clear beginning, middle, and end?

☐ use correct language, spelling, and conventions?

Writing About the Focus Question

USE EVIDENCE Remind students that they should use their graphic organizers as well as their annotations in the texts to write their responses.

Allow students to revisit the texts as frequently as they need to in order to support comprehension and to respond to the Focus Question.

MONITOR After students have completed their responses, have them review the Writing Checklist and revise their writing responses.

DIFFERENTIATE AND EXTEND

In addition to or instead of the writing response, consider having students complete one of the following assignments:

Write Beyond Have students assume the role of a big cat at a sanctuary and have them write thank you notes to a caregiver.

Read Beyond Have students read the full text of *Black Beauty* or another novel about the lives of animals.

Conduct an Interview Have students write a list of questions they would ask a person who works at an animal shelter, veterinarian's office, or sanctuary about how he or she cares for animals.

Create a Visual Text Have students choose an animal from one of the three texts and create a graphic that explains how to best care for it.

How Do I Use It? When giving feedback or asking for text evidence, use a checklist of all the texts under consideration. Continue asking for text evidence until every text has been checked off. Citing text evidence can also be a collaborative effort. Partners or small groups can divide texts among individuals. Combining the contributions into one argument or conclusion ensures that all texts will be considered. It will also provide for multiple perspectives in the analysis.

Unit 2 • 45

SELF-ASSESS and REFLECT

SELF-ASSESS Have students use the Writing Rubric on page 46 to self-assess their writing response. Tell them to assign themselves a score from 1–4 (with "4" being the highest) for each category in the first column.

REFLECT Use the Writing Rubric on Student Worktext page 46 to assess each student's writing. Record points for each category in the first column of the rubric. Have students remove the page from their Student Worktexts and place it in their writing portfolios, along with the drafts and final versions of their responses.

SELF-ASSESS and REFLECT

Focus Question What are the different ways people care for animals?

This is the rubric that your teacher will use to assess your writing. Refer to it as you revise your work. After you have finished your final version, review your writing and record your points for each category on the "Student" line in the first column.

	Accomplished (4 points)	Competent (3 points)	Developing (2 points)	Beginning (1 point)
RESPONSE Score: Student _____ Teacher _____	The response answers the question effectively and with insight.	The response answers the question effectively.	The response partially responds to the question but does not adequately address it.	The response addresses the texts but does not address the question.
ORGANIZATION Score: Student _____ Teacher _____	The main idea is convincingly stated. Ideas are organized in cohesive paragraphs that support the main idea.	The main idea is clearly stated. Ideas are organized in logical paragraphs.	The main idea is weak. Ideas are organized in a somewhat logical and cohesive way.	The main idea is missing. The organization of the paragraphs is not logical.
TEXT EVIDENCE Score: Student _____ Teacher _____	Response includes more than one piece of appropriate text evidence from each text. Evidence supports the main idea in a thorough way.	Response includes one piece of text evidence from each text. Evidence supports the main idea clearly.	Response does not include at least one piece of text evidence from each text. Text evidence does not adequately support the main idea.	Response does not contain relevant evidence.
LANGUAGE Score: Student _____ Teacher _____	Writing includes precise and sophisticated vocabulary related to the topic.	Writing includes appropriate vocabulary related to the topic.	Writing includes imprecise and inaccurate vocabulary.	Writing does not include vocabulary that appropriately reflects the topic of the response.
SPELLING AND CONVENTIONS Score: Student _____ Teacher _____	Response includes correct spelling, grammar, and punctuation consistently.	Response includes mostly correct spelling, grammar, and punctuation.	Response has many errors in spelling, grammar, and punctuation.	Response's errors in spelling, grammar, and punctuation make it extremely difficult to understand the response.

UNIT 3

Focus Question How are things that live in an ecosystem connected?

Texts for Close Reading

Unit 3 • 47

GENRE STUDY

Discuss with students the genres of "10 Interesting Things About Ecosystems" and "On Frogless Pond."

Remind students that *genre* refers to the format and features of a text and typically falls into one of two categories—literature or informational text. Literature is a creative work that doesn't necessarily rely on facts, and informational text contains factual information. Both texts in this unit are informational. A fact sheet is an explanatory text that consists of a list of facts and supporting information about a specific topic. An explanatory text presents information about a topic in greater depth. With the class, list the features of fact sheets and explanatory texts. Have students identify the characteristics shared by these subgenres and those that differ.

Focus Question

Have students read the Focus Question on Worktext page 47. Tell them that the texts and illustrations in this unit will help them answer this question.

Texts for Close Reading

Have students read to themselves the descriptions of the texts in this unit.

There is no need to explain what students should expect to find in their close readings or to do any preteaching about the subject matter.

TEXT COMPLEXITY

Food Chain
- Style: diagrammatic
- Knowledge demands: medium
- Levels of meaning: literal/ inferential

10 Interesting Things
Quantitative: 760L
Qualitative
- Structure: conventional
- Language: academic
- Knowledge demands: medium
- Levels of meaning: literal

On Frogless Pond
Quantitative: 780L
Qualitative
- Structure: conventional and diagrammatic
- Language: familiar
- Knowledge demands: medium
- Levels of meaning: literal

Unit 3 • 47

Food Chain

Set a Purpose

Explain to students that they will look at the image on page 48 to begin to gain a deeper understanding of how things living in an ecosystem are connected.

Visual Text Analysis

Remind students that an image can be analyzed as a text by looking at its details and making inferences. Direct students' attention to the image on Student Worktext page 48.

Encourage students to annotate the Visual Text. Suggest they use arrows, labels, circles, margin notes, and other markings to highlight details that will help them gain a better understanding of the meaning of the image.

1. Have students record their first impressions about the image. Lead them to discuss as a whole class, in small groups, or with a partner what they think is being shown in the diagram.

2. Encourage students to make note of the details that support their observations in question 1. Encourage them to identify the individual organisms shown in the diagram and to consider what the arrows indicate. If students miss them, point out the red-and-green shapes below the mushrooms and have students suggest what they might be. Have students explain as a whole class, in small groups, or with a partner what details they noted and what those details might tell them about the connections between things living in an ecosystem.

3. Guide students to synthesize all the details they see in the diagram to draw conclusions about the artist's message.

Food Chain

Look at this Visual Text, and make annotations on the image. Review the image or parts of the image as many times as necessary to answer the following questions.

1. What is your first impression of what's going on in this diagram?

Sample answer: A series of images show the food chain in nature. A grasshopper feeds on grass. That grasshopper is eaten by a mouse, and the mouse is eaten by a snake. Finally, a large bird of prey eats the snake. All of them are connected to the mushrooms in some way.

PROFESSIONAL DEVELOPMENT

Visual Text: ELL

What Is It? Visual Text analysis requires identifying an image's details, subject, structural components, meaning, and purpose.

Why Is It Important? Visual Texts allow ELL students to apply close-reading techniques and analytical thinking without a language barrier. However, Visual Text analysis will present challenges to ELL students, as they will be expected to express and support ideas about the images in English.

How Do I Use It? The accessibility of a Visual Text may give ELL students greater confidence. Elicit responses that allow them to "translate" visual impressions into the English

2. What details in the diagram help give you that impression?

Sample answer: There are arrows going from one thing to another. The grass has
an arrow going toward the insect. The insect has an arrow going to the rodent, the
rodent has an arrow going toward the snake. The snake has an arrow going to the
bird. They each depend on the other for survival.

I don't know what the arrows pointing to the mushrooms mean. Maybe the
mushrooms depend on all of these species for survival.

3. What do you conclude is the message of the diagram?

Sample answer: The message is that everything living in the ecosystem is connected.
Different species depend on each other to survive. They are linked in a chain.

Text-Dependent Questions

As necessary, encourage discussion
with such prompts as:

1. What do you notice about the
arrows in the diagram? (Sample
answer: The arrows connect each plant
or animal with the living thing that
eats it. For example, the arrow pointing from the plants to the grasshopper shows that the grasshopper eats
the plants.)

2. How is the grasshopper connected to the snake? (Sample
answer: The grasshopper is eaten by
the mouse, which is then eaten by
the snake. Even though they are not
directly connected by an arrow, the
grasshopper and the snake are connected in the food chain.)

3. What do you notice about the
mushrooms? (Sample answer: All of
the other living things in the diagram
are connected to the mushrooms.
They all must feed the mushrooms in
some way.)

4. What do you predict will happen if the grass is removed from
this food chain? (Sample answer: If
the grass is removed, the grasshoppers
will have nothing to eat and die. If the
grasshoppers die, the mice will lose
a food source, and so on through the
food chain.)

expression with which they are most comfortable. Pair ELL
students with native English speakers to encourage the former
to express complex thoughts using basic English. Use the
Visual Text on Student Worktext page 48 as an opportunity to
model and reinforce the academic language of text analysis.
Provide models or sentence frames to give students practice
with terms such as *diagram, details, composition, style,
purpose,* and *audience.* For example: *The directions of the
arrows in the diagram indicate* _____ . Understanding the
diagram fully will also rely on knowledge of content-specific
vocabulary that you might introduce to ELL students briefly
at this point: *ecosystem, energy, food chain.*

10 Interesting Things

Tell students that they will read to learn about the connections between things living in an ecosystem.

1st READ

Set a Purpose

Explain to students that they will read to get a general understanding of what the text is about.

Have students read "10 Interesting Things About Ecosystems" independently, annotating the text as they read. Remind students that suggested annotation symbols appear on page 8 of the Getting Started with Close Reading unit. Circulate and observe students' markings and notes, especially questions and anything they found confusing. The observations and annotations may be used to inform instruction. Based on students' needs, you may want to meet with them in small groups.

Use the Text-Dependent Questions to prompt students to engage with the text.

Text-Dependent Questions

1. What is this text about? (This fact sheet is about the different kinds of ecosystems around the world.)

Scaffolded Support Use the following scaffolded question and sentence frame as necessary to support comprehension.

> What is being described in this fact sheet?
>
> Ecosystems are found _____ .

> ✔ **Self-Monitoring Strategies** can help you check your understanding and clarify a text. Use them as you read.
>
> ☐ Visualize.   ☐ Ask yourself questions.   ☐ Draw conclusions.   ☐ Reread to clarify.

Read this fact sheet to learn about the connections between things living in an ecosystem. Make annotations as you read. You may want to review Annotating a Text on page 8.
Sample annotations appear throughout the text.

10 Interesting Things About Ecosystems

1   **Coral reefs are beautiful and fragile.** Coral reefs are busy underwater ecosystems. Some people call them the "rainforests of the sea." The corals look like rocks but are animals with hard skeletons. They **?** form a base for many organisms to live. You'll find crabs, sea stars, worms, clams, sponges, jellyfish, sea turtles, and lots of fish. Coral reefs are very fragile and easily affected by pollution.

2   **Half the world's species live in tropical rain forests.** Tropical rain forests are near the equator. Because it's warm and wet, there are lots of lush plants and trees. Half of the world's species live in these busy **?** ecosystems. Many kinds of plants, animals, fungi, and microscopic organisms live here and nowhere else. The plants in tropical rain forests produce 40 percent of Earth's oxygen.

3   **To live in the desert, you have to save water.** The world's deserts have little rain and are very dry. Here, living things have ways of finding and saving water. Cactuses store water. They can live without rain for months. The kangaroo mouse gets all its water from the seeds it eats.

4   **!** **Grasslands are all around.** Every continent except Antarctica has grasslands. These are areas with medium rainfall. Tall grasses, herbs, and flowers are all mixed together. Grasslands are home to lots of different species that live in the soil, feed on the grass, or eat the animals that eat the grass. In the United States, that could be buffalos and cows. In Africa, it's gazelles, lions, and elephants.

PROFESSIONAL DEVELOPMENT

Layered Questions: Scaffolding

What Is It? Layered questions are a series of Text-Dependent Questions related to the same topic. The first layered question requires a surface understanding, such as a general understanding of what the text is about. Next, ask students to identify key details of information needed to arrive at a deeper understanding. The intent is to support the student so that he or she can answer the original Text-Dependent Question.

Make notes here about your annotations from each read. You will refer to these notes later when you return to your annotations. **Sample notes appear below.**

ANNOTATION NOTES

Key Ideas and Details:

There are many very different kinds of ecosystems on Earth. Coral reefs are located underwater. Corals are actually animals. Tropical rain forests are warm and wet. There are many animals here that can't be found anywhere else. Forty percent of Earth's oxygen is produced here. Deserts are very dry with little rain. Every continent except Antarctica has grasslands.

Language and Text Structure:

fragile, organisms, lush, microscopic—use context to figure out meaning

Connections and Inferences:

Many animals live in unexpected or unusual places. The ways that animals relate to where they live are very interesting!

Unit 3 • 51

2. What are some of the key details each paragraph includes? (Sample answer: Most of the paragraphs describe the weather, animal life, and vegetation in each of the ecosystems.)

3. How is the kangaroo mouse able to survive in its harsh ecosystem? (Sample answer: Paragraph 3 says the kangaroo mouse lives in the desert, where there is very little water. The mouse gets all the water it needs from the seeds it eats.)

Think Aloud *I'm confused by the idea that corals "form a base" where "lots of other organisms" live. How can living creatures form a place where other creatures live? I'll reread paragraph 1 to see if I can get a better understanding. I see that "corals look like rocks" and "have hard skeletons." Now I understand that, even though they are alive, corals are hard enough that plants and animals can live on and around their bodies.*

Partner Talk Have partners review together the locations and the animals found in each of the ecosystems mentioned in the fact sheet.

Why Is It Important? Layered Text-Dependent Questions provide a scaffold for students to answer questions about the text that they cannot answer on their own. Layered questions model how to think through a difficult question by breaking up a complex idea into easier-to-manage chunks.

How Do I Use It? When students are unable to answer a question about the text, ask several focused layered questions related to the question. For example, to support students in answering Text-Dependent Question 3 on this page, begin with a question that requires a basic understanding, such as, *What is life like in the desert?* Next, you might ask, *How have living things adapted to survive in the desert?*

10 Interesting Things

2nd READ

Set a Purpose

Students will return to "10 Interesting Things About Ecosystems" to understand the text structure and the effects of the language used in the text.

Text-Dependent Questions

1. How does the organization of the text help you understand its meaning? **(Each paragraph follows a boldfaced sentence that states a fact about an ecosystem. The text in each paragraph gives more information about the fact in bold.)**

2. What is the tone of this text? What language creates the tone? **(The text has more than one tone. Scientific words like *ecosystems, organism, species*, and *microscopic* give it a serious and educational tone. The text also uses informal phrases like "lots of" and "all mixed together" and contractions like "it's" instead of "it is," so the text doesn't sound like a textbook.)**

3. Vocabulary: Multiple-Meaning Word Discuss contextual meanings of words with more than one meaning in the text.

Paragraph 9: What does *needles* mean in this context? What words or phrases in the item are clues to its meaning? **(*Needles* means "sharp, short, and stiff leaves." The clues are "green all year-round" and "instead of leaves." Pine and fir trees have needle-like leaves instead of large, flat leaves like the leaves on an oak tree.)**

Partner Talk Have partners identify academic language used in the text and discuss how it contributed to their understanding.

5   **Freshwater ecosystems have rare species.** Ponds, lakes, streams, and rivers are home to lots of different species that can't live in salty ocean water. There are freshwater ecosystems all over the world. They are home to some amazing creatures. There are many kinds of frogs, fish, insects, and microscopic organisms like amoebas. And there are rare species like river dolphins in Asia and South America, beavers in North America and Europe, and platypuses in Australia.

6   ! **In the tundra, life is tough.** In the tundra, it feels like winter all the time. Tundra occurs near the north and south poles of our planet: the Arctic tundra and the Antarctic tundra. There is also alpine tundra at the top of the world's tallest mountains. It's a hard place to live. In the Arctic tundra, there are polar bears, foxes, and reindeer. In the Antarctic tundra, there are seals and penguins resting on the shores between swims in the ocean.

7   **The bottom of the ocean has thriving communities.** At the bottom of
?   the ocean, there are small underwater volcanoes. They spew scalding hot water, gases, and chemicals. They're called hydrothermal vents. It's a dark place to live, but some animals love it there. Giant tube worms over six feet long, clams, and shrimp call these vents home.

8   **Wetlands are home to baby fish.** Swamps, marshes, and bogs are types of wetlands. Wetlands can have freshwater, salt water, or a mixture of both. They are home to lots of different aquatic plants and animals. Fish, frogs, alligators, and crocodiles lay eggs here. It's a great place for the babies to hatch and grow. They are also home to many different kinds of insects.

9   ? **Boreal forests are home to lots of trees.** Much of North America, Europe, and Asia are in a temperate region, between the Arctic and subtropics. Here, the weather is generally not too hot, not too cold. There are also distinct seasons. There are many big forests. The trees here are green all year-round and have needles instead of leaves. Animals like bears, porcupines, and eagles make homes in these vast forests.

10 **There are ecosystems even in big cities.** Big cities around the world have interesting ecosystems too. There are many animals that share living spaces with people. Raccoons, coyotes, opossums, skunks, foxes, and birds are common neighbors. In some places, people build special bridges over roads for animals. It lets them move between places without getting hurt.

PROFESSIONAL DEVELOPMENT

Self-Monitoring Strategies: Drawing Conclusions

What Is It? A conclusion is a reasoned judgment. It differs from an observation, which is simply a recognition or restatement of an existing idea, and an inference, which is an assumption drawn from existing facts and/or background knowledge. A conclusion is a logical next thought or a rational interpretation. Conclusions can differ, depending on the general knowledge, life experiences, and prejudices of the reader.

Why Is It Important? Drawing conclusions enables readers to extend the facts presented in a text, to predict possible outcomes of events, to connect concepts, to identify details

Make notes here about your annotations from each read. You will refer to these notes later when you return to your annotations. Sample notes appear below.

ANNOTATION NOTES

Key Ideas and Details:

Special ecosystems include freshwater ecosystems, the tundra, the

bottom of the ocean, wetlands, boreal forests—and even big cities!

Language and Text Structure:

"Scalding" must mean something like "very hot."

"Aquatic" must have something to do with water.

"Temperate" means "not too hot and not too cold."

Connections and Inferences:

Ecosystems have many surprises. Who would guess there are so many

animals living at the bottom of the ocean? I was amazed that many

animals can live right in the middle of big cities.

Unit 3 • 53

---

10 Interesting Things

3rd READ

Set a Purpose

Students will read to draw inferences from the text and make connections.

Text-Dependent Questions

1. What inference can you draw about why a large number of animal species live in tropical rain forests? (Paragraph 2 says rain forests have "lots of lush plants and trees" that provide places to live and food for all those different species.)

2. What connection can you make between tropical rain forests and grasslands? (Paragraph 2 says rain forests are only near the equator, and paragraph 4 says grasslands are everywhere. In both places the plants the animals depend on for food are dependent on the amount of rain that falls in the area.)

3. What connections can you make between paragraph 4 and the Visual Text? (The Visual Text shows how living things in a food chain are connected. Paragraph 4 explains how species in the grassland ecosystem "live in the soil, feed on the grass, or eat the animals that eat the grass.")

Think Aloud *As I read paragraph 6, I asked myself how the animals living in the tundra adapted to the "tough" life there. I visualized some of the animals mentioned and they all have very thick fur. So, many tundra animals have adapted to the cold by growing fur to keep warm.*

Partner Talk Ask students to discuss how making inferences helped them to understand the text's central message.

Unit 3 • 53

---

that are missing from the text, and to analyze unspoken assumptions in the text.

How Do I Use It? Consistently require students to provide evidence for their conclusions about a text. For example, in discussing the challenges of urban ecosystems for animals, students might conclude that many animals living in cities are endangered by cars and trucks even more than animals in the country are. Encourage students to support this conclusion with text evidence. Ask, *What sentence made you think that?* In discussion of paragraph 10, draw attention to the purpose of the special bridges over roads for animals. Ask, *How do people know where a bridge just for animals is needed?* Record and discuss students' conclusions.

Respond to Reading

You may want to check students' understanding by having them complete page 54 in the Student Worktext.

1. Remind students that a summary should only include the key ideas and details essential to understanding what the text is about. Point out that they can use the graphic organizer on Student Worktext page 54 to capture and organize those key ideas and details. The graphic organizer should then guide them in writing their summaries.

2. Refer students to pages 12 and 13 in Getting Started to help them write their individual summaries.

Have students work independently to answer the questions on page 54 of their Worktexts.

COLLABORATE Have students exchange their final summaries with their partners and review each other's summaries. Remind pairs that when they review and discuss their partners' summaries, they should consider whether or not the summary has the following elements:

- contains only important information
- answers as many of the following as possible: Who? What? When? Where? and How?

REFLECT Have students share the sections of the text they reread to improve their understanding.

Return to the TEXT

Respond to Reading: 10 Interesting Things About Ecosystems

Review the annotations and notes you made while reading "10 Interesting Things About Ecosystems." Think about how they can help you understand the text.

1. Use this Summary Chart to help you summarize the text.

Summary Chart		
	Informational Text	
Who?	the people or subjects	plants and animals
What?	the topic or problem	different kinds of ecosystems
Where?	the location or region where the events occur	all over the planet
When?	the date, year, or time	the present
How?	the events, steps, or process	Hot, cold, rainy, or dry weather make some ecosystems right for some animals and plants.

2. Use the completed graphic organizer from Item 1 to help you write a summary of "10 Interesting Things About Ecosystems."

Sample answer: There are many different ecosystems on Earth. Ecosystems have many different plants and animals all in the same area. Animals live in tough places, like the tundra and the bottom of the ocean. Different kinds of weather make ecosystems right for certain plants and animals.

REFLECT In the text, where did you reread in order to improve your understanding?

Sample answer: I had to reread paragraph 7 to understand "hydrothermal vents." I was able to imagine them as small underwater volcanoes.

PROFESSIONAL DEVELOPMENT

Collaboration: Partner Discussion

What Is It? Working with partners allows for a brief, planned conversation between pairs of students on a specific topic. Partner discussions can be a response to either a question or a prompt.

Why Is It Important? Working with a partner allows for short-term sharing in a setting that can be less stressful than whole-class or small-group speaking. It also allows for targeted peer interaction in which partners who have a deeper understanding of the text to work with partners whose comprehension is not as advanced. It provides an opportunity for collaboration between partners with different levels of language or thinking skills.

Comprehension Check: 10 Interesting Things About Ecosystems

Answer the questions to demonstrate an understanding of what the text means.

1. How does the photograph support the author's claim in paragraph 1 that coral reefs are "beautiful and fragile"? Give evidence from the text to support your answer.

   Sample answer: The hard skeletons of coral reefs "form a base for many organisms to live." Reefs are fragile because they are "easily affected by pollution." The photograph shows what coral looks like and all the jellyfish and fish that they attract. The colorful reef is very beautiful. I understand how pollution would destroy its beauty and harm the animals.

2. What inferences can you make about how life in the tundra (paragraph 6) might be similar to life in the desert (paragraph 3)? Cite at least two examples of text evidence that support your answer.

   Sample answer: In both these ecosystems, animals face tough challenges. Paragraph 3 says deserts are "very dry" and animals must have "ways of finding and saving water." In the tundra, it is so cold that "it feels like winter all the time." Paragraph 6 says it is "a hard place to live." It must be hard to find food and water in both ecosystems.

3. What does the author want us to understand about the different places where animals live on Earth? Give at least two pieces of text evidence to support your answer.

   Sample answer: By using bold subheadings, the author wants us to understand that the differences between these places make them interesting. We also need to understand the ways in which animals adapt to their surroundings. For example, raccoons, bears, and water animals adapt to the different ecosystems they call home, such as big cities, boreal forests, and wetlands.

Stop and Assess

Use the following rubrics to assess your students' understanding of the text.

	Item 1 answers indicate:
2	how the photo supports the description of coral reefs in the text. Two pieces of text evidence support the answer.
1	some understanding of how the photo supports the text, but text evidence supports only part of the answer.
0	no understanding of how the photograph supports the text, without any relevant text evidence.

	Item 2 answers indicate:
2	inferences about how life in the tundra and desert are difficult. Two pieces of text evidence are cited to support the claim.
1	only what the text states explicitly and don't include inferences.
0	no understanding of how life in the tundra and life in the desert are similar, and no relevant text evidence is cited.

	Item 3 answers indicate:
2	that each ecosystem is different and that animals have adapted to survive in each. Two pieces of evidence support the answer.
1	that each ecosystem is different but not that animals have adapted to survive in each. Insufficient text evidence supports the answer.
0	no understanding of what the text says about ecosystems and the animals that live in them. No relevant text evidence provided.

How Do I Use It? For summary review, pair partners with varied skill levels. Remind students how to use academic language while providing constructive feedback. Then, have students take turns sharing their reviews. Encourage students to point out strengths in each other's summaries, as well as what needs revision. Circulate to ensure that students are taking proper turns and contributing fairly. You can observe partner discussions as an ongoing informal assessment.

On Frogless Pond

Students will read an explanatory text and diagram to learn more about the way ecosystems work.

Read this explanatory text and diagram to learn more about the way ecosytems work. Make annotations as you read. You may make different annotations each time you read.
Sample annotations and notes appear throughout the text.

On Frogless Pond

1   Everything is connected in an ecosystem. The diagram shows some connections between residents living in or near a pond. Groups of
?   animals and plants are linked in a web. Any sudden changes in this web of relationships may upset the balance of nature.

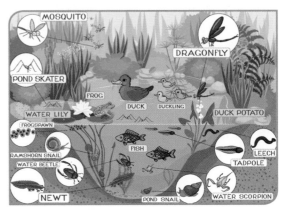

Pond Ecosystem

2   Take the frog shown near the left side of the diagram, for example. Frogs
?   and their tadpole offspring have become less and less common. Scientists are not sure about all the reasons why. Diseases, pollution, pesticides, and climate change may all play a role. What happens to the ecosystem of a frogless pond? For example, tadpoles help to control algae with their eating habits. Algae are plantlike growths in the water. Think pond slime! Without tadpoles, more algae will grow and spoil the pond for fish and ducks. Adult frogs also help. They eat lots of insect pests. Frogs and tadpoles are also important food for birds, snakes, fish, and other animals.

3   Finally, let's remember that human beings are probably also part of the ecosystem at most ponds. Without frogs in that ecosystem, we would lose the benefits that frogs give us for education and natural beauty.

Set a Purpose

Explain to students that they will read to find out what "On Frogless Pond" is about.

Have students read "On Frogless Pond" independently, annotating the text as they read. Remind students that suggested annotation symbols appear on page 8 of the Getting Started with Close Reading unit. Circulate and observe students' markings, especially questions and anything they found confusing. The observations and annotations may be used to inform instruction. Based on students' needs, you may want to meet with them in small groups.

Text-Dependent Questions

1. What are the text and diagram about? (The text and diagram are about a pond's ecosystem.)

2. What happens when frogs disappear from a pond's ecosystem? (Paragraph 2 says that without frogs, insects grow in number, and animals that eat frogs have less food.)

Think Aloud *I can add lines to the picture to visualize connections between some of the organisms. I see a line between the frog and the mosquito because frogs eat insects. I see another line between the fish and the tadpole because the fish eat tadpoles.*

Partner Talk Have students identify the organisms in the diagram.

PROFESSIONAL DEVELOPMENT

Annotations: Key Words and Phrases

What Is It? Annotations are marks that students make as they read the text, such as highlighting, underlining, and circling key words. Students add annotations in layers as they read and reread.

Why Is It Important? Making annotations helps keep students' attention focused on specific words. They can mark places of confusion, note questions to ask, or write their own reactions to text information. Making their own marks on a page makes the reading experience personal.

Make notes here about your annotations from each read.
You will refer to these notes later when you return to
your annotations. Sample notes appear below.

Key Ideas and Details:

For many reasons, frogs are becoming less common. If frogs are removed

from a pond ecosystem, algae and insect pests may get out of control and spoil

the pond for fish and ducks. Birds, snakes, and fish will have to go without

some of their favorite food. Humans will not have frogs for education and

beauty.

Language and Text Structure:

"residents," "web," and "offspring"— Context helped me to figure out the

meanings of these words.

Diagram shows what is being described in the text.

Connections and Inferences:

If one part of an ecosystem changes, the whole web will change—like

the food chain diagram that showed that each animal depends on

another to survive.

How Do I Use It? As you introduce "On Frogless Pond," model
how to annotate. Read paragraph 1 aloud and circle the
phrase "balance of nature." Think aloud to demonstrate that
annotations can be used to keep track of questions and key
terms. *The text says that when sudden changes happen in an
ecosystem, the "balance of nature" can be upset. I'm not exactly
sure what "balance of nature" is, but I think it's important. So,
I'm going to circle the phrase and come back to it later to see
if I understand it better after I read the whole text.* Encourage
students to circle or list the many examples of domain-specific
language in this text (e.g. *ecosystem, pesticides, algae*) and
make sure they understand the terms' meanings.

On Frogless Pond

2nd READ

Set a Purpose
Students will examine how language and the diagram reveal meaning in this text.

Text-Dependent Questions
1. What is the tone of this text, and what language creates the tone? (The tone is informative but familiar. "Take the frog shown" and "let's remember" help readers feel they are in a conversation.)

2. How does the diagam help you understand the text? (The diagram shows how many organisms are part of the pond ecosystem, including ones the text doesn't mention.)

Partner Talk Have partners discuss ways in which the diagram builds on the information provided in the text.

3rd READ

Set a Purpose
Students will read to make inferences about the text.

Text-Dependent Questions
1. What is the "balance of nature"? (It is the balance between all the parts of an ecosystem that depend on each other.)

2. How does this text help you better understand the Visual Text? (The text explains how everything in an ecosystem is connected. I understand how and why the arrows connect the living things in the Visual Text.)

Partner Talk Have students discuss inferences they made while reading the text.

Respond to Reading

You may want to check students' understanding by having them complete page 58 in the Student Worktext.

1. Have students reread the text to identify causes for the decline in frog populations. Then have them reread the text to identify the effects of frog decline on a pond ecosystem. Students should use the information in the text to complete the graphic organizer.

2. Have students use the information they recorded on their graphic organizers to describe how information is organized in the text.

3. Refer students to pages 12 and 13 of Getting Started to help them write their individual summaries.

Have students work independently to answer the questions on page 58 of their Worktexts.

COLLABORATE When finished, have students exchange summaries with their partners and review each other's summaries. Remind pairs that when they review and discuss their partners' summaries, they should consider whether or not the summary has the following elements:

- contains only important information
- answers as many of the following as possible: Who? What? When? Where? and How?

REFLECT Suggest that students review their annotations and Annotation Notes to remind themselves when they visualized the text to aid their understanding.

Return to the TEXT

Respond to Reading: On Frogless Pond

Review the annotations and notes you made while reading "On Frogless Pond." Think about how your annotations can help you answer the questions.

1. Use information from the text and diagram to complete the graphic organizer.

Causes for Decline in Frog Numbers	Effects of Decline in Frog Numbers
Sample answer: diseases pollution pesticides climate change	Sample answer: buildup of algae too many insect pests less food for birds, snakes, fish fewer tadpoles

2. Use your graphic organizer to identify the way the author organizes the text.

Sample answer: The author organizes this text by cause and effect. The author explains in paragraph 2 reasons why there are fewer frogs. The author then explains the effects on the ecosystem of a frogless pond.

3. Write a short summary of "On Frogless Pond."

Sample answer: Everything in an ecosystem is connected. If there were no frogs or tadpoles in a pond, for example, algae and insect pests would build up. There would also be less food for birds, fish, and snakes.

REFLECT What words, phrases, or sections did you have to visualize to make sure you understood?

Sample answer: I visualized the buildup of algae in the pond, with the plants covering over the surface of the water.

PROFESSIONAL DEVELOPMENT

Classroom Management: Partner Work

What Is It? When you manage your classroom, you organize the flow of both work and students. One classroom management challenge is moving from whole-class instruction to partner work.

Why Is It Important? Partner discussions allow the teacher to circulate and give personal attention to more students. Partner work provides opportunities for students to teach each other.

How Do I Use It? Pair partners with varied skill levels. Assign a prompt—for example, the Collaborate activity on this page—and allow students time to think before responding.

Comprehension Check: On Frogless Pond

Answer the questions to demonstrate an understanding of what the text means.

1. What connection can you make between the diagram and the text about pond ecosystems? Provide text evidence to support your answer.

   Sample answer: The diagram shows what it says in paragraph 1, that "animals and plants are linked in a web." The diagram makes it clear that the animals include insects, birds, and fish. It shows where in a pond the plants and animals can be found and how they might be linked to each other.

2. How does the diagram support the information in paragraph 2 about tadpoles and their part in the ecosystem? Provide text evidence in your answer.

   Sample answer: The diagram shows how the tadpoles swim around among the pond vegetation. Paragraph 2 says tadpoles "control algae with their eating habits." If frogs disappear from the pond, there will be no tadpoles, and then lots of algae will "spoil the pond for fish and ducks."

3. What inference can you make about the role of human beings as part of the pond ecosystem? Provide text evidence to support your answer.

   Sample answer: According to the text, human beings are probably part of the ecosystem "at most ponds." Humans can damage a pond ecosystem by polluting and using pesticides. In paragraph 3, the author comments on how human beings might be affected by a frogless pond. I can infer that while humans are not portrayed in the diagram, there is a place for them in a pond ecosystem.

Unit 3 • 59

Stop and Assess

Use the following rubrics to assess your students' understanding of the text.

Item 1 answers indicate:	
2	that the diagram supports the text information that living things in a pond ecosystem are connected, with text evidence to support the answer.
1	that the diagram shows that all living things in a pond ecosystem are connected, but do not provide text evidence.
0	no understanding of what the text and diagram show about a pond's ecosystem, and no text evidence.

Item 2 answers indicate:	
2	that the diagram shows how tadpoles can prevent algae from building up and spoiling the pond for fish and ducks, with supporting text evidence.
1	that the diagram shows how tadpoles prevent algae from building up and spoiling the pond, but text evidence is inadequate.
0	a lack of understanding of the role tadpoles play in the pond's ecosystem, and don't cite any relevant text evidence.

Item 3 answers indicate:	
2	an inference about humans' role in a pond's ecosystem, with text evidence to support the claim.
1	an understanding that humans can affect a pond's ecosystem, with no text evidence to support the inference.
0	no understanding of humans' role in a pond's ecosystem and no text evidence.

Then, have students take turns explaining their ideas and/or suggestions, each allowing the other time to share his or her thoughts. Circulate to ensure that students are taking proper turns and contributing fairly.

If necessary, remind students of their goal: to review each other's summaries and offer suggestions on where the summary needs strengthening or revision.

Return to the Focus Question

Explain to students that they will fill out a graphic organizer that will help them answer the Focus Question: How are things that live in an ecosystem connected?

CONNECT TEXTS Have small groups of students discuss how each text they read helps them answer the Focus Question. Have small groups share and compare their discussion notes with another small group.

Scaffolded Support You may provide the following sentence frames to support students in their use of academic language:

> In the text _____, the author/artist makes the point that _____ . He/she does this by _____ .

Remind students to use their annotations and summaries to support their answers. They can also reread portions of the texts, if necessary.

Have students complete their graphic organizers individually and then answer the Focus Question.

REFLECT Remind students that each text provides different information about ecosystems. Ask, *How did reading all three texts give you a greater understanding of how things living in an ecosystem are connected?*

Return to the Focus Question: How are things that live in an ecosystem connected?

Review your answers to questions about the texts as well as your annotations and Annotation Notes. Think about the discussions you've had about the texts. How does that information help you answer the Focus Question?

Use the graphic organizer to organize information about the texts.

1. In the boxes, record the details from each text that help you answer the Focus Question.

2. Make connections between those details to help you answer the Focus Question. Write your answer in the box provided.

10 Interesting Things About Ecosystems
Sample answer: Animals and plants adapt to conditions in their ecosystems.

Food Chain (Visual Text)
Sample answer: Animals depend on other living things in their ecosystem for food.

On Frogless Pond
Sample answer: Taking frogs out of a pond ecosystem affects other living things in the pond.

How are things that live in an ecosystem connected?
Sample answer: Animals, birds, plants, insects, and humans are closely linked together in an ecosytem. Members of an ecosystem depend on one another. If you change any part of it, there will be one or more effects on the other parts.

REFLECT How did making connections between the three texts help you to answer the Focus Question?

Sample answer: All the texts showed me how connected different parts of nature

are. In Text 1 I learned about some different types of ecosystems. The Visual Text

and Text 2 showed how animals in an ecosystem depend on other living things.

PROFESSIONAL DEVELOPMENT

Differentiation: End-of-Unit Writing Assignment

What Is It? An end-of-unit writing assignment is a form of differentiation that calls upon students to take what they have learned throughout the unit and expand upon it. For example, the optional Write Beyond assignment invites students to write about one of the texts in the unit from a different point of view.

Why Is It Important? Writing beyond a reading encourages creativity and develops writing skills. When writing beyond, students present information and ideas in the original texts from a different perspective, which leads to deeper insights into the text's meaning.

Writing About the Focus Question

Now that you have answered the Focus Question using all three texts, develop your ideas into a longer piece of writing.

USE EVIDENCE

- Explain how things that live in an ecosystem are connected. Use at least one piece of evidence from each text to support your answer.
- If you need more room, use additional paper.

MONITOR

- Use the Writing Checklist as you work to make sure your writing has all of the important pieces of information.
- Use the rubric on page 62 when you have completed your first draft to help you evaluate, revise, and edit your work.

WRITING CHECKLIST ✔

Does my writing . . .

☐ answer the Focus Question?

☐ provide text evidence to support my ideas?

☐ have a clear beginning, middle, and end?

☐ use correct language, spelling, and conventions?

Unit 3 • **61**

Writing About the Focus Question

USE EVIDENCE Remind students that they should use their graphic organizers as well as their annotations in the texts to write their responses.

Allow students to revisit the texts as frequently as they need to in order to support comprehension and to respond to the Focus Question.

MONITOR After students have completed their responses, have them review the Writing Checklist and revise their writing responses.

DIFFERENTIATE AND EXTEND

In addition to or instead of the writing response, consider having students complete one of the following assignments:

Write Beyond Have students assume the role of a pond-dwelling animal or insect and write journal entries describing the changes it sees in its habitat when the frog population drops in number.

Read Beyond Have students read more in-depth articles about the ecosystems mentioned in this unit.

Research Have students choose an ecosystem and research the food webs in that ecosystem.

Create a Visual Text Have students create a graphic that shows the organisms living in the immediate environment of your school. The graphic should indicate relationships among the organisms.

How Do I Use It? You may want to assign the Write Beyond assignment on page 61 of this guide. Encourage students to have fun and use their creativity in this assignment, but point out that they need to include evidence from the text to support their ideas. Students may want to make a list of the changes they would see (e.g., algae blooms, insect numbers increase) when frog populations decline, and then use that information as they write their journal entries. Students may want to write several shorter entries to chronicle changes they would note over time.

Unit 3 • **61**

SELF-ASSESS and REFLECT

SELF-ASSESS Have students use the Writing Rubric on page 62 to self-assess their writing response. Tell them to assign themselves a score from 1–4 (with "4" being the highest) for each category in the first column.

REFLECT Use the Writing Rubric on Student Worktext page 62 to assess each student's writing. Record points for each category in the first column of the rubric. Have students remove the page from their Student Worktexts and place it in their writing portfolios, along with the drafts and final versions of their responses.

Focus Question How are things that live in an ecosystem connected?

This is the rubric that your teacher will use to assess your writing. Refer to it as you revise your work. After you have finished your final version, review your writing and record your points for each category on the "Student" line in the first column.

	Accomplished (4 points)	Competent (3 points)	Developing (2 points)	Beginning (1 point)
RESPONSE Score: Student ____ Teacher ____	The response answers the question effectively and with insight.	The response answers the question effectively.	The response partially responds to the question but does not adequately address it.	The response addresses the texts but does not address the question.
ORGANIZATION Score: Student ____ Teacher ____	The main idea is convincingly stated. Ideas are organized in cohesive paragraphs that support the main idea.	The main idea is clearly stated. Ideas are organized in logical paragraphs.	The main idea is weak. Ideas are organized in a somewhat logical and cohesive way.	The main idea is missing. The organization of the paragraphs is not logical.
TEXT EVIDENCE Score: Student ____ Teacher ____	Response includes more than one piece of appropriate text evidence from each text. Evidence supports the main idea in a thorough way.	Response includes one piece of text evidence from each text. Evidence supports the main idea clearly.	Response does not include at least one piece of text evidence from each text. Text evidence does not adequately support the main idea.	Response does not contain relevant evidence.
LANGUAGE Score: Student ____ Teacher ____	Writing includes precise and sophisticated vocabulary related to the topic.	Writing includes appropriate vocabulary related to the topic.	Writing includes imprecise and inaccurate vocabulary.	Writing does not include vocabulary that appropriately reflects the topic of the response.
SPELLING AND CONVENTIONS Score: Student ____ Teacher ____	Response includes correct spelling, grammar, and punctuation consistently.	Response includes mostly correct spelling, grammar, and punctuation.	Response has many errors in spelling, grammar, and punctuation.	Response's errors in spelling, grammar, and punctuation make it extremely difficult to understand the response.

62 • Unit 3

UNIT 4

Focus Question
In what ways would time travel be a positive or negative experience?

Texts for Close Reading

Unit 4 • 63

GENRE STUDY

Discuss with students the genres of *A Connecticut Yankee in King Arthur's Court* and "Sonal's Time Machine."

Remind students that *genre* refers to the format and features of a text and typically falls into one of two categories—literature or informational text. Literature is a creative work that doesn't necessarily rely on facts, and informational text is based on factual information. Fantasy incorporates magic or supernatural elements in the plot, while science fiction incorporates science and imagined technology of the future. With the class, list the features of fiction, being sure to include the elements of fantasy and science fiction. Have students identify characteristics these two subgenres share and characteristics that are different.

Focus Question

Have students read the Focus Question on Worktext page 63. Tell them that the texts and illustrations in this unit will help them answer this question.

Texts for Close Reading

Have students read to themselves the descriptions of the texts in this unit.

There is no need to explain what students should expect to find in their close readings or to do any preteaching about the subject matter.

TEXT COMPLEXITY

Are those dinosaurs . . . *alive*?
- Style: documentary
- Knowledge demands: low
- Levels of meaning: literal/ inferential

A Connecticut Yankee
Quantitative: 560L
Qualitative
- Structure: narrative
- Language: archaic/familiar
- Knowledge demands: medium
- Levels of meaning: literal

Sonal's Time Machine
Quantitative: 810L
Qualitative
- Structure: narrative
- Language: familiar
- Knowledge demands: low
- Levels of meaning: literal

Are those dinosaurs . . . alive?

Set a Purpose

Explain to students that they will look at the image on page 64 to begin to gain a deeper understanding of the ways time travel would be a positive or negative experience.

Visual Text Analysis

Remind students that an image can be analyzed as a text by looking at its details and making inferences. Direct students' attention to the image on Student Worktext page 64.

Encourage students to annotate the Visual Text. Suggest they use arrows, labels, circles, margin notes, and other markings to highlight details that will help them gain a better understanding of the meaning of the image.

1. Have students discuss as a whole class, in small groups, or with a partner their first impression of the photograph.

2. Encourage students to make note of the details that support their observations in question 1. Encourage them to try to identify the two dinosaurs in the photograph, ways in which they are similar and different, and the relationship between the child and the dinosaurs. Have students explain as a whole class, in small groups, or with a partner what details they noted and what those details might tell them about the ways time travel could be a positive or negative experience.

3. Guide students to synthesize all the details they see in the photograph to express their understanding.

Are those dinosaurs . . . alive?

Look at this Visual Text, and make annotations on the image. Review the image or parts of the image as many times as necessary to answer the following questions.

1. What is your first impression of this photograph?

Sample answer: A small boy is at a museum. He is looking at two dinosaurs in an

area with plants and leaves.

_____

_____

_____

_____

_____

_____

PROFESSIONAL DEVELOPMENT

Visual Text: ELL

What Is It? Incorporating information from a Visual Text can present extra challenges for English-language learners and students who have difficulty reading. Such students need help in "translating" their visual impressions into verbal descriptions.

Why Is It Important? Students can understand an image without verbalizing it, but they need words to analyze the image and to describe it to others. Looking at images and talking about what they see helps students develop fluency in reading and writing and speaking about nonverbal texts. Such activities also work the other way around: as they build

2. What details in the photograph helped give you this impression?

Sample answer: At first, the fence made me think it is a zoo, but I know this must be a museum and not a zoo because dinosaurs no longer exist. The museum has tried to show people what the dinosaurs and their world looked like. The tyrannosaurus rex looks ready to strike. The dinosaurs are lit with a weird green light.

_____

_____

_____

_____

_____

_____

3. What does this photograph help you understand about what time travel would be like?

Sample answer: The photograph is showing what it would be like to come face to face with dinosaurs. I can't help feeling nervous for the boy. The photograph helps me imagine what it would be like if people could travel through time to see real dinosaurs.

_____

_____

_____

_____

_____

_____

_____

Unit 4 • **65**

Text-Dependent Questions

As necessary, encourage discussion with such prompts as:

1. What do you notice about the dinosaurs in the photograph? (Sample answer: The dinosaurs are large and look real. They seem like they have just walked out of the forest. The green dinosaur is showing lots of large, sharp teeth. The brown dinosaur appears to be nibbling a plant.)

2. What do you notice about the child in the photograph? (Sample answer: The child is small compared to the dinosaurs. He is standing behind a fence, stretching to see over the top.)

3. What kind of world does the display show the dinosaurs lived in? (Sample answer: The display shows the dinosaurs on the edge of a forest of thick green plants. I see a mist in the air that makes me think it must be humid. It must be hot, too, for all of those plants to grow.)

4. What words would you use to describe the dinosaurs? (Sample answer: I would use the words *amazing, scary, ferocious,* and *incredible* to describe the dinosaurs.)

fluency with language, students are better able to create images from verbal descriptions.

How Do I Use It? Asking 5W (who, what, where, when, why) questions about an image can help students form the words and sentences they need to describe what they see. For example, the Visual Text for this unit shows a child looking at a life-like display of two dinosaurs. Start by pointing to details in the photograph (dinosaurs, ferns, fence, child) and having students name them. Then ask questions such as, *Where is this child? Why is there a fence?* and *Is the forest in the background real?* Have students write their answers. Work with students as they form their answers into complete sentences.

Unit 4 • **65**

A Connecticut Yankee

Tell students that they will read to learn about one author's ideas about time travel.

1st READ

Set a Purpose

Explain to students that they will read to get a general understanding of what the text is about.

Have students read the excerpt from *A Connecticut Yankee in King Arthur's Court* independently, annotating the text as they read. Remind students that suggested annotation symbols appear on page 8 of the Getting Started with Close Reading unit. Circulate and observe students' markings and notes, especially questions and anything they found confusing. The observations and annotations may be used to inform instruction. Based on students' needs, you may want to meet with them in small groups.

Use the Text-Dependent Questions to prompt students to engage with the text.

Text-Dependent Questions

1. What is this text about? (Sample answer: The text is about a man who travels back in time to King Arthur's Camelot in the year 528.)

Scaffolded Support Use the following scaffolded question and sentence frames as necessary to support comprehension.

Who is the narrator?

The narrator is from _____ .

In paragraph 18, a slim boy says the year is _____ .

✔ **Self-Monitoring Strategies** can help you check your understanding and clarify a text. Use them as you read.

☐ Visualize.　☐ Ask yourself questions.　☐ Draw conclusions.　☐ Reread to clarify.

Read this excerpt to learn about one author's ideas about time travel. Make annotations as you read. You may want to review Annotating a Text on page 8.
Sample annotations appear throughout the text.

A Connecticut Yankee in King Arthur's Court

by Mark Twain

1　I am an American. I was born and reared in Hartford, in the state
? 　of Connecticut. I am a Yankee of the Yankees. It was during a misunderstanding with a fellow we used to call Hercules. He laid me out with a punch. Then the world went out in darkness. I didn't feel anything any more. When I came to again, I was sitting under an oak tree, on the grass in a beautiful country landscape. A fellow on a horse looked down at me. He was in armor from head to heel. He had a helmet on his head, a shield, a sword, and a large spear. His horse had armor on, too.

2　? 　"Fair sir, will ye joust?" said this fellow.

3　　"Will I which?"

4　? 　"Will ye try a passage of arms for land or lady or for—"

5　　"What are you giving me?" I said. "Get along back to your circus, or I'll report you."

6　　Now what does this man do but come rushing at me with his long spear pointed straight ahead. He meant business, so I was
? 　up the tree when he arrived. He allowed that I was his property. I was to go with him and he would not hurt me. We marched comfortably along. We did not come to any circus or sign of a circus. So I gave up that idea. I asked him how far we were from Hartford. He said he had never heard of the place. At the end of an hour we saw a far-away town. Beyond it stood a vast gray fortress, with towers and turrets.

PROFESSIONAL DEVELOPMENT

Self-Monitoring Strategies: Reread to Clarify

What Is It? Rereading to clarify is one of the **Self-Monitoring Strategies** students can employ to ensure comprehension while reading.

Why Is It Important? When students return to a confusing portion of a text to reread, they are setting a goal: to make sense of something unclear. This sharpens their focus and hones the thinking process. Rereading to clarify develops critical thinking and independent learning and builds students' literacy confidence.

Make notes here about your annotations from each read. You will refer to these notes later when you return to your annotations. Sample notes appear below.

ANNOTATION NOTES

Key Ideas and Details:

The narrator has traveled in time and in space. He meets a man on a horse

who has a "helmet on his head, a shield, a sword, and a large spear." He

must be a knight.

Language and Text Structure:

The knight speaks English, but the narrator can't understand him.

"reared" in paragraph 1—can figure out meaning from context clues: "born,"

"in Hartford," and "Yankee of Yankees"

The knight's old-fashioned language makes the narrator think the knight is

crazy.

Connections and Inferences:

I think the narrator follows the knight because he is worried the knight will

hurt him if he does not go.

Unit 4 • 67

2. What happened in paragraph 1 that caused the narrator to travel through time? (Sample answer: The narrator, or "Yankee of the Yankees" was knocked out "with a punch" from a man he calls "Hercules." When he "came to again," he was in a place and time he did not recognize.)

3. Where do the events take place? (Sample answer: The events in paragraph 1 begin in Hartford, Connecticut, but then, after the narrator is punched, the rest of the events take place in King Arthur's Camelot.)

Think Aloud *I'm unsure what "When I came to again" means in paragraph 1. As I reread the paragraph, I note that the narrator explains that Hercules "laid me out with a punch," and the "world went out in darkness." I now see that Hercules's punch did more than knock the narrator down—he was knocked unconscious, which can happen if you get hit on the head. Then the world went "into darkness." Now I understand that "When I came to again" means the narrator woke up from being knocked out.*

Partner Talk Have students discuss the narrator's confusions about what he is seeing and experiencing.

How Do I Use It? Model rereading to clarify a section of text for students. Read aloud paragraph 6 from the text on Student Worktext page 66. *After reading this paragraph, I'm a bit confused. The narrator says he was "up the tree," but then he and the knight are marching "comfortably along." After rereading, I realize that after the knight stated that the narrator "was his property" the narrator climbs out of the tree—this action is just not clearly stated by the narrator himself. Now I understand.*

Unit 4 • **67**

A Connecticut Yankee

2nd READ

Set a Purpose

Students will return to *A Connecticut Yankee at King Arthur's Court* to understand the language in the text.

Text-Dependent Questions

1. What is the effect of the dialogue in paragraphs 3 to 5? (The dialogue shows the narrator's personality and adds humor. "Will I which?" in paragraph 3 and "Get along back to your circus, or I'll report you" in paragraph 5 show the Yankee's confusion and grumpy personality and makes the story funny.)

2. How does the illustration help you better understand the text? (The illustration helps me see what the narrator is wearing and how his appearance differs from the other character. It helps me understand why the girl's "mouth dropped open" and people "went into the huts and fetched their families" when he passed by.)

3. Vocabulary: Multiple-Meaning Word Discuss contextual meanings of familiar and unfamiliar words and phrases.

Paragraph 1: What does *reared* mean in this context? What words or phrases in the paragraph are clues to its meaning? (*Reared* means "brought up" or "raised." The narrator says he "was born and reared in Hartford," and that he is a "Yankee of Yankees" so he must have never lived anywhere else.)

Partner Talk Have partners discuss how the language helped them understand the text and the time period in which it takes place.

7   "Bridgeport, Connecticut?" said I, pointing.

8 ! "Camelot," said he.

9   "Camelot," said I to myself. "I don't seem to remember hearing of it before."

10   It was a soft summer landscape—as lovely as a dream. The air was full of the smell of flowers, the buzzing of insects, the twittering of birds. There were no people, no stir of life. Presently a girl with golden hair came along. Around her head she wore a hoop of red poppies. The circus man paid no attention to her. He didn't even seem to see her and she was not startled at his fantastic dress. But when she noticed me, then there was a change! Her mouth dropped open and she became the picture of curiosity touched with fear. She stood gazing until we were lost to her view.

11   As we approached the town, signs of life began to appear. There were small fields and garden patches and people, too. The people wore long coarse linen robes. All of them stared at me and went into the huts and fetched their families. But nobody ever noticed that other fellow. In the town dogs and children played in the sun. Presently there was a distant blare of music. It came nearer, and soon a noble parade of soldiers wound into view. We followed them through one winding alley and then another. Then we climbed and climbed till we saw the huge castle. There was an exchange of bugle blasts. The great gates were flung open and the
?   drawbridge was lowered. Soon we were in a great paved court. All about us there was noise and confusion. A slim boy in tights came over to me. He
?   wore a plumed satin cap tilted over his ear. He said he had come for me. As we walked along we chatted and he happened to mention that he was
!   born in the year 513. It made the cold chills creep me! I stopped and said, a little faintly,

12   "Maybe I didn't hear you just right. What year was it?"

13   "513."

14   "513! Come, my boy, be honest with me. Now tell me, honest and true, where am I?"

15   *In King Arthur's Court.*

16   I waited a minute, to let that idea shudder its way home.

17   "And what year is it now?"

18   "528—nineteenth of June."

19   I felt a sinking of the heart. I shall never see my friends again. They will
!   not be born for more than thirteen hundred years yet."

PROFESSIONAL DEVELOPMENT

Text-Dependent Questions

What Is It? Text-Dependent Questions are those that can be answered only by referring to the text. They keep students grounded in the text and reliant on only the content the author provides. Text-Dependent Questions require students to use evidence from the text to justify their answers.

Why Is It Important? Too often, teachers' questions take students away from the text too quickly, asking them what they think or feel. While we want to get students' reactions, we must first start with what they know using only the details in the text. This close examination of the text aids in comprehension and the development of skills students need to understand and analyze other rigorous texts.

Make notes here about your annotations from each read.
You will refer to these notes later when you return to
your annotations. Sample notes appear below.

Key Ideas and Details:

Narrator has never heard of Camelot.

finds out date—he went back in time to year 528

He's sad he won't see his friends again.

Language and Text Structure:

The narrator says the landscape is "as lovely as a dream."

The experience "made cold chills creep" him. The location is beautiful, but

he is scared.

What do "court" and "plumed" mean?

Connections and Inferences:

Narrator will never see his friends again. Time travel can cause loneliness and

homesickness.

"not be born for more than thirteen hundred years" = he went back 1300 years

At first he thought the knight looked strange, but to the people of Camelot

he is the only one who looks strange.

How Do I Use It? In addition to the optional Think Alouds provided in the unit, you can also explicitly model strategies to address comprehension issues. Many students need support in identifying effective strategies in specific reading situations. Modeling these strategies will expand students' strategy repertoire. For example, support Text-Dependent Question 2 in the third read of *A Connecticut Yankee* with a Think Aloud: *To answer this question, I reread paragraphs 10 and 11. I note that while the narrator has a positive experience viewing the landscape, which he describes "as lovely as a dream," all his other experiences are strange and upsetting. For example, the girl views him with "curiosity" and "fear," and villagers stare at him. I conclude his time travel experience is mostly negative.*

A Connecticut Yankee

3rd READ

Set a Purpose
Students will read to draw inferences from the text.

Text-Dependent Questions
1. Why does the narrator repeatedly mention the circus? (I infer that the narrator has seen circus performers dressed up in odd costumes. When the oddly dressed knight rushed at him "with his long spear," the narrator believed he was just a performer from a nearby circus.)

2. What were the positive and negative things about time travel for the narrator? (The landscape was described as being "as lovely as a dream," but he finds it hard to communicate with the people since they speak differently. His odd appearance makes others view him "with fear.")

3. What can you infer about the narrator based on his reactions to learning he's traveled through time? (I can infer that the narrator will miss his friends. In paragraph 19, he reveals that he "felt a sinking of the heart" when he learned he'd "never see [his] friends again." He doesn't mention his home or possessions, just his friends.)

Think Aloud *I wasn't sure why the narrator asked if he was being taken to Bridgeport, Connecticut. He still doesn't know he has traveled through time and space, so I can conclude that he thinks he is in a part of Connecticut that he hasn't seen before.*

Partner Talk Have partners share inferences they drew from the text about how the narrator felt in this unusual situation.

Return TO THE TEXT

Respond to Reading

You may want to check students' understanding by having them complete page 70 in the Student Worktext.

1. Remind students that a summary should only include the key ideas and details essential to understanding what the text is about. Point out that they can use the graphic organizer on Student Worktext page 70 to capture and organize those key ideas and details. The graphic organizer should then guide them in writing their summaries.

2. Refer students to pages 12 and 13 in Getting Started to help them write their individual summaries.

Have students work independently to answer the questions on page 70 of their Worktexts.

COLLABORATE Have students exchange their final summaries with their partners and review each other's summaries. Remind pairs that when they review and discuss their partners' summaries, they should consider whether or not the summary has the following elements:

- contains only important information
- answers as many of the following as possible: Who? What? When? Where? and How?

REFLECT Have students share ways they were able to clarify and better understand a confusing word or phrase.

Return to the TEXT

Respond to Reading: A Connecticut Yankee in King Arthur's Court

Review the annotations and notes you made while reading *A Connecticut Yankee in King Arthur's Court*. Think about how they can help you understand the text.

1. Use this Story Map to help you summarize the text.

Characters (Who)	Setting (Where and When)
the Connecticut Yankee (narrator), a knight in armor, a girl with golden hair, a slim boy in tights, townspeople and soldiers	Camelot and area around it June 19, 528

Conflict (What)	Main Events (How)
Narrator has gone back in time 1300 years. The knight takes the narrator prisoner.	The narrator is knocked out, wakes up, and is challenged to a joust; finds out he is in Camelot; and learns that the year is 528.

2. Use the completed graphic organizer from item 1 to help you write a summary of *A Connecticut Yankee in King Arthur's Court*.

Sample answer: The "Yankee" is knocked out in a fight and wakes in a place he doesn't know. When he wakes up, a knight challenges him to joust and then takes him prisoner. When they arrive in Camelot, he learns that the year is 528. He has traveled back in time 1300 years.

REFLECT What word or phrase did you find confusing? What Self-Monitoring Strategy did you use to gain a better understanding of it?

Sample answer: At first I didn't understand what "the world went out in darkness" meant. I reread and understood that the author was knocked unconscious during a fight.

70 • Unit 4

PROFESSIONAL DEVELOPMENT

Classroom Management: Peer Leadership in Small-Group Activities

What Is It? Peer leadership involves placing students in leadership roles during paired and small-group activities.

Why Is It Important? Leading an activity gives students practice in peer and self-management and social interaction. It encourages leadership and motivation. Having students lead group discussions and activities frees you up to closely observe students at work.

How Do I Use It? Provide ample structure for student leaders. Assign an activity with a clear and deliverable goal, and stick to a short time frame. For example, have small groups retell

Comprehension Check: A Connecticut Yankee in King Arthur's Court

Answer the questions to demonstrate an understanding of what the text means.

1. What clues in the text help the reader to know that the narrator has traveled through time before it is revealed at the end of the story? Provide text evidence to support your answer.

   Sample answer: The narrator is knocked out and wakes up to see a knight and

   horse in armor. The knight uses old-fashioned language that the narrator cannot

   understand. The narrator travels to a place with "a vast gray fortress, with

   towers and turrets." The townspeople dress differently and find his clothing

   strange. Finally, the narrator discovers that he is in the year "528."

2. What inference can you make about what effect time travel has had on the narrator's life?

   Sample answer: I can infer that time travel has mostly had a negative effect

   on the narrator. First, he does not know where he is. Second, he is in danger

   when a knight challenges him to a joust and makes the narrator "his property."

   Then the townspeople "stared" at him. Finally, he realizes that because he has

   traveled through time, he will not see his friends again.

3. How does the narrator's mood change throughout the story? Provide text evidence to support your answer.

   Sample answer: At first he is annoyed because he cannot understand the knight.

   In paragraph 5 he says, "I'll report you." Then he is confused by all he sees as

   they walk along and he tries to figure out where he is. In paragraph 19 when

   the Yankee realizes he has gone back in time and that he will not see his

   friends again, his mood becomes sad and he feels "a sinking of the heart."

Unit 4 • 71

Stop and Assess

Use the following rubrics to assess your students' understanding of the text.

Item 1 answers indicate:	
2	the author hints at the time travel through the language and dress of the characters, and the setting. Several pieces of text evidence are cited to support the answer.
1	one way the author hints that the narrator has traveled through time, but supporting evidence is insufficient.
0	no understanding of how the author hints that the narrator has traveled through time. No relevant text evidence is provided.

Item 2 answers indicate:	
2	that traveling through time has been mostly a negative experience for the narrator. At least two pieces of text evidence support the answer.
1	some understanding of how the narrator's experience has been negative, but insufficient text evidence is cited.
0	no understanding of how the narrator's experience has been, and don't cite any relevant text evidence.

Item 3 answers indicate:	
2	the narrator's mood changes from annoyed to confused to sorrowful; at least two pieces of evidence support the answer.
1	only a partial understanding of how the narrator's mood changes throughout the text. Supporting evidence is insufficient.
0	no understanding of how the narrator's mood changes throughout the text. No text evidence is cited.

A Connecticut Yankee in King Arthur's Court from different characters' points of view. Give groups 10 minutes to find details in the text that support their characters' viewpoints. Assign group leaders and give them the responsibilities of keeping discussions on topic and assuring that all group members have opportunities to participate. Observe student leadership and provide one-to-one coaching with suggestions or corrections. After the activity, allow peer leaders and other students in the group time to share their ideas with the class. Keep student reflections or take notes to help prepare for future peer-led activities.

Unit 4 • **71**

Sonal's Time Machine

Students will read a science fiction story to learn about the effects of time travel.

1st READ

Set a Purpose

Explain to students that they will read to find out what "Sonal's Time Machine" is about.

Have students read "Sonal's Time Machine" independently, annotating the text as they read. Remind students that suggested annotation symbols appear on page 8 of the Getting Started with Close Reading unit. Circulate and observe students' markings, especially questions and anything they found confusing. The observations and annotations may be used to inform instruction. Based on students' needs, you may want to meet with them in small groups.

Text-Dependent Questions

1. What is the text about? (It is about a girl, Sonal, who builds a time machine and travels into the future.)

2. What does Sonal see when she arrives in the future? (Sonal's neighborhood looks very different. There are no roads or cars. Houses are replaced with "flowers and fruit trees," and an ancient castle stands where "the Takahashis' house once stood.")

Scaffolded Support Use the following scaffolded question and sentence frame as necessary to support comprehension.

Where is Sonal in the future?

Everything looks _____.

Partner Talk Have students compare and contrast the world in Sonal's time to the world in the future.

Read this science fiction story to learn about the effects of time travel. Make annotations as you read. You may make different annotations each time you read.
Sample annotations and notes appear throughout the text.

Sonal's Time Machine

1   No one had seen Sonal since the last day of school. Sonal hadn't said much to her friends, so they were surprised to learn about her summer plans. "I'm going to build a time machine," she said.

2   Six weeks later, in the shed that Sonal called her "laboratory," she and her friends examined her finished time machine.

3   "I'm going to travel into the future by way of the fourth dimension—time. Sonal waved and the time machine disappeared. Inside the time machine, Sonal watched the sun rise and set thousands of times as she hurtled her way into the future. She seemed to see the future as a sped-up film, showing brief glimpses of major events before she finally arrived at her destination 800,000 years in the future.

4   She tumbled out the folding door of her machine onto the exact spot where her shed had stood 800,000 years ago. Instead of the suburban neighborhood crowded with houses, the land was covered with flowers and fruit trees. The air was warmer and the sun seemed brighter. Far in the distance, where the Takahashis' house once stood, she saw a castle of green marble. Behind Sonal was a huge and ancient statue.

5   "Where are the people and animals? Roads? Cars?" Sonal was surprised. She thought the future would have more of all these things, not less.

6   The sound of laughter caught her ear. "People!" she thought. Down in the valley, where once the Main Street ran, she could see beautiful people dressed in colorful robes. They were throwing flower petals at one another. "The future seems to be all peace and beauty," she said to herself.

7   Behind her, a secret door opened in the base of the statue. Had Sonal been alert and turned around, she would have seen slim, ugly, pale figures creeping out and carrying her time machine into the base of the statue.

8   "Yes," Sonal thought. "I like it here very much. But I'm feeling a bit hungry, and it is getting late. I wonder if those pretty people will help." She had thought the people of the future would have plenty of supplies and had not brought any of her own. It now began to dawn on her that, unprepared as she was, she would be in a lot of danger if anything happened to the time machine.

PROFESSIONAL DEVELOPMENT

Intertextual Analysis: Comparing and Contrasting Themes

What Is It? When analyzing more than one text, the deepest level of analysis is to compare themes, or overarching messages, and how each text treats them.

Why Is It Important? While topics, opinions, and techniques may be shared by multiple texts, each text's treatment of a theme is different. Since the theme constitutes the deepest meaning of a text, comparing and contrasting themes allows students to understand a text's meaning on multiple levels and from multiple perspectives.

How Do I Use It? Thematic comparison should take place after students have completed their analysis of individual texts.

Make notes here about your annotations from each read. You will refer to these notes later when you return to your annotations. Sample notes appear below.

ANNOTATION NOTES

Key Ideas and Details:
Sonal tells her friends that she will build a time machine and travel

through time.

Time is the fourth dimension.

She goes 800,000 years into the future.

She doesn't have food or water.

Something has stolen her time machine.

Language and Text Structure:
The writer uses chronological order but jumps over 800,000 years.

The story is told in the third person but is mostly about Sonal's experience.

"began to dawn"—figurative language

Connections and Inferences:
"air was warmer" —the climate has changed

Sonal's back is turned when her time machine is taken—she does not

know she is in danger.

Sonal's Time Machine

2nd READ

Set a Purpose
Students will examine the text structure and how the language used in the text reveals meaning.

Text-Dependent Questions
1. How does the text show the passage of time as Sonal travels through time? (Sample answer: The phrase in paragraph 3, "Sonal watched the sun rise and set thousands of times" shows the many days that pass as Sonal "hurtles into the future.")

Partner Talk Have partners discuss the author's use of language to describe the setting.

3rd READ

Set a Purpose
Students will read to make inferences to determine the text's meaning.

Text-Dependent Questions
1. What can you infer about the figures who take Sonal's time machine? (Sample answer: They are described as "slim, ugly, pale figures," so they are not the same "beautiful people" Sonal sees in the valley. The pale figures don't want Sonal to see them because they are "creeping" out of the statue when she's not looking to move the time machine. I can infer that they are not going to be friendly or helpful to Sonal.)

Partner Talk Have students make inferences about the text's meaning.

Since themes and their comparisons can be abstract, scaffold instruction by allowing students to name and note the themes of each text. Graphic organizers that help students compare and contrast or make connections (Venn diagrams, T charts, webs) can help students visualize the connections between themes. Writing is often a helpful tool for analyzing the deeper connections between texts. Encourage students to write a sentence stating the theme of *A Connecticut Yankee in King Arthur's Court* and another for "Sonal's Time Machine." Have students write a paragraph comparing and contrasting the themes. Provide multiple writing scaffolds, including frames, outline forms, and model paragraphs using a main-idea/supporting-detail structure.

Respond to Reading

You may want to check students' understanding by having them complete page 74 in the Student Worktext.

1. Have students reread the text to search for major points to record in the left column of the graphic organizer and supporting details to record in the right column.

2. Refer students to pages 12 and 13 of Getting Started to help them write their individual summaries.

3. Encourage students to think about how the text would be different if Sonal knew her time machine had been stolen.

Have students work independently to answer the questions on page 74 of their Worktexts.

COLLABORATE When finished, have students exchange summaries with their partners and review each other's summaries. Remind pairs that when they review and discuss their partners' summaries, they should consider whether or not the summary has the following elements:

- contains only important information
- answers as many of the following as possible: Who? What? When? Where? and How?

REFLECT Suggest that students review their annotations and Annotation Notes to remember conclusions they drew as they read.

Return to the TEXT

Respond to Reading: Sonal's Time Machine

Review the annotations and notes you made while reading "Sonal's Time Machine." Think about how your annotations can help you answer the questions.

1. Use information from the text to complete the graphic organizer.

Major Points	Supporting Details
Sonal builds a time machine. travels 800,000 years into future future different than she expected Sonal's time machine is stolen.	builds the machine in six weeks Her friends watch her first run. Her neighborhood is very different. She has not brought any supplies.

2. Use your graphic organizer to write a brief summary of "Sonal's Time Machine."

Sample answer: Sonal builds a time machine. She gathers her friends for her

first time travel. The machine works, and she arrives 800,0000 years in the

future. The future is much different than she expected. She has not brought

supplies, and her time machine is stolen when her back is turned.

3. What is the effect of the reader knowing Sonal's time machine is gone before Sonal realizes it is gone?

Sample answer: It makes me feel sorry for Sonal and it increases the tension. I

think the "slim, pale figures" are bad and that Sonal might be in danger. Sonal

doesn't realize it, and I am nervous for her!

REFLECT How did drawing conclusions help you better understand the text?

Sample answer: Based on the information in paragraph 8, I conclude

that Sonal does not realize her time machine has been taken.

74 • Unit 4

PROFESSIONAL DEVELOPMENT

Collaboration: Small Groups

What Is It? Collaboration is constructive conversation between students during which they share questions about and understandings of a text to enhance comprehension. Collaboration can take place among a whole class, in small groups, or between pairs but is most effective when you predetermine which size group is best for a particular topic and proceed accordingly.

Why Is It Important? Choosing the properly sized group for a collaborative discussion is critical. Larger groups allow more students to hear one another's ideas, while smaller groups allow students to delve deeper into their

Comprehension Check: Sonal's Time Machine

Answer the questions to demonstrate an understanding of what the text means.

1. Sonal ends up in the exact same location 800,000 years into the future. What inference can you make about how the time machine works? Provide text evidence to support your answer.

   Sample answer: I can infer that the time machine can travel through "the fourth

   dimension—time," but not through space. Sonal is in her own neighborhood in

   the future. In paragraph 4, she sees a castle "where the Takahashis' house once

   stood." Paragraph 6 says "Down in the valley, where once the Main Street ran,

   she could see beautiful people dressed in colorful robes."

2. What does the author want you to understand about the world that Sonal finds in the future? Use text evidence in your answer.

   Sample answer: I can infer that the world appears to be a very peaceful and

   beautiful place, but that there are hidden dangers. Sonal arrives in a world that

   appears "all peace and beauty" but behind her pale figures creep out and steal

   her time machine.

3. What inferences can you make about Sonal's personality based on the information in the text? Provide evidence from the text to support your answer.

   Sample answer: She is very smart to think of building a time machine and to

   successfully build one. She must also be very brave to test the machine herself

   and set her "destination 800,000 years into the future." But she is also a little

   careless. She has not "brought any of her own" supplies. When her time

   machine is taken, she doesn't even notice. She is not "alert" and on her guard.

Stop and Assess

Use the following rubrics to assess your students' understanding of the text.

Item 1 answers indicate:	
2	that the time machine travels through time but not space, and provides text evidence to support the claim.
1	that the time machine travels through time but not space, but text evidence is insufficient.
0	no understanding of what the time machine can and can't do, and no text evidence.

Item 2 answers indicate:	
2	inferences that the future world is not all it appears to be, and provides text evidence to support the claim.
1	only what the text says explicitly, and provide no text evidence.
0	a lack of understanding that the beauty of the future world hides dangers, and don't cite any relevant text evidence.

Item 3 answers indicate:	
2	inferences about Sonal's personality and ability, with text evidence to support the claim.
1	inferences about Sonal's personality and/or abilities, with no text evidence to support the inference.
0	no understanding of Sonal and no text evidence.

understanding of a text. Collaborative discussion develops speaking and listening skills and encourages students to consider a text from more than one perspective.

How Do I Use It? Once students complete their summaries of "Sonal's Time Machine," pair them up for collaboration. Instruct pairs to discuss the details they included in their summaries and note which details their summaries have in common. Have the students consider adding or deleting details from their summaries based on their discussions.

Return to the Focus Question

Explain to students that they will fill out a graphic organizer that will help them answer the Focus Question: In what ways would time travel be a positive or negative experience?

CONNECT TEXTS Have small groups of students discuss how each text they read helps them answer the Focus Question. Have small groups share and compare their discussion notes with another small group.

Scaffolded Support You may provide the following sentence frames to support students in their use of academic language:

In the text _____ , the author/photographer makes the point that _____ . He/she does this by _____ .

Remind students to use their annotations and summaries to support their answers. They can also reread portions of the texts, if necessary.

Have students complete their graphic organizers individually and then answer the Focus Question.

REFLECT Remind students that each text provides different information about what it is like to travel through time. Ask, *How did reading all three texts give you a greater understanding of the ways time travel would be a positive and/or negative experience?*

Return to the Focus Question: In what ways would time travel be a positive or negative experience?

Review your answers to questions about the texts as well as your annotations and Annotation Notes. Think about the discussions you've had about the texts. How does that information help you answer the Focus Question?

Use the graphic organizer to organize information about the texts.

1. In the boxes, record the details from each text that help you answer the Focus Question.

2. Make connections between those details to help you answer the Focus Question. Write your answer in the box provided.

> **Are those dinosaurs . . . alive?** (Visual Text)
> Sample answer: Seeing dinosaurs face-to-face would be scary but fascinating.

> **A Connecticut Yankee in King Arthur's Court**
> Sample answer: traveler separated from family, friends forever; confusing to be in a different time

> **Sonal's Time Machine**
> Sample answer: unable to prepare for the distant future because it is unknown

> **In what ways would time travel be a positive or negative experience?**
> Sample answer: A positive is that the time traveler could see what life was like in the past or will be like in the future. There are negatives, too. A time traveler doesn't know what he or she will find or how to prepare for life in the time period he or she visits. Also, there is a danger of being stuck in a different time.

REFLECT How did making connections between the three texts help you to answer the Focus Question?

Sample answer: The texts showed how time travel can be dangerous and

confusing. Also we cannot know what the distant future is like so we don't know

how to prepare for it. The photo showed that travel to the past can be interesting.

PROFESSIONAL DEVELOPMENT

Differentiation: Graphic Organizers

What is It? Graphic organizers are tools that assist students in recording their understandings of the texts they read. They include main idea charts, summary charts, Venn diagrams, and other visual resources.

Why Is It Important? Graphic organizers aid in the comprehension of a text's ideas, assist in recognizing a text's structure, and help structure ideas for writing.

How Do I Use It? Use graphic organizers to assist students in analyzing and synthesizing information from one or more texts before they answer the Focus Question. A summary organizer at the end of each unit provides space for students

Writing About the Focus Question

Now that you have answered the Focus Question using all three texts, develop your ideas into a longer piece of writing.

USE EVIDENCE

- Explain the ways in which time travel would be a positive or negative experience. Use at least one piece of evidence from each text to support your answer.
- If you need more room, use additional paper.

MONITOR

- Use the Writing Checklist as you work to make sure your writing has all of the important pieces of information.
- Use the rubric on page 78 when you have completed your first draft to help you evaluate, revise, and edit your work.

WRITING CHECKLIST ✔

Does my writing . . .

☐ answer the Focus Question?

☐ provide text evidence to support my ideas?

☐ have a clear beginning, middle, and end?

☐ use correct language, spelling, and conventions?

Writing About the Focus Question

USE EVIDENCE Remind students that they should use their graphic organizers as well as their annotations in the texts to write their responses.

Allow students to revisit the texts as frequently as they need to in order to support comprehension and to respond to the Focus Question.

MONITOR After students have completed their responses, have them review the Writing Checklist and revise their writing responses.

DIFFERENTIATE AND EXTEND

In addition to or instead of the writing response, consider having students complete one of the following assignments:

Write Beyond Have students assume the role of someone who witnesses a visitor from the future. Have them describe their observations in a letter to a friend.

Read Beyond Have students read a work of science fiction that involves time travel, such as *A Wrinkle in Time*.

Research Ask students to choose and research a period and place in time they would visit if they could time travel.

Create a Visual Text Using graphic applications on a computer or electronic device or traditional poster board, have students create a visual display that answers the Focus Question.

to answer the unit's Focus Question individually and then collectively. After students fill in the answers for each text, ask them to find commonalities between the four summaries. Encourage them to fill out the organizers using sentence frames to make connections by using parallel language. For example, *The Yankee's time travel experience is negative because _____ / Sonal's time travel experience is negative because _____.* Encourage students to include one or two supporting details from each text in the graphic organizer.

SELF-ASSESS and REFLECT

SELF-ASSESS Have students use the Writing Rubric on page 78 to self-assess their writing response. Tell them to assign themselves a score from 1–4 (with "4" being the highest) for each category in the first column.

REFLECT Use the Writing Rubric on Student Worktext page 78 to assess each student's writing. Record points for each category in the first column of the rubric. Have students remove the page from their Student Worktexts and place it in their writing portfolios, along with the drafts and final versions of their responses.

Focus Question In what ways would time travel be a positive or negative experience?

This is the rubric that your teacher will use to assess your writing. Refer to it as you revise your work. After you have finished your final version, review your writing and record your points for each category on the "Student" line in the first column.

	Accomplished (4 points)	Competent (3 points)	Developing (2 points)	Beginning (1 point)
RESPONSE Score: Student _____ Teacher _____	The response answers the question effectively and with insight.	The response answers the question effectively.	The response partially responds to the question but does not adequately address it.	The response addresses the texts but does not address the question.
ORGANIZATION Score: Student _____ Teacher _____	The main idea is convincingly stated. Ideas are organized in cohesive paragraphs that support the main idea.	The main idea is clearly stated. Ideas are organized in logical paragraphs.	The main idea is weak. Ideas are organized in a somewhat logical and cohesive way.	The main idea is missing. The organization of the paragraphs is not logical.
TEXT EVIDENCE Score: Student _____ Teacher _____	Response includes more than one piece of appropriate text evidence from each text. Evidence supports the main idea in a thorough way.	Response includes one piece of text evidence from each text. Evidence supports the main idea clearly.	Response does not include at least one piece of text evidence from each text. Text evidence does not adequately support the main idea.	Response does not contain relevant evidence.
LANGUAGE Score: Student _____ Teacher _____	Writing includes precise and sophisticated vocabulary related to the topic.	Writing includes appropriate vocabulary related to the topic.	Writing includes imprecise and inaccurate vocabulary.	Writing does not include vocabulary that appropriately reflects the topic of the response.
SPELLING AND CONVENTIONS Score: Student _____ Teacher _____	Response includes correct spelling, grammar, and punctuation consistently.	Response includes mostly correct spelling, grammar, and punctuation.	Response has many errors in spelling, grammar, and punctuation.	Response's errors in spelling, grammar, and punctuation make it extremely difficult to understand the response.

UNIT 5

Focus Question Why does Earth support life and other planets do not?

Texts for Close Reading

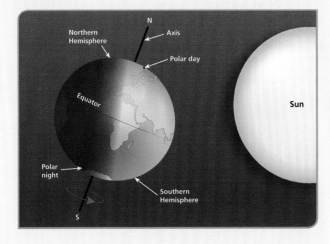

Unit 5 • 79

GENRE STUDY

Discuss with students the genres of "What Is Earth?" and "Life on Mars?"

Remind students that *genre* refers to the format and features of a text and typically falls into one of two categories—literature or informational text. Literature is a creative work that doesn't necessarily rely on facts, and informational text is based on factual information. "What Is Earth?" is a straightforward, explanatory text. Its purpose is to explain its topic and educate readers. "Life on Mars?" has explanatory elements, but it is also intended to entertain readers. Have students identify characteristics shared by explanatory texts and magazine articles as well as characteristics unique to each genre.

Focus Question

Have students read the Focus Question on Worktext page 79. Tell them that the texts and illustrations in this unit will help them answer this question.

Texts for Close Reading

Have students read to themselves the descriptions of the texts in this unit.

There is no need to explain what students should expect to find in their close readings or to do any preteaching about the subject matter.

TEXT COMPLEXITY

Planets of the Solar System
- Style: illustrative
- Knowledge demands: medium
- Levels of meaning: literal

What is Earth?
Quantitative: 530L
Qualitative
- Structure: conventional
- Language: academic
- Knowledge demands: high
- Levels of meaning: literal

Life on Mars?
Quantitative: 690L
Qualitative
- Structure: conventional
- Language: academic
- Knowledge demands: high
- Levels of meaning: literal

Unit 5 • 79

Planets of the Solar System

Set a Purpose

Explain to students that they will look at the image on page 80 to begin to gain a deeper understanding of why Earth supports life.

Visual Text Analysis

Remind students that an image can be analyzed as a text by looking at its details and making inferences. Direct students' attention to the image on Student Worktext page 80.

Encourage students to annotate the Visual Text. Suggest they use arrows, labels, circles, margin notes, and other markings to highlight details that will help them gain a better understanding of the meaning of the image.

1. Have students record their first impressions about the image. Lead them to discuss as a whole class, in small groups, or with a partner what they think is happening in the illustration.

2. Encourage students to make note of the details that support their observations in question 1. Have them name the planets they have identified and compare their features. Have students explain as a whole class, in small groups, or with a partner what details they noted and what those details might tell them about why the planets in our solar system other than Earth don't support life.

3. Guide students to synthesize all the details they see in the illustration to draw conclusions about what the picture tells them about why other planets might not support life.

Planets of the Solar System in Orbit

Look at this Visual Text, and make annotations on the image. Review the image or parts of the image as many times as necessary to answer the following questions.

1. What's your first impression of what's going on in this picture?

Sample answer: The planets of our solar system are going around the sun.

_____
_____
_____
_____
_____
_____
_____
_____

PROFESSIONAL DEVELOPMENT

Intertextual Analysis: Incorporating Information from a Visual Text

What Is It? To incorporate information from a visual text, students follow the same process as close reading written texts. Their first look at the image is the First Read. Its purpose is to describe what the image shows. During the Second Read, students look at visual details and composition. During the Third Read, students analyze the message the image is trying to convey.

Why Is It Important? Because so much of what we learn is now conveyed in images, analyzing visual elements is a critical comprehension skill. Image comprehension also enhances

2. What do you see that makes you think that?

Sample answer: I recognized the sun first. I identified Earth by its oceans and

continents, Saturn by its rings, and Mars because it is "the red planet." I infer that

the other planets are the rest of our solar system. Since each white line that runs

through each planet circles the sun, I conclude that the white lines represent

the planets' orbits.

_____

_____

_____

_____

_____

3. How does the picture help you understand why Earth supports life and other planets do not?

Sample answer: The picture shows that every planet is a different size and is a

different distance from the sun. Earth is the third planet: not too far from the sun,

but not too close. I also see blue oceans only on Earth. The water and distance

from the sun are clues to why Earth supports life and others do not.

_____

_____

_____

_____

_____

_____

_____

Text-Dependent Questions

As necessary, encourage discussion with such prompts as:

1. What is the biggest object in the picture? (Sample answer: the sun)

2. Where can you find our location in this picture? (Sample answer: We are on Earth, the third planet out from the sun.)

3. What inference can you make about the difference between planets closer to the sun compared to Earth? (Sample answer: They must be warmer than Earth as they are closer to the sun, which looks fiery and hot in this illustration.)

4. How big are other planets compared to Earth? (Sample answer: Some planets are bigger, and some planets look smaller.)

our comprehension of the written texts they accompany. For example, advertising imagery and copy can interact in complex ways to affect viewers.

How Do I Use It? Prompt students to identify the main idea of an image from the title and any labels. Then, have them analyze the image's details. In this image, have students identify the objects in the illustration and their relationships to one another. Have students identify what the curved lines represent (each planet's path around the sun). Students can then use details from the image to draw conclusions, for example, about the relative temperatures of the planets given their distances from the sun.

What Is Earth?

Tell students that they will read to learn about planet Earth.

1st READ

Set a Purpose

Explain to students that they will read to get a general understanding of what the text is about.

Have students read "What is Earth?" independently, annotating the text as they read. Remind students that suggested annotation symbols appear on page 8 of the Getting Started with Close Reading unit. Circulate and observe students' markings and notes, especially questions and anything they found confusing. The observations and annotations may be used to inform instruction. Based on students' needs, you may want to meet with them in small groups.

Use the Text-Dependent Questions to prompt students to engage with the text.

Text-Dependent Questions

1. What is this text about? (Sample answer: The text is about the features of Earth and how it supports life.)

Scaffolded Support Use the following scaffolded sentence frames and question as necessary to support comprehension.

Earth moves around _____.

Earth's _____ takes a year.

How do scientists learn about Earth?

✔ **Self-Monitoring Strategies** can help you check your understanding and clarify a text. Use them as you read.

☐ Visualize.　☐ Ask yourself questions.　☐ Draw conclusions.　☐ Reread to clarify.

Read this article to learn about planet Earth. Make annotations as you read. You may want to review Annotating a Text on page 8. Sample annotations appear throughout the text.

What Is Earth?

1　　Earth is our home planet. Four planets in the solar system are bigger than Earth. Three planets are smaller. It is the third-closest planet to the sun. Earth has been called the "Goldilocks planet." In the story "Goldilocks and the Three Bears," Goldilocks liked everything just right. Her porridge couldn't be too hot or too cold, and her bed couldn't be too hard or too soft. On Earth, everything is just right for living things. It's warm, but not too warm. It has water, but not too much water. Earth is the only planet known to have lots of liquid water, and liquid water is important for life. Earth is the only planet where life has been found.

2　　**What Does Earth Look Like?** From space, Earth looks like a blue marble with white swirls and brown, yellow, green, and white parts. The blue part is water, and the white swirls are clouds. The brown, yellow, and green parts are land, and the white parts are ice and snow.

3　　**How Does Earth Move?** Earth travels around the sun on a path called an *orbit.* Earth takes 365 days to travel once around the sun. We call one trip around the sun a *year.* Earth spins as it travels around the sun. Earth makes a full spin once every 24 hours. We call this a *day.* When places on Earth are facing toward the sun, it is daytime. When they are facing away, it is nighttime.

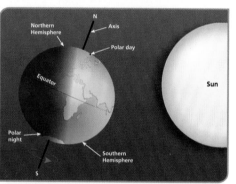

The tilt of Earth's axis. The Northern and Southern Hemispheres experience opposite seasons. One part of the planet is more directly exposed to the rays of the sun.

PROFESSIONAL DEVELOPMENT

Think-Aloud Modeling: Using Different Strategies

What Is It? One of the goals of close reading is to develop real-reader behaviors in your students—that is, to provide students with opportunities to approach a text the way a skilled, proficient reader would, taking full advantage of the repertoire of **Self-Monitoring Strategies** these readers use. To do this, it is important to model the strategies skilled readers use when confronted with text challenges. These include drawing conclusions, asking yourself questions, rereading to clarify, and visualizing.

Why Is It Important? Modeling the strategies using Think Alouds demonstrates your thinking to students and allows them repeated opportunities to see how skilled

Make notes here about your annotations from each read.
You will refer to these notes later when you return to
your annotations. Sample notes appear below.

ANNOTATION NOTES

Key Ideas and Details:

Earth is the planet where we live. It has lots of water in liquid form.

Earth is the only planet in our solar system that supports life.

Earth takes 365 days to travel once around the sun, which is a year.

Earth makes a full spin once every 24 hours, or a full day.

facing the sun = daytime

facing away from the sun = nighttime

Language and Text Structure:

Author compares life on Earth to Goldilocks in the bears' house: the

conditions are perfect. The comparison helps me understand that for life

to develop on a planet, the conditions have to be just right.

Connections and Inferences:

Seen from space, Earth looks unlike any other planet in the solar system.

The blue oceans, moving white clouds, and frozen white polar regions

show the presence of water.

2. What is a "Goldilocks Planet"?
(Sample answer: Based on the information in the first paragraph, it is a
planet where things are "just right"
for life.)

3. What four things make up
Earth? (Sample answer: Paragraph
6 describes how Earth is made up of
land, air, water, and life.)

Think Aloud *As I read the
text, I'm asking myself, "What
are all the things that people
and animals need to survive?"
Paragraph 6 gives the parts of the
planet, including land, air, and
water. Those are three things that
living things need for survival.*

Partner Talk Have pairs of students discuss what they learned
about planet Earth.

readers approach comprehension difficulties. With repeated
exposures, students will begin to internalize and use these
strategies while reading on their own.

How Do I Use It? Use the Think Alouds provided in the lessons.
Reinforce the specific Think Alouds from each read during
reflection at the end of each text. You may repeat or return
to the main points of prior Think Alouds to jog students'
memories. Have students describe their own use of strategies,
using your Think Aloud as a model. Have classmates volunteer
how they used a different strategy to understand the same
difficult concept or passage in a text, or how they applied the
same strategy to a different part of the text.

What Is Earth?

2nd READ

Set a Purpose

Students will return to "What Is Earth?" to understand the text structure.

Text-Dependent Questions

1. How does the author clue you in to what paragraph 3 is about with the boldfaced question "How Does Earth Move?" (Sample answer: I expect to find facts about how the planet moves through space.)

2. What text structure does the section "Why Does Earth Have Seasons?" use? (Sample answer: Paragraph 4 uses a cause-and-effect structure.)

Scaffolded Support Use the following scaffolded question as necessary to support comprehension.

> What does the word *because* tell you in the first sentence of the section "Why Does Earth Have Seasons?"

3. Vocabulary: Compound Words Have students analyze how combining words can modify their meaning.

Paragraph 3: How is "daytime" different from "day"? (Sample answer: In this text, a day is one full spin of Earth. Daytime is when the sun is shining on one part of Earth. Daytime is only about half of a day.)

Partner Talk Have students discuss how the boldfaced questions in each paragraph help organize the text.

4   **Why Does Earth Have Seasons?** Earth has seasons because it is tilted. The season depends on whether a place is tilted toward or away from the sun. In the summer, the Northern Hemisphere is tilted toward the sun. The sun's rays hit the Northern Hemisphere in a straight line, and the days are long and hot. The opposite happens in winter, when the north is tilted away from the sun, and the days are short and dark. When it is summer in the northern half of Earth, it is winter in the southern half. In the spring and fall, the sun shines evenly on both hemispheres.

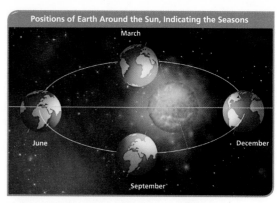

Positions of Earth Around the Sun, Indicating the Seasons

March

June

December

September

Earth rotates on its axis as it orbits the sun, but the axis always points in the same direction. Earth has seasons because its axis is tilted.

5   The equator is a make-believe line around the center of Earth. Mapmakers use the line to divide Earth into two halves: the Northern Hemisphere and the Southern Hemisphere. The northernmost point on Earth is called the North Pole. The southernmost point is the South Pole.

6   **What Are Earth's Different Parts?** Earth is made up of land, air, water, and life. Mountains, valleys, and flat places make up the land. The air is made of different gases. One of the gases is oxygen. Oceans, lakes, rivers, streams, rain, snow, and ice are made of water. Earth has many different kinds of life. People, animals, and plants live on Earth. Some living things are very tiny and some are very large. Each part of Earth connects to and works with the other parts.

7   **Why and How Does NASA Study Earth?** NASA studies Earth to learn how it changes. Scientists want to know how Earth has changed in the past and how it is changing now to help them predict how Earth might change in the future. NASA studies Earth with satellites, which look toward Earth from space and take pictures of Earth. They collect facts about Earth's parts that help scientists predict weather and climate. Knowing more about Earth helps people take better care of it.

84 • Unit 5

PROFESSIONAL DEVELOPMENT

Annotations: Confusions

What Is It? Annotations are text markups that record a reader's thoughts, ideas, and understandings while reading. Students can indicate a confusing area of the text with a question mark, an underline, or a written question in the margin.

Why Is It Important? Making annotations is a metacognitive strategy for self-monitoring comprehension. Emphasizing the use of confusion-related annotations can encourage persistence with difficult texts.

How Do I Use It? Encourage students to mark a difficult or confusing text on the first read with a question mark and

Make notes here about your annotations from each read.
You will refer to these notes later when you return to
your annotations. Sample notes appear below.

ANNOTATION NOTES

Key Ideas and Details:

The seasons, nighttime, and daytime are created by Earth's orbit, tilt,

and rotation.

The "equator is a make-believe line" mapmakers use to divide Earth.

When it is summer in the northern half, it is winter in the southern half.

NASA uses satellites to study Earth.

Earth's features: life, land, water, and air

Language and Text Structure:

The text is a series of questions and answers.

The image helps me understand how Earth is tilted and why that causes

seasons to happen.

Connections and Inferences:

NASA's work is not all about distant planets and outer space.

TV weatherpeople can predict the weather because of Earth's satellites.

to include questions in their annotation notes to come back
to during their second and third reads. Model annotating a
confusion: *In paragraph 4, I have trouble picturing how or
why Earth would tilt toward or away from the sun. I'll put a
question mark near some of the words I didn't understand,
like hemisphere. As I read again, I see that the north or south
halves of Earth are hemispheres. I can connect the confusing
parts to the diagram. It helps me see that Earth is always
tilted, but as it moves around the sun, different parts end up
angled toward or away from the sun.*

What Is Earth?

3rd READ

Set a Purpose
Students will read to draw
inferences from the text.

Text-Dependent Questions
1. What inference can you make
about the relationship between
Earth's movement and weather?
(I can infer from the information in
paragraph 3 that Earth's movement
has a big effect on weather. Paragraph
4 says that the way Earth is tilted
combined with its movement around
the sun causes the seasons, and the
weather changes as the seasons
change.)

Scaffolded Support Use the following scaffolded question and
sentence frame as necessary to
support comprehension.

   What changes are caused
   by Earth's movements?

   When the northern half
   of Earth tilts toward the
   sun _____.

2. What can you infer about
NASA scientists' interest in Earth?
(Paragraph 7 says NASA scientists are
collecting information so humans can
take better care of Earth, so they must
want to find ways to keep the planet
healthy and safe.)

Partner Talk Have students discuss
the inferences they drew from
the text about how other planets
might be different from Earth.

Respond to Reading

You may want to check students' understanding by having them complete page 86 in the Student Worktext.

1. Remind students that a summary should only include the key ideas and details essential to understanding what the text is about. Point out that they can use the graphic organizer on Student Worktext page 86 to capture and organize those key ideas and details. The graphic organizer should then guide them in writing their summaries.

2. Refer students to pages 12 and 13 in Getting Started to help them write their individual summaries.

Have students work independently to answer the questions on page 86 of their Worktexts.

COLLABORATE Have students exchange their final summaries with their partners and review each other's summaries. Remind pairs that when they review and discuss their partners' summaries, they should consider whether or not the summary has the following elements:

- contains only important information
- answers as many of the following as possible: Who? What? When? Where? and How?

REFLECT Have students use their annotations to identify points of confusion and the Self-Monitoring Strategies they used to clarify them.

Return to the TEXT

Respond to Reading: What Is Earth?

Review the annotations and notes you made while reading "What is Earth?" Think about how they can help you understand the text.

1. Use this Summary Chart to help you summarize the text.

Summary Chart		
	Informational Text	
Who?	the people or subjects	planet Earth, the solar system
What?	the topic or problem	Earth is a planet with living things.
Where?	the location or region where the events occur	Earth and our solar system
When?	the date, year, or time	the present time
How?	the events, steps, or process	Earth's spin creates day and night. Everything works together so living things have oxygen and water.

2. Use the completed graphic organizer from Item 1 to help you write a summary of "What Is Earth?"

Sample answer: Earth is one of the eight planets that make up our solar system. The temperature, the amount of water, and many other things make Earth ideal for the development of life. NASA studies Earth to learn how it changes.

REFLECT What word or phrase did you find confusing? What Self-Monitoring Strategy did you use to gain a better understanding of it?

Sample answer: At first I did not understand the difference between "orbit" and "spin." When I reread "How Does Earth Move?" I understood that Earth's "orbit" is its path around the sun, and its "spin" refers to the way it turns on its axis.

PROFESSIONAL DEVELOPMENT

Text Complexity: Reader and Task Factors

What Is It? The complexity of a given text depends, in part, on readers' skills and knowledge. Readers vary greatly in their cognitive and reading skills, motivations, prior knowledge, life experiences, and familiarity with the tasks required of them. By analyzing students and their varying needs, teachers can provide the appropriate scaffolding that supports full comprehension for all.

Why Is It Important? Complex texts tend to have more domain-specific language and grasping their meaning requires more inferencing and connecting ideas than simpler texts. For students used to skimming and scanning,

Comprehension Check: What Is Earth?

Answer the questions to demonstrate an understanding of what the text means.

1. How does the example of Goldilocks and the Three Bears help you understand how Earth is different from other planets? Give two examples of text evidence to support your answer.

   Sample answer: The story helped me understand that Earth is different because it is "just right." It is not "too hot or too cold." The first paragraph says that Earth is "the only planet known to have lots of liquid water." Because everything is "just right" on Earth and not on other planets, Earth is the only planet that is known to support life.

2. How do paragraphs 3 and 4 and the diagrams help you understand the relationship between Earth's tilt and the seasons? Provide text evidence to support your answer.

   Sample answer: The seasons are created by Earth's tilt combined with its orbit around the sun. Paragraph 4 says "The season depends on whether a place is tilted toward or away from the sun." The diagram helps me understand how the planet tilts and how it brings some places closer to or farther away from the sun.

3. How do paragraphs 3 and 4 and the diagram on page 84 help you understand how the planet's orbit relates to how we measure time? Provide text evidence to support your answer.

   Sample answer: We measure time by the movement of our planet. A day is the time it takes Earth to spin once on its axis as it orbits the sun. Paragraph 3 says that we call "one trip around the sun a *year*." The diagram shows the position of Earth around the sun at four different times of the year. I can see that it takes a full year for Earth to orbit the sun.

Unit 5 • 87

Stop and Assess

Use the following rubrics to assess your students' understanding of the text.

Item 1 answers indicate:	
2	Earth has conditions that are "just right" to support life, with specific text examples.
1	Earth has water and a mild climate, with text support.
0	no understanding of Earth's differences, and no text support.

Item 2 answers indicate:	
2	that Earth's tilt combined with its orbit around the sun causes seasons, with strong text support from the text and the diagram.
1	that Earth's tilt combined with its orbit around the sun causes seasons, with some support.
0	no understanding of how the tilt causes seasons, and no text support.

Item 3 answers indicate:	
2	that we measure time by how Earth moves, with specific evidence from the text and the diagram.
1	that we measure time by how Earth moves, with some text evidence.
0	no understanding of why or how the orbit affects how we measure time, and no evidence.

slowing down to read every word or line requires extra practice, as well as learning how to focus on content.

How Do I Use It? As you prepare for close reading assignments, identify words or passages for which your students might need scaffolding, Think-Aloud modeling, or similar support. Students may benefit from the use of dictionaries or glossaries to grasp domain-specific terms (for example, in this text: *hemisphere, solar, orbit, equator, satellites*). Students can benefit from peer-led activities in which students more familiar with a subject can offer explanations to students less familiar with the subject. Use productive conversation techniques such as revoicing to ensure that students with less background knowledge can make connections to the text.

Unit 5 • 87

Life on Mars?

Students will read to learn about Mars.

1st READ

Set a Purpose

Explain to students that they will read to find out what "Life on Mars?" is about.

Have students read "Life on Mars?" independently, annotating the text as they read. Remind students that suggested annotation symbols appear on page 8 of the Getting Started with Close Reading unit. Circulate and observe students' markings, especially questions and anything they found confusing. The observations and annotations may be used to inform instruction. Based on students' needs, you may want to meet with them in small groups.

Text-Dependent Questions

1. What is the text about? (Sample answer: The text is about what conditions on Mars are like and whether there is water and life on Mars.)

Scaffolded Support Use the following scaffolded question and sentence frame as necessary to support comprehension.

What are the first two paragraphs about?

The section "Latest Research" is about finding _____ on _____.

Partner Talk Have students discuss the facts about Mars presented in the article.

Read this magazine article to learn about Mars. Make annotations as you read. You may make different annotations each time you read.
Sample annotations and notes appear throughout the text.

Life on Mars?

What goes on upon all those distant globes? Are they worlds? It is in this that lies the peculiar interest of Mars. —Percival Lowell, astronomer (1855–1916)

The Planet Next Door

1   ! Earth is the third planet from the sun. Mars is the fourth from the sun and almost 150 million miles from it. Since it was first identified in the night sky in ancient times, Mars has been identified by its characteristic redness.

Exploring Mars

2   The telescope was invented in 1608. It enabled astronomers to examine
? the solar system in more detail than before. Mars was of special interest to them. They could see that it had dark patches that they thought must be oceans. They knew water supports life. They wondered if there could be life on Mars. People have been wondering the same thing ever since.

3   What if those astronomers could go to Mars and settle the question? What would they find when they get there? They would not get a warm welcome. The surface of Mars is cold, dry, and almost airless. The average
! temperature is minus 80 degrees Fahrenheit. That's about 40 degrees colder than the average winter temperature at the North Pole. Mars is rocky. There are canyons, extinct volcanoes, and craters. A layer of red dust covers the surface. Strong winds cause dust storms that cover the planet. The atmosphere on Mars is almost 96% carbon dioxide, which would be poisonous to humans. The air can also have up to 100% humidity at night.

Latest Research

4   New research has transformed our understanding of Mars. There are clouds. Snow falls at the planet's poles as the air warms during the day. Robotic exploration has revealed ancient water channels cut deep into the planet's surface. Areas of fossilized dust reveal extinct oceans. There are
! signs of a great flood 3.5 billion years ago. There is evidence that Mars had a warmer, wetter climate once—the kind of climate that supports life.

5   Where did all the water go? Many NASA scientists believe it went underground. If there ever has been life on Mars, could it still exist in water hidden beneath the planet's surface?

PROFESSIONAL DEVELOPMENT

Teacher Observation: Student Annotations

What Is It? Circulating as students independently annotate a text provides an opportunity to observe and record key ideas they highlight, misunderstandings that arise, places where background information is lacking, and points of confusion. You can use students' notes to create Text-Dependent Questions, identify places in the text to model strategies, and modify your plans for upcoming close readings of the text.

Why Is It Important? The most helpful scaffolding will arise from the comprehension needs of your students. Circulating and observing students while they annotate texts can provide you with this valuable information and give you insights into how your students are thinking about texts.

Make notes here about your annotations from each read.
You will refer to these notes later when you return to
your annotations. Sample notes appear below.

ANNOTATION NOTES

Key Ideas and Details:

People have wondered for a long time if there is life on Mars.

Recent research shows water on the surface of Mars = possibility of

underground oceans and life on Mars.

NASA's most recent ideas about Mars are based on "robotic exploration."

Language and Text Structure:

The quotation that begins the article previews what we will be reading

about by saying that people have been interested in Mars for a long time.

"Exploring Mars" tells what we know so far, and "Latest Research" tells

what we are doing to learn more.

The article ends with a question.

Connections and Inferences:

The more we understand why some planets are able to create life and some

are not, the better we will know what we are looking for.

Unit 5 • **89**

How Do I Use It? Record your findings by annotating your
copy of the text. In addition, you can create a simple three-
column note-taking form. Use the headings: "Preplanned
Text-Dependent Questions"; "Observations of Students: Name/
Misunderstanding"; and "New Text-Dependent Questions."
Use your observations and insights from student annotations
to develop scaffolded Text-Dependent Questions or probe
the meaning of the annotations. You might probe the sample
annotations on pages 88–89 by asking, *You added lots of
annotations to the paragraph about telescopes. How does
this paragraph connect to how we understand Mars today?*

Life on Mars?

2nd READ

Set a Purpose
Students will examine how the
text is organized.

Text-Dependent Questions
1. How is information organized in
this text? How does this structure
contribute to your understanding?
(The text is organized with headings
for each different section. The text
structure prepares me for what each
section will be about, and I know
where to look for specific information.)

2. What is the purpose of the quotation in the introduction? (It sets
up the text by quoting an astronomer
from over a hundred years ago, showing that people have been fascinated
by Mars for a long time.)

Partner Talk Have students
discuss how the text is organized.

3rd READ

Set a Purpose
Students will read to identify
the text's message.

Text-Dependent Questions
1. How has new research affected
our understanding of life on
Mars? (Paragraph 4 describes new
research that shows several signs
that Mars once had and may still have
water. A planet must have water to
support life.)

2. What conclusion does the text
reach about life on Mars? (It doesn't
reach a firm conclusion, but it says
that Mars may have hidden life.)

Partner Talk Have partners discuss
the text's message.

Unit 5 • **89**

Respond to Reading

You may want to check students' understanding by having them complete page 90 in the Student Worktext.

1. Suggest that students identify specific facts about Mars provided by the text and try to assign them to the categories given in the graphic organizer.

2. Have students use the information they recorded on their graphic organizers to describe the conditions on Mars as we know them.

3. Refer students to pages 12 and 13 of Getting Started to help them write their individual summaries.

Have students work independently to answer the questions on page 90 of their Worktexts.

COLLABORATE When finished, have students exchange summaries with their partners and review each other's summaries. Remind pairs that when they review and discuss their partners' summaries, they should consider whether or not the summary has the following elements:

- contains only important information

- answers as many of the following as possible: Who? What? When? Where? and How?

REFLECT Ask students to return to unfamiliar vocabulary noted in their annotations and to be sure that they have clarified the terms' meanings.

Return to the TEXT

Respond to Reading: Life on Mars?

Review the annotations and notes you made while reading "Life on Mars?" Think about how your annotations can help you answer the questions.

1. Use information from the text to complete the graphic organizer.

Mars Conditions That Do Not Support Life	Mars Conditions That Support Life
Sample answer: cold almost airless strong winds	Sample answer: possibility of water underground water in atmosphere (humidity)

2. Use your graphic organizer to describe conditions on Mars that support life and those that do not.

Sample answer: Most of the conditions on Mars make life there impossible. It is cold. There is no air that humans can breath. There are strong winds that create dust storms. Scientists believe the water on Mars is in underground oceans, and that there is water in the atmosphere. If that is true, it may support life.

3. Write a short summary of "Life on Mars?"

Sample answer: The disappearance of water from the surface of Mars is a mystery. Some scientists believe there might have been oceans below the planet's surface, and that there is still a possibility of life on Mars.

REFLECT What words, phrases, or sections did you ask yourself questions about to be sure you understood?

Sample answer: I asked myself what it would be like to live in a place that can be minus 80 degrees, and has wind storms and 100% humidity. I think it would be very difficult.

PROFESSIONAL DEVELOPMENT

Differentiation: Multiple Graphic Organizers

What Is It? Graphic organizers are flow charts, grids, and other diagrams used to organize and connect ideas. Using multiple graphic organizers can be an effective strategy for tackling complex informational texts with high knowledge demands.

Why Is It Important? Using multiple graphic organizers helps students connect ideas in multiple ways. For example, a branching graphic organizer might help students identify main ideas and details, while a two-column grid or Venn diagram might help students compare those ideas. The more connections students make, the more deeply they will comprehend what they read.

Return to the TEXT

Comprehension Check: Life on Mars?

Answer the questions to demonstrate an understanding of what the text means.

1. What information in "Life on Mars?" shows that Mars is not a "Goldilocks planet" like Earth?

Sample answer: Text 1 says Earth is the "Goldilocks planet" because it is

"warm, but not too warm," "has water, but not too much water," and has

"lots of liquid water." Text 2 says Mars has an average temperature of "minus

80 degrees Fahrenheit" and that the atmosphere is "poisonous to humans."

Conditions on Mars are not "just right" for life as they are on Earth.

2. What impact did the invention of the telescope have on people's ideas about Mars? Provide evidence from the text to support your answer.

Sample answer: When astronomers looked through telescopes for the first

time, they saw things "in more detail than before." They thought the

"dark patches" on the planet "must be oceans." The oceans would be the

source of life on Mars. The invention of the telescope was an early step in the

exploration for life on Mars.

3. What conclusion can you draw about life on Mars based on the information in paragraphs 4 and 5? Provide evidence from the text to support your answer.

Sample answer: I conclude that, while scientists still do not know for sure if

Mars can support life, there is enough evidence of life for them to keep

researching. They have found "clouds," "snow," "ancient water channels,"

and the possibility of "water hidden beneath the planet's surface," which gets

us closer to finding out if there is life on Mars.

Unit 5 • **91**

Stop and Assess

Use the following rubrics to assess your students' understanding of the text.

	Item 1 answers indicate:
2	that Mars cannot support life the way Earth supports life, based on information from the text.
1	that Mars cannot support life, with no text support.
0	no understanding of why Mars is different from Earth, and no text support.

	Item 2 answers indicate:
2	how telescopic views led to the assumption of life on Mars, with support from the text.
1	how early astronomers thought they saw life on Mars, with some text support.
0	no understanding of how telescopes led to the idea of life on Mars, and no text support.

	Item 3 answers indicate:
2	the ongoing mystery of life on Mars, with supporting ideas from the text.
1	the possibility of life on Mars, with some text support.
0	no understanding of the purpose of the question, and no text support.

How Do I Use It? Different texts with different purposes and organizations may need different graphic organizers. Select organizers to suit each text in this unit, such as a cause-and-effect organizer for "What Is Earth?" and a Venn diagram for "Life on Mars?" to compare what we used to know about Mars and what we now know about Mars. When students analyze and synthesize across texts, encourage them to use a third graphic organizer, such as a Venn diagram, to compare and contrast the major ideas they wrote down in the first two graphic organizers. Students can even compare and contrast the graphic organizers themselves, noting that the first text uses one structure, while the second text uses a different structure.

Unit 5 • **91**

Return to the Focus Question

Explain to students that they will fill out a graphic organizer that will help them answer the Focus Question: Why does Earth support life and other planets do not?

CONNECT TEXTS Have small groups of students discuss how each text they read helps them answer the Focus Question. Have small groups share and compare their discussion notes with another small group.

Scaffolded Support You may provide the following sentence frames to support students in their use of academic language:

> In the text _____, the author/artist makes the point that _____. He/she does this by _____.

Remind students to use their annotations and summaries to support their answers. They can also reread portions of the texts, if necessary.

Have students complete their graphic organizers individually and then answer the Focus Question.

REFLECT Remind students that each text provides information about planetary conditions. Ask, *How did reading all three texts give you a greater understanding of why Earth supports life and other planets do not?*

ANALYZE and SYNTHESIZE ACROSS TEXTS

Return to the Focus Question: Why does Earth support life and other planets do not?

Review your answers to questions about the texts as well as your annotations and Annotation Notes. Think about the discussions you've had about the texts. How does that information help you answer the Focus Question?

Use this graphic organizer to organize information about the texts.

1. In the boxes, record the details from each text that help you answer the Focus Question.

2. Make connections between those details to help you answer the Focus Question. Write your answer in the box provided.

Planets of the Solar System in Orbit (Visual Text)
Sample answer: Earth has an ideal spot near the sun.

What Is Earth?
Sample answer: Earth has water, oxygen, and the right temperature.

Life on Mars?
Sample answer: Mars is cold and airless.

Why does Earth support life and other planets do not?
Sample answer: To support life, a planet must have the right conditions. Mars does not now have the conditions to support life. Earth is the only planet we know of with the air, water, and temperature to support life.

REFLECT How did making connections between the three texts help you to answer the Focus Question?

The Visual Text shows that Earth has perfect conditions for life because of its water

and distance from the sun. Text 1 says that a planet must have the right degree of

warmth to support life. Text 2 describes what a planet needs to support life.

PROFESSIONAL DEVELOPMENT

Intertextual Analysis: Citing Evidence from Multiple Sources

What Is It? Students compare two or more texts in terms of purpose, point of view, or other specific aspects. The more specific the comparison being made, and the greater the variety of texts, the more useful it is for helping students develop reading and writing skills. Comparisons may be made across genres, as in comparing a photo to a written text, or across media, as in comparing a graph to a bulleted list.

Why Is It Important? Being able to approach a topic from multiple vantage points is an important higher-order

Writing About the Focus Question

Now that you have answered the Focus Question using all three texts, develop your ideas into a longer piece of writing.

USE EVIDENCE

- Explain why Earth supports life and other planets do not. Use at least one piece of evidence from each text to support your answer.
- If you need more room, use additional paper.

MONITOR

- Use the Writing Checklist as you work to make sure your writing has all of the important pieces of information.
- Use the rubric on page 94 when you have completed your first draft to help you evaluate, revise, and edit your work.

WRITING CHECKLIST ✔

Does my writing . . .

- ☐ answer the Focus Question?
- ☐ provide text evidence to support my ideas?
- ☐ have a clear beginning, middle, and end?
- ☐ use correct language, spelling, and conventions?

Unit 5 • **93**

Writing About the Focus Question

USE EVIDENCE Remind students that they should use their graphic organizers as well as their annotations in the texts to write their responses.

Allow students to revisit the texts as frequently as they need to in order to support comprehension and to respond to the Focus Question.

MONITOR After students have completed their responses, have them review the Writing Checklist and revise their writing responses.

DIFFERENTIATE AND EXTEND

In addition to or instead of the writing response, consider having students complete one of the following assignments:

Write Beyond Have students assume the role of a space explorer in search of life on other planets and describe the planetary conditions they are hoping to find in a speech to an audience of scientists.

Create a Visual Text Have students use the library or online resources to create a slideshow of photographs of the surfaces of other planets or solar-system bodies, such as large moons.

Research Have students research "extra-solar planets," or planets outside the solar system, and whether scientists think they could support life.

Design a Brochure Have students work independently to create a brochure advertising a planet that is "ideal for human life."

thinking skill. Comparing texts helps students learn to distinguish between facts and opinions, analyze how authors use facts, and find details to support their own ideas.

How Do I Use It? In this unit, different texts tackle different but related facets of the Focus Question. Students will have to draw conclusions by linking each of the texts and making connections among the texts' details. Have students break down the Focus Question into subquestions such as, "Why does Earth support life?" and "What are conditions like on other planets?" Students can search for answers from individual texts, and then synthesize how these pieces help answer the Focus Question.

Unit 5 • **93**

SELF-ASSESS and REFLECT

SELF-ASSESS Have students use the Writing Rubric on page 94 to self-assess their writing response and write a final version. Tell them to assign themselves a score from 1–4 (with "4" being the highest) for each category in the first column.

REFLECT Use the Writing Rubric on Student Worktext page 94 to assess each student's writing. Record points for each category in the first column of the rubric. Have students remove the page from their Student Worktexts and place it in their writing portfolios, along with the drafts and final versions of their responses.

SELF-ASSESS and REFLECT

Focus Question Why does Earth support life and other planets do not?

This is the rubric that your teacher will use to assess your writing. Refer to it as you revise your work. After you have finished your final version, review your writing and record your points for each category on the "Student" line in the first column.

	Accomplished (4 points)	Competent (3 points)	Developing (2 points)	Beginning (1 point)
RESPONSE Score: Student _____ Teacher _____	The response answers the question effectively and with insight.	The response answers the question effectively.	The response partially responds to the question but does not adequately address it.	The response addresses the texts but does not address the question.
ORGANIZATION Score: Student _____ Teacher _____	The main idea is convincingly stated. Ideas are organized in cohesive paragraphs that support the main idea.	The main idea is clearly stated. Ideas are organized in logical paragraphs.	The main idea is weak. Ideas are organized in a somewhat logical and cohesive way.	The main idea is missing. The organization of the paragraphs is not logical.
TEXT EVIDENCE Score: Student _____ Teacher _____	Response includes more than one piece of appropriate text evidence from each text. Evidence supports the main idea in a thorough way.	Response includes one piece of text evidence from each text. Evidence supports the main idea clearly.	Response does not include at least one piece of text evidence from each text. Text evidence does not adequately support the main idea.	Response does not contain relevant evidence.
LANGUAGE Score: Student _____ Teacher _____	Writing includes precise and sophisticated vocabulary related to the topic.	Writing includes appropriate vocabulary related to the topic.	Writing includes imprecise and inaccurate vocabulary.	Writing does not include vocabulary that appropriately reflects the topic of the response.
SPELLING AND CONVENTIONS Score: Student _____ Teacher _____	Response includes correct spelling, grammar, and punctuation consistently.	Response includes mostly correct spelling, grammar, and punctuation.	Response has many errors in spelling, grammar, and punctuation.	Response's errors in spelling, grammar, and punctuation make it extremely difficult to understand the response.

UNIT 6

Focus Question What kinds of relationships do people have with their dogs?

Texts for Close Reading

Unit 6 • **95**

GENRE STUDY

Discuss with students the genres of "Why the Indian Loves His Dog" and "From Wolf into Dog."

Remind students that *genre* refers to the format and features of a text and typically falls into one of two categories—literature or informational text. Literature is a creative work that doesn't necessarily rely on facts, and informational text is based on factual information. This unit includes both literature and an informational text: a short story based on a myth and a factual article. Each tells a different version of the same process of dog domestication. One is meant to be interpreted figuratively, the other literally, and both suggest some larger themes about the topic. Have students identify characteristics a story and an article might share and characteristics unique to each genre.

Have students read the Focus Question on Worktext page 95. Tell them that the texts and illustrations in this unit will help them answer this question.

Texts for Close Reading

Have students read to themselves the descriptions of the texts in this unit.

There is no need to explain what students should expect to find in their close readings or to do any preteaching about the subject matter.

TEXT COMPLEXITY

Fire House Dog
- Style: documentary
- Knowledge demands: medium
- Levels of meaning: literal/inferential

Why the Indian Loves His Dog
Quantitative: 590L
Qualitative
- Structure: conventional
- Language: archaic
- Knowledge demands: medium
- Levels of meaning: literal/inferential

From Wolf into Dog
Quantitative: 760L
Qualitative
- Structure: conventional
- Language: academic
- Knowledge demands: high
- Levels of meaning: literal/inferential

Unit 6 • **95**

Fire House Dog

Set a Purpose

Explain to students that they will look at the image on page 96 to begin to gain a deeper understanding of people's relationships with dogs.

Visual Text Analysis

Remind students that an image can be analyzed as a text by looking at its details and making inferences. Direct students' attention to the image on Student Worktext page 96.

Encourage students to annotate the Visual Text. Suggest they use arrows, labels, circles, margin notes, and other markings to highlight details that will help them gain a better understanding of the meaning of the image.

1. Have students record their first impressions about the image. Lead them to discuss as a whole class, in small groups, or with a partner what they think is happening in the photograph.

2. Encourage students to make note of the details that support their observations in question 1. Have them identify the figures in the image and how they relate to each other. Have students explain as a whole class, in small groups, or with a partner what details they noted and what those details might tell them about relationships between people and dogs.

3. Guide students to synthesize all the details they see in the photograph to draw conclusions about what the image tells them about the relationship between dogs and humans.

Fire House Dog

Look at this Visual Text, and make annotations on the image. Review the image or parts of the image as many times as necessary to answer the following questions.

1. What is your first impression of this photograph?

Sample answer: There are five firefighters and a white dog with black spots. All the firefighters are looking at the dog and smiling. The dog looks as if he enjoys the attention. They are all happy.

PROFESSIONAL DEVELOPMENT

Academic Language: Language Frames

What Is It? Academic language plays a vital role in academic success. It is more formal than casual conversation and employs academic and domain-specific vocabulary. Students should practice using academic language to become "fluent." Language frames, sentences with intentional blank spaces that students complete, can help students effectively use academic language.

Why Is It Important? Language frames facilitate critical thinking and encourage students to cite details from the text to support their answers. They can provide the basis for productive class discussion.

2. What details in the photograph helped give you that impression?

Sample answer: The people are all dressed in firefighter suits. The firefighters are

all kneeling close to the dog at the dog's level. They are all laughing or smiling.

At the front of the photo, two firefighters are petting the dog. The dog seems

happy, like he is enjoying the closeness and attention of the firefighters.

_____

_____

_____

_____

_____

_____

3. How does the image help you understand the relationships between dogs and humans?

Sample answer: The image shows that the humans and the dog are happy in one

another's company. The humans feel friendly toward the dog, and the dog feels the

same. The firefighters are dressed for work, so I can infer that this dog may be a part

of their work as well as a friend.

_____

_____

_____

_____

_____

_____

_____

Text-Dependent Questions

As necessary, encourage discussion with such prompts as:

1. Who are the people in the photograph? (Sample answer: They are firefighters.)

2. Where was the photograph taken? (Sample answer: It is in a fire house; there are trucks behind the firefighters, and the title mentions a fire house.)

3. What do you notice about the relationship the firefighters have with the dog? (Sample answer: The firefighters are all smiling at the dog, and the dog even seems to be smiling back at them. I think the firefighters really love the dog. They probably rely on the dog for some things, too, and the dog must trust the people, because they all work together in a dangerous job.)

How Do I Use It? Use language frames to assist students as they analyze the Visual Text _Fire House Dog._ Use frames that guide students to cite evidence from the image. _The figures in the photo are _____. They are positioned _____. Their facial expressions are _____. Based on this information, I can infer that _____._

Why the Indian Loves His Dog

Tell students that they will read to learn about one man's relationship with dogs.

1st READ

Set a Purpose

Explain to students that they will read to get a general understanding of what the text is about.

Have students read "Why the Indian Loves His Dog" independently, annotating the text as they read. Remind students that suggested annotation symbols appear on page 8 of the Getting Started with Close Reading unit. Circulate and observe students' markings and notes, especially questions and anything they found confusing. The observations and annotations may be used to inform instruction. Based on students' needs, you may want to meet with them in small groups.

Use the Text-Dependent Questions to prompt students to engage with the text.

Text-Dependent Questions

1. What is this text about? (This text is about the relationship between a man and his dogs. They are partners, but the man does not want to live the violent way of animals. So the man and the dogs can no longer speak, but they remain loyal friends.)

Scaffolded Support Use the following scaffolded question and sentence frame as necessary to support comprehension.

What goal do the man and the dogs share?

When the man lives by the law of dogs, he _____ .

✔ **Self-Monitoring Strategies** can help you check your understanding and clarify a text. Use them as you read.

☐ Visualize. ☐ Ask yourself questions. ☐ Draw conclusions. ☐ Reread to clarify.

Read this story to learn about one man's relationship with dogs. Make annotations as you read. You may want to review Annotating a Text on page 8.
Sample annotations appear throughout the text.

Why the Indian Loves His Dog

from *Stories the Iroquois Tell Their Children,* Retold by Mabel Powers, 1917

1 ? The dog is the Indian's best friend. He is the comrade by day and the protector by night.

2 Here is how this came to be.

3 An Indian and his dogs went into the woods to hunt. It was in the days when dogs and men could talk together, and each understood
! the language of the other.

4 When they reached the woods, the dogs began to talk. They told the Indian many wonderful things about the woods. They taught him
? how to scent and track the game, and where to look for trails.

5 The man listened to what the dogs said, and he did as they told him. Soon the ground was piled high with deer and other game.

6 Never had the Indian's arrows brought him so much game. He was so pleased that he said to the dogs, "Always shall I listen to what you say, and be one of you."

7 "Ah, but listen!" said the dogs. "If you wish to be one of us, you must live under the law of dog. Animals have different laws. When two dogs meet, they use their strength to see which is the better dog.

8 "But men do not fight when strangers meet. They shake hands. As we fight strange dogs, so you, too, must fight strange men to see which is the best man. You must do this if you are to live under the law of dogs."

PROFESSIONAL DEVELOPMENT

Annotations: Connections

What Is It? As students annotate a text or multiple texts, they circle or otherwise highlight key terms or ideas that link ideas, events, characters, or themes. They use graphic organizers and other strategies to connect this information and achieve a global view of the topic.

Why Is It Important? Making connections throughout a literary text helps students track characters, plot lines, and, eventually, themes and unstated meanings. Making connections between texts allows for a more thorough analysis of a topic.

Make notes here about your annotations from each read. You will refer to these notes later when you return to your annotations. Sample notes appear below.

ANNOTATION NOTES

Key Ideas and Details:

In this story, humans and dogs understand each other's language.

The man's dogs tell him he needs to obey the law of dogs: When dogs

meet, they fight to test each other to see who is stronger. When men

meet, they shake hands.

Language and Text Structure:

"comrade" means "companion" or "friend"?

"scent and track the game" = "game" must be what you get when you go

hunting—maybe an animal used for food

Connections and Inferences:

Dogs have different laws and customs than humans. They fight to see who

is stronger. I infer that men developed a more peaceful way of life.

2. Why doesn't the man like the "law of dog"? (Sample answer: Paragraph 13 says that when the man fights the strangers, which he must under the "law of dog," he gets hurt.)

Scaffolded Support Use the following scaffolded question and sentence frame as necessary to support comprehension.

> What happens when the man fights the strangers?

> The man thinks it is better to _____.

3. What do the dogs agree to do for the man when he says he will once more "live under the law of men"? (Sample answer: In paragraph 15 the dogs say they will no longer be able to talk to the man, but they will remain his loyal friends.)

Think Aloud *I'm not sure why the man has to fight strangers, so I'll reread to clarify. Here in paragraph 7 is the explanation. To be one with the dogs, the man must follow their laws. When two dogs meet, they fight "to see which is the better dog." So the man needs to fight people he doesn't know when he meets them if he follows the law of dogs.*

Partner Talk Have partners discuss the relationship between the man and the dogs.

How Do I Use It? As students read, they are encouraged to mark connections or surprising information with an exclamation point. For example, an important element of this story is that people and dogs once communicated with language. A student might make a connection between this idea and ideas in other stories they have read in which animals speak and place an exclamation point next to the phrase "each understood the language of the other" in paragraph 3. Encourage students to reference specific lines or paragraphs they have annotated in annotation notes. This will help them recall their connections upon later rereading or analysis.

Why the Indian Loves His Dog

2nd READ

Set a Purpose

Students will return to "Why the Indian Loves His Dog" to understand how the text structure supports the author's purpose.

Text-Dependent Questions

1. How does the dialogue help you understand the text? (Sample answer: The dogs are speaking to the human in the beginning of the story, so I can tell this is a made-up story and not a true story about "why the Indian loves his dog.")

2. How does the information about the Happy Hunting Ground support the author's purpose? (Sample answer: Paragraphs 17–20 help the reader understand "why the Indian loves his dog." Dogs are in control of a "great log upon which the souls pass" to the Happy Hunting Ground.)

3. Vocabulary: Multiple-Meaning Words Discuss unfamiliar meanings of words in context.

Paragraph 4: What does *game* mean in this text, and how can you tell? (Sample answer: *Game* means "animals people hunt." I can tell because the text describes deer as one kind of game.)

Partner Talk Have students discuss the author's word choice and how the author's purpose is expressed in the story.

---

9   The man said he would think it over. Next morning, the man said he would live under the law of animals.

10   The following day, the man made ready to
?   leave the woods. He made a strong harness for the dogs, so that they could help bring the game back to the camp.

11   When the sun was high, the man and the dogs left. They had not gone far before they saw two strange Indians coming.

12   "Now," said the dogs to the man, "remember you are living under the dog's law. You must fight these strange men."

13   The man attacked first one Indian and then the other. When they left him, he was badly injured. Seeing this, the dogs leaped upon the Indians and drove them away. Then the dogs came back to where their friend lay on the ground. They began to lick his face.

14   The man could not speak for some time. But then he said to the dogs, "No longer do I wish to live under the law of animals. No more shall I fight strangers. I shall shake hands with strangers and will bid them welcome. From this time, I shall be a man and live under the law of men."

15   "Then," said the dogs sadly, "we shall no longer be able to talk with you. We won't tell you the things we know. But we will always stand by you. We will fight for you, when you need us."

16   This is why the Indian and his dog are no longer able to speak each other's language. This is also why an Indian's dog will fight for his friend.

17   The dog is a true friend to the Indian. The soul of an Indian on its
?   journey to the Happy Hunting Ground must cross a deep, swift-running stream. On either side, two dogs hold in their teeth a great log upon which the souls pass.

18   The soul of the Indian who has been kind to his dog crosses the log easily.

19   But if the soul of an Indian who has been unkind to his dog comes to the river, the dogs say, "This man was cruel to his dog. This man shall not cross."

20   Then when the soul of the unkind Indian is halfway across, they turn
!   the log quickly. The soul is thrown into the deep, dark river.

100 ● Unit 6

PROFESSIONAL DEVELOPMENT

Productive Conversation: Reasoning

What Is It? Reasoning is the use of logic, inferences, and connections to draw conclusions. It is a critical thinking skill.

Why Is It Important? Reasoning is the process by which we find deeper meaning and connections within and between texts. It is also a metacognitive skill; when students are able to identify and analyze their own and others' reasoning, they are better able to apply it to new situations.

How Do I Use It? When asked, "Why do you think that?" students are likely to volunteer their reasoning. Drawing students back to the text can allow you to help students untangle their reasoning by identifying what the student

Make notes here about your annotations from each read. You will refer to these notes later when you return to your annotations. **Sample notes appear below.**

ANNOTATION NOTES

Key Ideas and Details:

Turning point of the story = when the man fights the two strangers.

They injure him. He then changes his mind about living under the law of dogs.

Language and Text Structure:

Happy Hunting Ground—souls must cross river to get here.

Connections and Inferences:

Message: Man had to go his separate way from the animals.

Some animals, like dogs, remain very loyal to humans if humans are kind

to them. Being kind to animals is important for human beings. Their

future may depend on the way they treat animals.

Unit 6 • **101**

thought vs. what was stated in the text. For example: *Why do you say the man gave up on his agreement? (Paragraph 14 says that he no longer wants to live under the law of animals.) Does the author say that he "gave up"? (The man says, "no longer do I wish.") How do the dogs see it? (They seem disappointed, but they are still his friends.) Do you think the author intended that the man was "giving up"? (No; it sounds more like he changed his mind after trying it.)*

Why the Indian Loves His Dog

3rd READ

Set a Purpose
Students will read to make inferences from the text.

Text-Dependent Questions
1. What inference can you make about the relationship between the man and his dogs? (Sample answer: Based on the events in paragraphs 13 and 14, I can infer that the man loves the dogs. They share how to hunt and they always defend him, but even though he loves them, he cannot be one of them.)

Scaffolded Support Use the following scaffolded sentence frame and question as necessary to support comprehension.

The dogs shared their knowledge of _____ with the man.

When the man is hurt by a stranger, what do the dogs do?

2. What is one theme of this story? (Sample answer: One theme is that kindness is rewarded and cruelty is punished. Paragraph 20 says that the souls of the kind pass over the log bridge, but the souls of the cruel are "thrown into the deep, dark river.")

Partner Talk Have pairs talk about inferences they made about the relationships between people and dogs.

Respond to Reading

You may want to check students' understanding by having them complete page 102 in the Student Worktext.

1. Remind students that a summary should only include the key ideas and details essential to understanding what the text is about. Point out that they can use the graphic organizer on Student Worktext page 102 to capture and organize those key ideas and details. The graphic organizer should then guide them in writing their summaries.

2. Refer students to pages 12 and 13 in Getting Started to help them write their individual summaries.

Have students work independently to answer the questions on page 102 of their Worktexts.

COLLABORATE Have students exchange their final summaries with their partners and review each other's summaries. Remind pairs that when they review and discuss their partners' summaries, they should consider whether or not the summary has the following elements:

- contains only important information
- answers as many of the following as possible: Who? What? When? Where? and How?

REFLECT Have students look for question marks in their annotation notes in order to identify any confusing words or phrases.

Return to the TEXT

Respond to Reading: Why the Indian Loves His Dog

Review the annotations and notes you made while reading "Why the Indian Loves His Dog." Think about how they can help you understand the text.

1. Use this Story Map to help you summarize the text.

Characters (Who)	Setting (Where and When)
storyteller, "an Indian and his dogs," "two strange Indians"	the woods in legendary time, long ago

Conflict (What)	Main Events (How)
fight between the main character and two strangers; the law of dogs vs. the law of men	Dogs convince man to live under the law of dogs. Man loses fight with strangers, so he changes his mind. Then dogs lose the power to talk to him, but they will stand by man. Man must be kind to dogs.

2. Use the completed graphic organizer from item 1 to help you write a summary of "Why the Indian Loves His Dog."

Sample answer: A man tries to live under the law of dogs (to fight strangers). He fought two strangers and lost. The man said he would now live under the law of men and shake hands. The dogs said that they would not talk to him anymore. But they would stand by him. The man is kind to dogs.

REFLECT What word or phrases did you find confusing? What Self-Monitoring Strategy did you use to gain a better understanding of it?

Sample answer: I didn't know at first what the "Happy Hunting Ground" was. But then I visualized the dogs holding the great log over the river. The soul of a kind man could cross, but the soul of a cruel man could not.

PROFESSIONAL DEVELOPMENT

Small-Group Discussion: Hearing Multiple Perspectives

What Is It? Pairs and groups of 3–6 students work independently to have informal discussions of the text or an assigned topic. The teacher circulates to monitor, motivate, and keep the discussion on topic.

Why Is It Important? Partner and small-group discussion can help ease the pressure individuals may feel when speaking in front of an entire class but can continue to give students practice in hearing multiple perspectives and negotiating group conversations.

Comprehension Check: Why the Indian Loves His Dog

Answer the questions to demonstrate an understanding of what the text means.

1. How does the text answer the question of "why the Indian loves his dog"? Give evidence from the text to support your answer.

   The text shows the ways in which the man depends on dogs and why he
   loves them. First, the man and the dogs work together to hunt. Then, the dogs
   help the man after he is injured in a fight. The man says he cannot live "under
   the law of animals." Finally, if a man is kind to his dogs, man will still receive
   help from dogs on the "journey to the Happy Hunting Ground."

2. What inferences can you make about the difference between the law of dogs and the law of men? Cite text evidence to support your answer.

   Sample answer: The law of dogs is based on force and violence and great
   loyalty. The law of men is based on being kind and polite. Dogs fight strangers
   "to see which is the best." Men "shake hands with strangers and will bid
   them welcome." That way men avoid attacks and injury.

3. What does the final agreement between the man and his dogs tell you about the relationship of humans with animals? Give text evidence to support your answer.

   Sample answer: At the end of the story, dogs and humans are "no longer able
   to speak each other's language," but they are still friends. The dogs promise to
   "stand by" the humans. The humans must be kind to dogs if they expect their
   souls to travel to the Happy Hunting Ground. So the dogs will be loyal, and
   the humans will be kind.

Unit 6 • **103**

Stop and Assess

Use the following rubrics to assess your students' understanding of the text.

Item 1 answers indicate:	
2	the text shows how the man depends on dogs, with ample text evidence.
1	the dogs are the man's friend, with some text evidence.
0	no understanding of the dogs' relationship with the man, and no text evidence.

Item 2 answers indicate:	
2	an inference about the difference between the law of dogs and the law of men, with specific supporting examples.
1	a contrast of how dogs and men live, with some text support.
0	no understanding of the contrast, and no text support.

Item 3 answers indicate:	
2	a close relationship across species, with sufficient text support.
1	a close friendship, with some text support.
0	no explanation of the relationship, and no text support.

How Do I Use It? Partner and small-group discussions work best when planned. Choose groups based on the purpose of the discussion. For example, the Collaborate activity on page 102 involves peer review of student writing and clearly works best with pairs. During discussions, note individual participation, including whether students are reluctant or domineering. Record data and use it for future groupings. During discussions, encourage students to allow their peers to contribute, even if opinions differ. Model productive conversation by asking students to find evidence for their ideas and opinions in the text.

From Wolf into Dog

Students will read an article to learn about wolves and dogs.

1st READ

Set a Purpose

Explain to students that they will read to find out what "From Wolf into Dog" is about.

Have students read "From Wolf into Dog" independently, annotating the text as they read. Remind students that suggested annotation symbols appear on page 8 of the Getting Started with Close Reading unit. Circulate and observe students' markings, especially questions and anything they found confusing. The observations and annotations may be used to inform instruction. Based on students' needs, you may want to meet with them in small groups.

Text-Dependent Questions

1. What is this text mainly about? (It is about how wolves changed over time to become domestic dogs.)

2. What details does the text describe about this change? (In paragraph 5 it says wolves followed humans and started to depend on humans for food and shelter.)

Scaffolded Support Use the following scaffolded sentence frame and question as necessary to support comprehension.

Wolves began to _____ humans.

What did the wolves get from the humans?

Partner Talk Have partners summarize for each other what happened when wolves became domesticated.

Read this article to learn about wolves and dogs. Make annotations as you read. You may make different annotations each time you read.
Sample annotations and notes appear throughout the text.

From Wolf into Dog

1 Dogs are such amazing creatures. We tend to think that they must always have been with us. But the long-ago ancestors of dogs were wild
! animals, not pets or companions. They were almost certainly wolves.

2 **The Life of Wolves** Wolves are larger than most breeds of dog. Their warm coat allows them to live in cold weather. They are strong and clever hunters. They eat deer, bison, and other smaller animals. Most wolves do
? not live alone. They live in groups called (packs). Living in a pack gives wolves protection. They usually have good relationships with other wolves.

3 ? **Domestication** Wild animals are domesticated when they become tame. Over many thousands of years, humans have domesticated many different animals. For example, cats, chickens, horses, camels, goats, sheep, and bees all now accept the company of humans. Humans depend on domestic animals for food, clothing, companionship, and help. It is hard to imagine our lives today without domestic animals.

4 **When, How, and Where?** Experts agree that dogs were the first wild animals to become domesticated. When, how, and where did wolves first become dogs? Many scientists think that domestication first took place about 15,000 years ago. But some experts believe that date is too recent.
! The process of domestication may be as much as 30,000 years old. The prehistoric cave paintings found in 1994 at Chauvet in France include an image of a child's footprints close to those of a dog or a wolf. The Chauvet paintings have been dated to about 35,000 years ago.

5 How did wolves become tame? We cannot know for sure. When humans lived in small hunter-gatherer groups, wolf packs probably followed the groups on hunts. They could have (scavenged) for meat left behind by the human hunters. They may have guarded human settlements by giving warning to other wolves of dangers in the area. Slowly, some wolves lost fear of humans and began to depend on their relationship with humans for their (food and shelter). Man began to understand how to benefit from the tamer wolves' presence.

6 Where did the first dogs develop from their wolf ancestors? Once again, there is no firm answer. Many experts think wolves developed into dogs at different times in different places.

PROFESSIONAL DEVELOPMENT

Text Complexity: High-Knowledge Demands

What Is It? Some informational texts have a concentration of domain-specific vocabulary and concepts that demand higher-order thinking from readers. Even the best readers must read slowly and closely, and additional domain-specific knowledge might be needed to achieve full comprehension.

Why Is It Important? The ability to work through complex texts and meet high-knowledge demands without discouragement is essential to students in education, in training for jobs that require technical knowledge, and in meeting the demands of a complex world.

Make notes here about your annotations from each read. You will refer to these notes later when you return to your annotations. Sample notes appear below.

ANNOTATION NOTES

Key Ideas and Details:

Dogs developed from wild wolves. Some wolves became tame over

thousands of years. Wolves lost their fear of humans and began to depend

on them.

Language and Text Structure:

ancestors = people who have gone before in a family

packs = groups

domestication = the process of becoming tame

List of animals in paragraph 3 helps me understand how important

domestic animals are to people.

Connections and Inferences:

Domestication of wolves must have been a slow process, and likely took

hundreds or thousands of years. Wolves must have changed in many ways

to turn into dogs, who are close companions to humans.

Unit 6 • 105

How Do I Use It? Help students comprehend the scientific meanings of the details and fit those details into a bigger picture. For "From Wolves into Dogs," suggest that students use unfamiliar words as a starting point for a graphic organizer or mind map about the topic. Have them define new words from the text and use the words to link to the topic of wolves, dogs, humans, and how people came to live and hunt with animals.

From Wolf into Dog

2nd READ

Set a Purpose
Students will examine how the text is structured.

Text-Dependent Questions
1. What is the main purpose of the first three paragraphs? (Sample answer: They give background information about wolves, dogs and domestic animals.)

2. How do paragraphs 5 and 6 connect to paragraphs 1 and 2? (Sample answer: These paragraphs describe what we understand about how wild wolves became domestic animals.)

Partner Talk Have partners consider how ideas build on each other in this text, such as the steps described in domestication.

3rd READ

Set a Purpose
Students will read to draw inferences from the text.

Text-Dependent Questions
1. What inference can you make about why humans domesticate animals? (Sample answer: I can infer that people domesticate animals so that they can use the animals for something people need. Some domesticated animals provide food and clothing. Some help people. For example, horses are used for transportation, and dogs can protect people.)

Partner Talk Have students discuss inferences they made about how and why wolves were domesticated.

Unit 6 • 105

Respond to Reading

You may want to check students' understanding by having them complete page 106 in the Student Worktext.

1. Have students reread the text and look for sentences that state the major ideas in each paragraph or section. Then have students locate details that support each major idea. They should use these to complete the graphic organizer.

2. Refer students to pages 12 and 13 of Getting Started to help them write their individual summaries.

3. Encourage students to think about what they now know that they didn't know before reading the text, and what that might tell them about the author's purpose for writing the text.

Have students work independently to answer the questions on page 106 of their Worktexts.

COLLABORATE When finished, have students exchange summaries with their partners and review each other's summaries. Remind pairs that when they review and discuss their partners' summaries, they should consider whether or not the summary has the following elements:

- contains only important information
- answers as many of the following as possible: Who? What? When? Where? and How?

REFLECT Suggest that students refer to their annotations to help them recall parts of the text that caused them confusion during their first read.

Return to the TEXT

Respond to Reading: From Wolf into Dog

Review the annotations and notes you made while reading "From Wolf into Dog." Think about how your annotations can help you answer the questions.

1. Use information from the text to complete the graphic organizer.

Major Ideas	Supporting Details
Sample answer: dogs descended from wolves domesticated 15,000–35,000 years ago hunted with humans	Sample answer: wolves live in packs cooperate with other wolves lost fear of humans

2. Use your graphic organizer to write a brief summary of "From Wolf into Dog."

Sample answer: Wolves were the long-ago ancestors of today's dogs and were domesticated many thousands of years ago. We know wolves live in packs and work together to hunt. Their willingness to work together with people probably led to wolves becoming tame.

3. What is the author's purpose in this text? Use text evidence to support your answer.

Sample answer: The author wants to explain that wild ancestors of today's dogs were wolves. Some wolves were domesticated into dogs many thousands of years ago. It is not clear exactly how, when, or where this happened.

REFLECT What words, phrases, or sentences did you have to reread to make sure you understood?

Sample answer: I needed to reread the paragraph about "Domestication" to make sure I understood what "domestication" is.

PROFESSIONAL DEVELOPMENT

Think-Aloud Modeling: Conversation

What Is It? In Think-Aloud Modeling, the teacher assumes the role of a student reader and models a thinking process or skill.

Why Is It Important? When given a topic to discuss, many students need help sharing ideas with others and listening to and learning from others. Acting out a conversation shows students how to use key ideas from the text in their comments and discussions. A conversational model also reminds students to give their answers and support their opinions using the text.

Comprehension Check: From Wolf into Dog

Answer the questions to demonstrate an understanding of what the text means.

1. How did the way people and wolves lived and hunted long ago influence their relationship? Provide text evidence to support your answer.

Sample answer: Since wolves and humans lived and hunted in groups, I can

infer that the two groups worked in similar ways, which made it easier for

wolves and humans to work together. Paragraph 2 says wolves live in packs

for protection. Living in packs may help them when they are hunting.

Paragraph 5 says that "humans lived in small hunter-gather groups."

2. In paragraph 3, the author says, "It is hard to imagine our lives today without domestic animals." What inference can you make based on this claim? What information from the text supports your answer?

Sample answer: The author states that "cats, chickens, horses, camels, goats,

sheep, and bees" are all domestic animals. Without them humans today would

lack many products and relationships we have had for a long time. For

example, we would not have dogs and cats as pets. We would go without

many different foods, such as eggs from chickens and honey from bees.

3. What inference can you make about how much experts know about domestication? Provide evidence from the text to support your answer.

Sample answer: I can infer that experts have discovered a lot of information

about the domestication of animals, but there is much more to find out.

Old ideas change as new discoveries are made. For example, scientists had

believed that "domestication first took place about 15,000 years ago." But

when cave paintings with animals were found in 1994, scientists discovered

animals may have been domesticated "about 35,000 years ago."

Stop and Assess

Use the following rubrics to assess your students' understanding of the text.

Item 1 answers indicate:	
2	that living and hunting in packs made it easy for them to work together, with relevant text evidence.
1	cooperation between the humans and the dogs, with references to the text.
0	no understanding of how people and wolves living together impacted their relationship, with no text support.

Item 2 answers indicate:	
2	the close relationship between humans and domestic animals, with relevant text support.
1	the benefits of domestic animals, with some text support.
0	no analysis of the importance of domestic animals, and no text support.

Item 3 answers indicate:	
2	experts have learned some things but there is much more to find out, with supporting language from the text.
1	experts have learned some things about domestication, with references to the text.
0	no understanding of what experts know, with no text evidence.

How Do I Use It? Model how to conduct a conversation. Say: *When having a conversation, I share my ideas, but I also listen to what the other person says and give comments or ask questions.* You might support the Collaborate activity on page 106 of this guide by acting out a dialogue with a student to demonstrate the process. After modeling, students can practice productive conversational skills as they review each other's summaries. Encourage students to remember the class discussion as a model for listening, speaking, and responding.

Return to the Focus Question

Explain to students that they will fill out a graphic organizer that will help them answer the Focus Question: What kinds of relationships do people have with their dogs?

CONNECT TEXTS Have small groups of students discuss how each text they read helps them answer the Focus Question. Have small groups share and compare their discussion notes with another small group.

Scaffolded Support You may provide the following sentence frames to support students in their use of academic language:

In the text _____, the author/photographer makes the point that _____. He/she does this by _____.

Remind students to use their annotations and summaries to support their answers. They can also reread portions of the texts, if necessary.

Have students complete their graphic organizers individually and then answer the Focus Question.

REFLECT Remind students that each text provides different information about people and their dogs. Ask, *How did reading all three texts give you a greater understanding of the kinds of relationships that exist between people and dogs?*

ANALYZE and SYNTHESIZE ACROSS TEXTS

Return to the Focus Question: What kinds of relationships do people have with their dogs?

Review your answers to questions about the texts as well as your annotations and Annotation Notes. Think about the discussions you've had about the texts. How does that information help you answer the Focus Question?

Use this graphic organizer to organize information about the texts.

1. In the boxes, record the details from each text that help you answer the Focus Question.

2. Make connections between those details to help you answer the Focus Question. Write your answer in the box provided.

Why the Indian Loves His Dog
Sample answer: Man relies on dogs for protection and help.

Fire House Dog (Visual Text)
Sample answer: Firefighters and the fire house dog are happy in each other's company.

From Wolf into Dog
Sample answer: Dogs and wolves helped humans hunt, and they protect each other.

What kinds of relationships do people have with their dogs?
Sample answer: Humans and dogs help each other. Dogs help people to hunt and give them protection. People help dogs by being kind to them and making them a part of their group.

REFLECT How did making connections between the three texts help you to answer the Focus Question?

Sample answer: I learned different ways that dogs and humans rely on each other. Texts 1 and 2 showed how man and dogs may have started helping each other, and the Visual Text shows man and dog being and working together.

PROFESSIONAL DEVELOPMENT

Intertextual Analysis: Analyzing Multiple Accounts of the Same Event or Topic

What Is It? A similar aspect can be compared across different texts. Many students are familiar with comparing and contrasting opposing viewpoints. They can build on this type of analysis by comparing subtle differences in genre, perspective, purpose, audience, structure, and language across multiple accounts of the same event or topic.

Why Is It Important? Analyzing texts on similar topics allows students to practice making intertextual connections, comparing genres, and synthesizing multiple ideas into a larger analysis. It can serve as a foundation for critical reading and evaluating sources.

Writing About the Focus Question

Now that you have answered the Focus Question using all three texts, develop your ideas into a longer piece of writing.

USE EVIDENCE

- Explain what kinds of relationships people have with their dogs. Use at least one piece of evidence from each text to support your answer.
- If you need more room, use additional paper.

MONITOR

- Use the Writing Checklist as you work to make sure your writing has all of the important pieces of information.
- Use the rubric on page 110 when you have completed your first draft to help you evaluate, revise, and edit your work.

WRITING CHECKLIST ✔

Does my writing . . .

☐ answer the Focus Question?

☐ provide text evidence to support my ideas?

☐ have a clear beginning, middle, and end?

☐ use correct language, spelling, and conventions?

Writing About the Focus Question

USE EVIDENCE Remind students that they should use their graphic organizers as well as their annotations in the texts to write their responses.

Allow students to revisit the texts as frequently as they need to in order to support comprehension and to respond to the Focus Question.

MONITOR After students have completed their responses, have them review the Writing Checklist and revise their writing responses.

DIFFERENTIATE AND EXTEND

In addition to or instead of the writing response, consider having students complete one of the following assignments:

Write Beyond Have students assume the role of a dog trainer. Have them write a blog for a group of coworkers about their relationship with dogs.

Read Beyond Have students find and read stories or novels that involve the bonds between people and dogs, such as *Lassie Come-Home*.

Research Have students use online resources to learn about medical service dogs and how they help people. Students can make a presentation to the class.

Create a Visual Text Have students create a storyboard for an animation based on "Why the Indian Loves His Dog." Encourage students to work toward a visual style that reflects the tone of the original story.

How Do I Use It? Graphic organizers can be a powerful tool for analyzing multiple accounts of the same event or topic. An interactive organizer can expand or contract to allow a visual representation of topic overlap. A T-Chart or Venn diagram can allow students to compare the mythic account of a man and dog forming a relationship with the factual account. Since students are comparing disparate genres, a customized graphic organizer may help. Headings could include "Beginning of Relationship," "How Dogs Help People," and "How People Help Dogs."

SELF-ASSESS and REFLECT

SELF-ASSESS Have students use the Writing Rubric on page 110 to self-assess their writing response and write a final version. Tell them to assign themselves a score from 1–4 (with "4" being the highest) for each category in the first column.

REFLECT Use the Writing Rubric on Student Worktext page 110 to assess each student's writing. Record points for each category in the first column of the rubric. Have students remove the page from their Student Worktexts and place it in their writing portfolios, along with the drafts and final versions of their responses.

SELF-ASSESS and REFLECT

Focus Question What kinds of relationships do people have with their dogs?

This is the rubric that your teacher will use to assess your writing. Refer to it as you revise your work. After you have finished your final version, review your writing and record your points for each category on the "Student" line in the first column.

	Accomplished (4 points)	Competent (3 points)	Developing (2 points)	Beginning (1 point)
RESPONSE Score: Student _____ Teacher _____	The response answers the question effectively and with insight.	The response answers the question effectively.	The response partially responds to the question but does not adequately address it.	The response addresses the texts but does not address the question.
ORGANIZATION Score: Student _____ Teacher _____	The main idea is convincingly stated. Ideas are organized in cohesive paragraphs that support the main idea.	The main idea is clearly stated. Ideas are organized in logical paragraphs.	The main idea is weak. Ideas are organized in a somewhat logical and cohesive way.	The main idea is missing. The organization of the paragraphs is not logical.
TEXT EVIDENCE Score: Student _____ Teacher _____	Response includes more than one piece of appropriate text evidence from each text. Evidence supports the main idea in a thorough way.	Response includes one piece of text evidence from each text. Evidence supports the main idea clearly.	Response does not include at least one piece of text evidence from each text. Text evidence does not adequately support the main idea.	Response does not contain relevant evidence.
LANGUAGE Score: Student _____ Teacher _____	Writing includes precise and sophisticated vocabulary related to the topic.	Writing includes appropriate vocabulary related to the topic.	Writing includes imprecise and inaccurate vocabulary.	Writing does not include vocabulary that appropriately reflects the topic of the response.
SPELLING AND CONVENTIONS Score: Student _____ Teacher _____	Response includes correct spelling, grammar, and punctuation consistently.	Response includes mostly correct spelling, grammar, and punctuation.	Response has many errors in spelling, grammar, and punctuation.	Response's errors in spelling, grammar, and punctuation make it extremely difficult to understand the response.

UNIT 7

Focus Question Why is Jackie Robinson a role model?

Texts for Close Reading

Unit 7 • 111

GENRE STUDY

Discuss with students the genres of "Jackie Robinson: Breaking the Color Barrier" and "Jackie Robinson at the Plate."

Remind students that *genre* refers to the format and features of a text and typically falls into one of two categories—literature or informational text. Literature is a creative work that doesn't necessarily rely on facts, and informational text is based on factual information. Some genres of informational text have some characteristics of literature. A biography is often considered to be literature even though it is a factual work. Most letters are informational texts, but letters can be written for a wide variety of reasons. With the class, list the features of a biography and a letter. Have students identify what characteristics they share and what characteristics are different.

Focus Question

Have students read the Focus Question on Worktext page 111. Tell them that the texts and illustrations in this unit will help them answer this question.

Texts for Close Reading

Have students read to themselves the descriptions of the texts in this unit.

There is no need to explain what students should expect to find in their close readings or to do any preteaching about the subject matter.

TEXT COMPLEXITY

Robinson with Teammates
- Style: documentary
- Knowledge demands: low
- Levels of meaning: literal/inferential

Breaking the Color Barrier
Quantitative: 780L
Qualitative
- Structure: conventional
- Language: familiar
- Knowledge demands: medium
- Levels of meaning: literal

Robinson at the Plate
Quantitative: 790L
Qualitative
- Structure: unconventional
- Language: familiar
- Knowledge demands: medium
- Levels of meaning: literal/inferential

Robinson with Teammates

Set a Purpose

Explain to students that they will look at the image on page 112 to begin to gain a deeper understanding of why Jackie Robinson is a role model.

Visual Text Analysis

Remind students that an image can be analyzed as a text by looking at its details and making inferences. Direct students' attention to the image on Student Worktext page 112.

Encourage students to annotate the Visual Text. Suggest they use arrows, labels, circles, margin notes, and other markings to highlight details that will help them gain a better understanding of the meaning of the image.

1. Have students record their first impressions about the image. Lead them to discuss as a whole class, in small groups, or with a partner what they think is happening in the photograph.

2. Encourage students to make note of the details that support their observations in question 1. Have them identify the setting and encourage them to examine figures in the photograph, what they're wearing, their postures, and their facial expressions. Have students explain as a whole class, in small groups, or with a partner what details they noted and what those details might tell them about Jackie Robinson.

3. Guide students to synthesize all the details they see in the photograph to draw conclusions about the message the photographer is trying to convey.

Brooklyn Dodgers infielder and slugger Jackie Robinson poses with teammates (L–R) Johnny "Spider" Jorgenson, Harold "Pee Wee" Reese, and Eddie Stanky on the steps of the Dodger's dugout.

Look at this Visual Text, and make annotations on the image. Review the image or parts of the image as many times as necessary to answer the following questions.

1. What is your first impression of what is happening in this photograph?

Sample answer: In this old photograph, four members of the Dodgers baseball team are posing for the camera on the steps of their dugout. Two players have their arms draped over their neighbors' shoulders. They look like they are friends and teammates.

PROFESSIONAL DEVELOPMENT

Collaboration: Whole Class

What Is It? Whole-class work involves all students working on a specific task as a group. Depending on class size and ability, whole-class collaboration may consist of call-and-response contributions or monitored discussions.

Why Is It Important? While whole-class instruction may not address targeted differentiation, the size and diversity of a full-class group can nonetheless be a tool to help students model, self-monitor, and observe.

2. What details support your answer?

Sample answer: The photograph is black and white. The activity in and around the

dugout shows the picture was taken at a game. The men are dressed in uniforms

that say "Dodgers" on the front. Dodgers is the team name and they are all on the

same team. The players' uniforms are clean, which shows the picture was taken

before the game started. They look happy and confident. Jackie Robinson is the

only black man shown in the picture.

3. What do you conclude is the photographer's message?

Sample answer: The photograph shows that these men work together as a team.

Text-Dependent Questions

As necessary, encourage discussion with such prompts as:

1. How would you describe the people in the photograph? (Sample answer: The four men are standing close together and some have their arms around their teammates' shoulders. They are all wearing Dodgers baseball uniforms. Three of them are smiling and one has a serious expression. Three of them are white and one of them is African American.)

2. Where was this photograph taken? (Sample answer: This photograph was taken in the place where the team sits in a baseball stadium.)

3. What is the relationship between the men? (Sample answer: Most of the men are smiling and three have their arms over each other's shoulders. They are teammates, but it looks like they are also friends.)

4. When was this photograph taken? (Sample answer: Based on the old fashioned-looking uniforms and the fact that the photograph is black and white, it looks like the photo was taken a long time ago.)

How Do I Use It? To facilitate collaboration, whole-class work should not function as a lecture. A teacher serves as both a participant and a moderator. Before lessons, plan the types of questions you might ask in a monitored discussion, including scaffolding where needed. It might be helpful to review the Visual Text on Student Worktext page 112 and anticipate students' prior knowledge and where the image might present comprehension or vocabulary challenges. Be flexible and accommodate unexpected developments, including difficulties and new areas of student inquiry.

Breaking the Color Barrier

Tell students that they will read to learn about Jackie Robinson.

1st READ

Set a Purpose

Explain to students that they will read to get a general understanding of what the text is about.

Have students read "Jackie Robinson: Breaking the Color Barrier" independently, annotating the text as they read. Remind students that suggested annotation symbols appear on page 8 of the Getting Started with Close Reading unit. Circulate and observe students' markings and notes, especially questions and anything they found confusing. The observations and annotations may be used to inform instruction. Based on students' needs, you may want to meet with them in small groups.

Use the Text-Dependent Questions to prompt students to engage with the text.

Text-Dependent Questions

1. What is this text about? (This text is about Jackie Robinson, the first African American to play on a major league baseball team.)

Scaffolded Support Use the following scaffolded sentence frames as necessary to support comprehension.

In 1947, Robinson _____ .

Robinson was the first African American to _____ .

✔ **Self-Monitoring Strategies** can help you check your understanding and clarify a text. Use them as you read.

☐ Visualize. ☐ Ask yourself questions. ☐ Draw conclusions. ☐ Reread to clarify.

Read this excerpt to learn about Jackie Robinson. Make annotations as you read. You may want to review Annotating a Text on page 8.
Sample annotations appear throughout the text.

Jackie Robinson: Breaking the Color Barrier
by Brian Heyman

1   On May 11, 1947, the Brooklyn Dodgers arrived at Shibe Park baseball stadium in Philadelphia, Pennsylvania. The team included a black player named Jackie Robinson.

2   For many Americans, the country still came in two shades—black and white. From their perspective, black people didn't deserve equal civil rights with whites.

3   Before the turn of the century, the major leagues in baseball were for white players only. For black players, there were the Negro Leagues. But then came Jackie Robinson. He burst through the color barrier on April 15, 1947. On that day he took the field for the Brooklyn Dodgers. The team represented the most racially diverse borough of New York City. It was a big first step in a career that went beyond sports. His teammate Ralph Branca explained how Robinson's achievement transcended the baseball diamond:

4   *I've often said that it changed baseball. But it also changed the country and eventually changed the world. Jackie made it easier for Rosa Parks. He made it easier for Martin Luther King Jr. And he made it easier for any black leader who was going to strive for racial equality. It basically changed the attitude of the whole country as far as looking at blacks went.*

5   *It happened on the team. We had southern guys who grew up looking down on blacks. They [African Americans] had to ride in the back of the bus. They couldn't drink at the same water fountains. They couldn't go to the same bathrooms. The white players eventually changed their minds.*

PROFESSIONAL DEVELOPMENT

Annotations: Avoiding Over-Annotating

What Is It? As students read, they may circle, underline, or highlight so many words that the sense of the text disappears, and they lose track of why they made the annotations. Over-annotating defeats the purpose of an annotation.

Why Is It Important? Over-annotating can be a sign that a student is not sufficiently distinguishing main ideas from supporting details. It may also be evidence that a student is encountering many new key words and phrases. If a student is reading and annotating word for word, he or she might need help with reading and comprehending whole phrases or with organizing information.

Make notes here about your annotations from each read.
You will refer to these notes later when you return to
your annotations. Sample notes appear below.

ANNOTATION NOTES

Key Ideas and Details:

The major leagues used to be for white players only. Black players played in

the Negro Leagues.

By becoming the first black player in baseball's major leagues, Jackie

Robinson helped change racial attitudes.

Robinson became an inspiration to African Americans.

Language and Text Structure:

The text uses phrases like "breaking the color barrier" and "burst through

the color barrier"—shows what a big deal it was at the time.

The third paragraph says his achievement "transcended the baseball

diamond." I think he means Robinson affected even people who weren't

interested in baseball.

Connections and Inferences:

Ralph Branca talks about Rosa Parks and Martin Luther King Jr.—Jackie

Robinson is one of the heroes of the civil rights movement.

How Do I Use It? When you notice that students are over-annotating, ask them to pause for self-monitoring. For example, students might underline every sentence in the second paragraph of "Jackie Robinson: Breaking the Color Barrier." Suggest that instead of underlining numerous sentences, they choose one sentence or phrase that clearly states the main idea of the paragraph. For example, they might underline "For many Americans" and "black people didn't deserve equal civil rights with whites." Discuss how carefully choosing which ideas to underline in the text can help students' gain a clearer and more precise understanding of the text.

2. What did Robinson do before joining the Dodgers? (In paragraph 6, the author says that Robinson attended the University of California, where he "excelled at four sports": baseball, football, basketball, and track. In 1942, he entered the U.S. Army, where he later "became a commissioned officer.")

3. How did Robinson become a member of the Brooklyn Dodgers? (Paragraph 7 says that, in 1945, the team's general manager, Branch Rickey, "scouted Robinson" for the Dodgers' minor-league team. In 1947, Robinson "was promoted to the Dodgers.")

Think Aloud *As I read paragraph 6, I was struck by what Robinson achieved before playing for the Dodgers. He was able to accomplish so much in both college and in the military. I thought about the fact that he "excelled at four sports" in college and that he refused to sit in the back of a military bus. I can draw the conclusion that Robinson was a strong man in every way. He had the physical strength to excel at multiple sports and the inner strength to stand up for his beliefs, even if it got him into trouble.*

Partner Talk Have students review the key details about Robinson's life.

Breaking the Color Barrier

2nd READ

Set a Purpose

Students will return to "Jackie Robinson: Breaking the Color Barrier" to understand how the language used in the text reveals meaning.

Text-Dependent Questions

1. What is the effect of the quotation in paragraphs 4 and 5? (The quotation from Ralph Branca supports the main idea that Robinson was a great man and makes the point stronger because Branca knew Robinson personally. Branca says that Robinson helped change the minds of racist teammates, which supports the statement that Robinson "touched many millions of lives, black and white.")

2. What does the language used throughout the text reveal about Robinson's character? (Words such as *transcended, excelled, honorable, dynamic, resilience,* and *dignity* show that Robinson was a special person with a character so strong he could "withstand the racism of players and fans" and be "an example to all Americans.")

3. Vocabulary: Multiple-Meaning Word Discuss contextual meanings of familiar and unfamiliar words and phrases.

Paragraph 3: What does *took* mean in this context? What words or phrases in the paragraph are clues to its meaning? (*Took* means "went onto." The clues are "the field" and "for the Brooklyn Dodgers.")

Partner Talk Have partners discuss how the author's use of language helped them understand Jackie Robinson.

6   Born in Georgia, on January 31, 1919, Robinson grew up in California. He excelled at four sports while in college at the University of California at Los Angeles. He played baseball, football, basketball, and ran track. The U.S. Army drafted him in 1942. The military was still segregated. He became a commissioned officer in 1943. Second Lieutenant Robinson refused to ride in the back of a military bus. He was charged with insubordination.

?   He was acquitted and earned an honorable discharge. "He was a person of action," says his widow, Rachel Isum Robinson.

7   When the war was over, the Brooklyn Dodgers'
!   general manager, Branch Rickey, decided it was time to integrate baseball. He started looking for a black player to add to the Dodgers roster. Rickey understood that his man would have to possess great strength of character to withstand the racism of players and fans. Rickey scouted Robinson in 1945. The new recruit spent the next season with the Dodgers' minor-league team in Montreal. He was promoted to the Dodgers for the 1947 season. It wasn't easy being a pioneer. Despite pressure experienced by no player before or since, Robinson excelled on the field.

8   In his first major-league season Robinson played first base. He compiled a .297 batting average. He displayed a dynamic style, and stole 29 bases to lead the National League. Baseball named him Rookie of the Year. He helped the team reach the World Series. Robinson's best season came in 1949, when he earned the league's Most Valuable Player award.

9   Robinson spent 10 seasons with the Dodgers. He made six World Series
!   appearances. In 1962, Robinson was inducted into the Baseball Hall of Fame. He was the first black player so honored.

10 After his playing career ended, Robinson continued to fight for racial equality. He played an active part in the civil rights movement.

11 In 1972, Jackie Robinson suffered a heart attack and died. He was only 53. Robinson had touched many millions of lives, black and white. His
?   resilience and dignity made him an example to all Americans. His actions helped African Americans in achieving their full rights as citizens of the United States.

12 "A life is not important," Robinson said, "except in the impact it has on other lives."

PROFESSIONAL DEVELOPMENT

Think-Aloud Modeling

What Is It? Remind students that close reading is not a passive activity. Skilled readers employ a variety of **Self-Monitoring Strategies** to ensure they fully comprehend a text's meaning. Model the use of one of these strategies with a Think Aloud to verbally "walk" through the thought process.

Why Is It Important? Think Alouds that model a strategy demonstrate how to close read. Frequent modeling of a variety of strategies demonstrates that some strategies work better than others for specific comprehension challenges.

Make notes here about your annotations from each read. You will refer to these notes later when you return to your annotations. **Sample notes appear below.**

ANNOTATION NOTES

Key Ideas and Details:

Robinson fought racism in the army and in baseball.

Brooklyn Dodgers coach integrated baseball when he chose Robinson

to be on the team.

Robinson was an example of courage to all Americans.

awards: Rookie of Year, MVP, Baseball Hall of Fame

Language and Text Structure:

words used to describe Robinson: person of action, great strength of

character, pioneer, dynamic style, resilience, dignity

lots of unknown words: insubordination, acquitted, honorable discharge,

inducted

"segregated" opposite of "integrated"

Connections and Inferences:

A person must be strong and courageous to make a difference.

Robinson believed that a person's life is important if you do good for others.

Unit 7 • **117**

Breaking the Color Barrier

3rd READ

Set a Purpose
Students will read to make inferences about the text.

Text-Dependent Questions

1. Why was the image of the stamp included in the text? (The image supports the statements that Robinson "excelled on the field" and was honored for his talent.)

2. Based on the text, what inferences can you make about Jackie Robinson's personality? (I can infer that Robinson was a hard worker because it takes dedication and hard work to excel "at four sports." I can also infer that he was a forgiving person because he didn't quit the Dodgers even though he experienced "racism of players and fans.")

3. How does this text add to your understanding of the Visual Text? (The sentence "The white players eventually changed their minds" in paragraph 5 helped me understand that not all the other players accepted Robinson or were friendly to him as his teammates are in the Visual Text.)

Think Aloud *I'm not sure what being "charged with insubordination" means in paragraph 6. I'll reread the paragraph and see if context clues can help me. I see that Robinson was charged because he "refused to ride in the back of a military bus." So, he broke a rule.* Insubordination *must mean "breaking a rule."*

Partner Talk Have students discuss the inferences they made about Jackie Robinson.

This exposure will help your students internalize and employ the strategies more often on their own.

How Do I Use It? Use the Think Alouds provided in the lessons. Use additional Think Alouds at points in the text where you predict a comprehension challenge or when you note one or more students are struggling, particularly in detail-dense paragraphs, such as paragraphs 3 and 4 in this text. Keep your Think Alouds brief and focused on a specific challenge and use a variety of Think Alouds to model different methods students can use to clarify confusing parts of the text.

Unit 7 • **117**

Respond to Reading

You may want to check students' understanding by having them complete page 118 in the Student Worktext.

1. Remind students that a summary should only include the key ideas and details essential to understanding what the text is about. Point out that they can use the graphic organizer on Student Worktext page 118 to capture and organize those key ideas and details. The graphic organizer should then guide them in writing their summaries.

2. Refer students to pages 12 and 13 in Getting Started to help them write their individual summaries.

Have students work independently to answer the questions on page 118 of their Worktexts.

COLLABORATE Have students exchange their final summaries with their partners and review each other's summaries. Remind pairs that when they review and discuss their partners' summaries, they should consider whether or not the summary has the following elements:

- contains only important information
- answers as many of the following as possible: Who? What? When? Where? and How?

REFLECT Have students share ways they were able to clarify and better understand a confusing word or phrase.

Respond to Reading: Jackie Robinson: Breaking the Color Barrier

Review the annotations and notes you made while reading "Jackie Robinson: Breaking the Color Barrier." Think about how they can help you understand the text.

1. Use this Summary Chart to help you summarize the text.

Summary Chart		
	Informational Text	
Who?	the people or subjects	Jackie Robinson
What?	the topic or problem	first black player in the major leagues; withstood racism in baseball, the military, and American society
Where?	the location or region where the events occur	the United States
When?	the date, year, or time	1943–1972
How?	the events, steps, or process	refused to ride in back of military bus; withstood racism in baseball and had great career; played active part in the civil rights movement until his death

2. Use the completed graphic organizer from item 1 to help you write a summary of "Jackie Robinson: Breaking the Color Barrier."

   Sample answer: Jackie Robinson spent his life fighting racism. As the first black player in the major leagues, he overcame prejudice and became one of the greatest players of all time. Robinson continued to work with the civil rights movement and is an example to all Americans.

   REFLECT What word or phrase did you find confusing? What Self-Monitoring Strategy did you use to gain a better understanding of it?

   Sample answer: I wasn't sure what the last sentence meant. It seemed that Robinson's achievements were not as important to him as helping others. I concluded that he was a very modest man.

PROFESSIONAL DEVELOPMENT

Collaboration: Purposeful Partner Talk

What Is It? Purposeful partner talk is productive conversation between two students who are analyzing a text to increase comprehension.

Why Is It Important? Purposeful partner talk requires students to use academic language to further develop their speaking and listening skills and to understand a text from a different point of view. These skills will serve students well not only in an academic setting, but in life in general.

Return to the TEXT

Comprehension Check: Jackie Robinson: Breaking the Color Barrier

Answer the questions to demonstrate an understanding of what the text means.

1. What does the author want you to understand about how Jackie Robinson helped the cause of racial equality? Use two pieces of evidence from the text to support your answer.

Sample answer: The author explains that Robinson proved by his own example

that a black player could be the equal of any white player in baseball's major

league. The effect when Robinson "burst through the color barrier" went

beyond baseball. As Ralph Branca says in paragraph 4, he "made it easier for

any black leader who was going to strive for racial equality."

2. What inference can you make about the effect Jackie Robinson had on his teammates? Cite text evidence to support your answer.

Sample answer: I can infer that playing with Robinson inspired players like

Ralph Branca to speak out for Jackie Robinson and against inequality. Branca

says in paragraph 5, "guys who grew up looking down on blacks...

eventually changed their minds."

3. How does the author demonstrate that Jackie Robinson was an inspiration to all Americans? Use textual evidence to support your answer.

Sample answer: The author makes it clear that Robinson's success as a baseball

player and as an activist was an inspiration to everyone. He describes what

Robinson achieved by courage, resilience, and dignity in the face of abuse. He

says, "Robinson had touched many millions of lives, black and white. His

resilience and dignity made him an example to all Americans."

Stop and Assess

Use the following rubrics to assess your students' understanding of the text.

Item 1 answers indicate:	
2	that by proving black players were equal to whites, Robinson helped the civil rights movement and changed the nation's mind about race, with two pieces of supporting text evidence.
1	that Robinson proved that black players were equal to whites, and text evidence may be insufficient.
0	no understanding of how Robinson helped the cause of racial equality, and don't cite any relevant text evidence.

Item 2 answers indicate:	
2	that Robinson changed the minds of teammates who at first didn't think blacks were equal, with sufficient text evidence.
1	that Robinson changed the minds of his previously racist teammates, but text evidence is insufficient.
0	no understanding of the effect Robinson had on his teammates, and don't cite relevant text evidence.

Item 3 answers indicate:	
2	that Robinson's courage, resilience, and dignity were inspirational to all, with strong text evidence.
1	some understanding of how Robinson was inspirational to all Americans, but text evidence is insufficient.
0	no understanding of how Robinson was inspirational to all Americans, and don't cite any relevant text evidence.

How Do I Use It? Use language frames and various productive conversation techniques, such as restating, adding on, and extending, to model purposeful partner talk before partners discuss "Jackie Robinson: Breaking the Color Barrier" on Student Worktext pages 118–119. For example: *After rereading the text, I understand how, through his actions, resilience, and attitude, Jackie Robinson was able to _____. The details in paragraph _____ support my idea. I agree with your statement that _____. However, I'd like to add _____.*

Robinson at the Plate

Students will read a letter to learn about what it was like to see Jackie Robinson play.

1st READ

Set a Purpose

Explain to students that they will read to find out what "Jackie Robinson at the Plate" is about.

Have students read "Jackie Robinson at the Plate" independently, annotating the text as they read. Remind students that suggested annotation symbols appear on page 8 of the Getting Started with Close Reading unit. Circulate and observe students' markings, especially questions and anything they found confusing. The observations and annotations may be used to inform instruction. Based on students' needs, you may want to meet with them in small groups.

Text-Dependent Questions

1. What is the text about? (It is a letter about Jackie Robinson and the effect he had on a boy and his father.)

2. When did Robinson first play for the Dodgers? (Paragraph 6 says Robinson debuted for the Dodgers on April 15, 1947, which was also the author's tenth birthday.)

Scaffolded Support Use the following scaffolded sentence frame as necessary to support comprehension.

The author writes a _____ that tells about _____.

Partner Talk Have students discuss what they learned about watching Jackie Robinson play baseball.

Read this letter to learn about what it was like to see Jackie Robinson play. Make annotations as you read. You may make different annotations each time you read.
Sample annotations and notes appear throughout the text.

Jackie Robinson at the Plate

1   Dear Millie,

2   If you want me to tell you about Jackie Robinson, you need to know a few things about your great-grandfather. It makes me feel very old to call him "your great-grandfather." The times we watched baseball together seem like distant memories. But I still remember sitting in the bleachers at Ebbets Field, with my dad beside me and Jackie Robinson at the plate.

3   My dad knew about Jackie Robinson long before Robinson entered major league baseball. Dad served in the army in WWII. In 1945, he was stationed at Fort Leavenworth, about thirty miles from Kansas City. At that time, the Kansas City Monarchs were one of the biggest teams in the Negro League. My dad was in the ballpark for their season opener on May 6. That day, the Monarchs took the field with a rookie shortstop, Jackie Robinson, whose strong swing gave him a batting average over .400.

4   ? The Monarchs won. Robinson scored a run and stole a base. But statistics don't explain the impression he made on my dad. "He had a love of the game," Dad told me. "Every moment, you knew there was no place else he'd rather be. His concentration was intense, and his speed was phenomenal. Even as a rookie he raised the game of his teammates."

5   I was raised in Brooklyn, so the Brooklyn Dodgers were my team. I was proud when they signed the first black player in the major leagues.

6   Jackie Robinson made his debut for the Dodgers on my tenth birthday: April 15, 1947. My mom joked that my dad had been bending her ear for two years about Jackie Robinson. This was her chance to see him for herself.

7   The Dodgers won. But again, statistics don't tell you much. The real story was about Jackie Robinson's spirit and persistence. He faced a bombardment of racial abuse that day—some of it from his own teammates. But he never let it interfere with his concentration or his love of the game. It made me feel angry and ashamed. But my mom said something I've never forgotten. "If Mr. Robinson has the courage to stand up to that terrible behavior and win the game, you can too."

8   I hope these memories are helpful. Good luck with the book.

9   Love, Grandpa

PROFESSIONAL DEVELOPMENT

Teacher Observation: Scaffolding

What Is It? Scaffolds are questions, cues, prompts, and direct instruction teachers provide to students to help them answer difficult questions and arrive at new concepts. Scaffolding in class discussion often begins with factual questions and progresses to questions that require students to make increasingly complex inferences.

Why Is It Important? Scaffolded questions arranged in logical order help students develop the higher-order thinking skills they need to derive the full meaning from a text. Scaffolding can also clear up confusion and help students visualize what is happening in a narrative or grasp a concept presented in an explanatory text.

Make notes here about your annotations from each read.
You will refer to these notes later when you return to
your annotations. Sample notes appear below.

ANNOTATION NOTES

Key Ideas and Details:

A veteran baseball fan remembers Jackie Robinson in a letter to his

granddaughter, Millie. He explains the things about Robinson that made him

a great ball player and role model.

Language and Text Structure:

baseball terms: "shortstop," "scored a run," "stole a base"

"Raised the game" means Robinson played so well he made his team-

mates play better too.

look up "bombardment"

Connections and Inferences:

Based on paragraph 8, "Millie" must be writing a book about baseball

or Jackie Robinson.

Unit 7 • 121

How Do I Use It? Begin a series of questions with one that can
easily be answered from the text, such as *Who is "speaking"
in the letter?* Then use the answer in a prompt for the next
question: *Millie's grandfather tells her about _____. At
first he was _____ of the Dodgers but at the game he felt
_____ because other people _____.* Continue using
answers to construct succeeding questions or stems for
sentence frames: *The author's personal thoughts and feelings
about Robinson support the idea that Robinson _____.*

Robinson at the Plate

2nd READ

Set a Purpose
Students will examine how the
text's structure and language
reveal meaning.

Text-Dependent Questions

1. What is the structure of the
body of the letter? (It begins in
the present with a response to the
author's granddaughter. The author
then describes some memories in
chronological order.)

2. How does the author's point of
view help readers make a connection with the topic? (Telling the
memories from a first-person point of
view helps readers understand how
it felt to witness the unfair treatment
Robinson received.)

Partner Talk Have partners discuss
how the author's language reveals
the way he feels about Robinson.

3rd READ

Set a Purpose
Students will read to make
inferences about the text.

Text-Dependent Questions

1. What can you infer about the
author of this letter? (He believes in
equality. His statement "It made me
feel angry and ashamed" in paragraph
7 reveals he rejected racist words and
behavior toward Robinson.)

2. What is the letter writer's message? (The message is that we should
try to live up to the people we admire.)

Partner Talk Have students cite
text evidence that reveals the
text's central message.

Unit 7 • 121

Return TO THE TEXT

Respond to Reading

You may want to check students' understanding by having them complete page 122 in the Student Worktext.

1. Have students reread the text to find details that show the physical qualities that made Robinson a great baseball player. Then have them find details that show the mental qualities that made him a great baseball player. Have students use these details to complete the graphic organizer.

2. Have students use the information they recorded on their graphic organizers to explain how the combination of Robinson's physical and mental qualities helped him play baseball.

3. Refer students to pages 12 and 13 of Getting Started to help them write their individual summaries.

Have students work independently to answer the questions on page 122 of their Worktext.

COLLABORATE When finished, have students exchange summaries with their partners and review each other's summaries. Remind pairs that when they review and discuss their partners' summaries, they should consider whether or not the summary has the following elements:

• contains only important information

• answers as many of the following as possible: Who? What? When? Where? and How?

REFLECT Suggest that students review their annotations and Annotation Notes to help them remember what words, phrases, or sections they visualized to better understand the text.

122 • Unit 7

Return to the TEXT

Respond to Reading: Jackie Robinson at the Plate

Review the annotations and notes you made while reading "Jackie Robinson at the Plate." Think about how your annotations can help you answer the questions.

1. Use information from the text to complete the graphic organizer.

Physical qualities that made Robinson a great ballplayer	Mental qualities that made Robinson a great ballplayer
Sample answer: phenomenal speed strong swing	Sample answer: love of the game intense concentration persistence

2. Use your graphic organizer to explain how Jackie Robinson's qualities helped him on the ball field.

Sample answer: Jackie Robinson was a good hitter and had great speed that helped his team to victory. He also had a love of the game and great concentration, which helped him overcome the prejudice of fans and other ballplayers. He also showed persistence, which is important in team sports.

3. Write a brief summary of "Jackie Robinson at the Plate."

Sample answer: The author writes a letter to his granddaughter in reply to her request for information about Jackie Robinson. He tells her why his father admired Robinson and remembers attending Robinson's Dodgers debut with both his parents.

REFLECT What words, phrases, or sections did you have to visualize to make sure you understood?

Sample answer: I visualized Jackie Robinson at the plate, stealing bases, and scoring runs to help me understand his concentration and speed.

122 • Unit 7

PROFESSIONAL DEVELOPMENT

Productive Conversation: Revoicing Students' Responses

What Is It? Productive Conversation strategies include revoicing, restating, adding on, reasoning, extending, giving examples, and providing appropriate wait time. In revoicing a student's response, you use academic language to express his or her ideas. For example, after a student answers a question you might say, *So, let me see if I understand your thinking. You said _____. Is that right?*

Why Is It Important? Revoicing is beneficial for all students, but is especially important for English learners and slower readers. The strategy can guide students toward correct English expression. Revoicing also provides opportunities

Comprehension Check: Jackie Robinson at the Plate

**Answer the questions to demonstrate an understanding of what
the text means.**

1. How is the narrator's father affected by the opening game of the
Kansas City Monarchs' 1945 season? Provide text evidence to support
your answer.

Sample answer: He is impressed not only by Jackie Robinson's skills and

speed, but by his "love of the game" and his strength of mind. The

impression stayed with him because the author's mother says her husband

had been "bending her ear for two years about Jackie Robinson."

2. How do the narrator's feelings about the Dodgers and their fans
change after Jackie Robinson played his first game? Support your
answer with evidence from the text.

Sample answer: The Dodgers are his home team, and he says, "I was proud

when they signed the first black player in the major leagues." After the game

the author feels "angry and ashamed" by the way the fans and Robinson's

own teammates used racial insults to make him feel unwelcome.

3. What inferences can you make about the author's mother?
Provide text evidence to support your answer.

Sample answer: Paragraph 6 shows she has a good sense of humor. She joked

that her husband "had been bending her ear for two years" about Robinson.

Also she wants her son to learn from what others experience and to see

Robinson as a role model. In paragraph 7, she says, "If Mr. Robinson has the

courage to stand up to that terrible behavior and win the game, you can too."

Unit 7 ● 123

Stop and Assess

Use the following rubrics to assess
your students' understanding of
the text.

	Item 1 answers indicate:
2	he's impressed by Robinson's athletic skill, love of the game, and character, and provide text evidence to support the answer.
1	he's impressed by Robinson's skill, love of the game, and character, but does not provide text evidence.
0	no understanding of how the author's father was affected by the opening game, and no text evidence provided.

	Item 2 answers indicate:
2	the author is proud that Robinson was signed to the team but also upset at how fans and teammates treated him, with sufficient text evidence.
1	the author is proud Robinson is on the team but upset at the treatment he receives, but text evidence is insufficient.
0	a lack of understanding of the author's feelings after Robinson plays his first game, and don't cite any relevant text evidence.

	Item 3 answers indicate:
2	an inference about the author's mother with text evidence to support the claim.
1	only what is explicitly stated in the text with little or no text evidence to support the answer.
0	no inference made about the author's mother, and no text evidence.

and time to develop collaborative conversation behaviors
(e.g., listening and responding to or building on the responses
of others).

How Do I Use It? Visit small groups as students review and
discuss each other's summaries. When necessary, revoice
student answers in a manner that encourages further
discussion. This provides opportunities to build vocabulary,
develop language, and deepen comprehension. For example:
*You are correct—this summary includes information not directly
supported by the text. Or, I agree with your observation that
this summary doesn't answer the questions Who? and Where?
What should _____ do to strengthen his/her summary?*

Unit 7 ● **123**

Return to the Focus Question

Explain to students that they will fill out a graphic organizer that will help them answer the Focus Question: Why is Jackie Robinson a role model?

CONNECT TEXTS Have small groups of students discuss how each text they read helps them answer the Focus Question. Have small groups share and compare their discussion notes with another small group.

Scaffolded Support You may provide the following sentence frames to support students in their use of academic language:

> In the text _____ , the author/photographer makes the point that _____ . He/she does this by _____ .

Remind students to use their annotations and summaries to support their answers. They can also reread portions of the texts, if necessary.

Have students complete their graphic organizers individually and then answer the Focus Question.

REFLECT Remind students that each text provides different information about Jackie Robinson. Ask, *How did reading all three texts help you better understand why Jackie Robinson is a role model?*

124 • Unit 7

Return to the Focus Question: Why is Jackie Robinson a role model?

Review your answers to questions about the texts as well as your annotations and Annotation Notes. Think about the discussions you've had about the texts. How does that information help you answer the Focus Question?

Use the graphic organizer to organize information about the texts.

1. In the boxes, record the details from each text that help you answer the Focus Question.

2. Make connections between those details to help you answer the Focus Question. Write your answer in the box provided.

> **Jackie Robinson with Teammates (Visual Text)**
> Sample answer: was only black player on the Brooklyn Dodgers

> **Jackie Robinson: Breaking the Color Barrier**
> Sample answer: had courage to break the color barrier; fought for racial equality

> **Jackie Robinson at the Plate**
> Sample answer: showed spirit and love of the game despite racial discrimination, inspires boy

> **Why is Jackie Robinson a role model?**
> Sample answer: Jackie Robinson broke the color barrier when he became the first black player in the major leagues. He was a great athlete whose strength of character was an example of courage and an inspiration to the nation.

REFLECT How did making connections between the three texts help you to answer the Focus Question?

The Visual Text shows Robinson was a team player. Text 1 explains that he broke

the color barrier in baseball and used his talents to fight for racial equality. Text 2

showed the impression he made on the people who watched him play.

124 • Unit 7

PROFESSIONAL DEVELOPMENT

Academic Language: Conversation

What Is It? Academic language is the language used in the classroom. It's more formal than casual, everyday conversation and employs academic vocabulary. It takes practice to become "fluent" in the use of academic language, particularly during classroom conversation where students may be tempted to slip into a more casual and informal way of communicating.

Why Is It Important? Using academic language in classroom discussion is essential for students to succeed in school. Students who use academic language during conversations with peers develop academic confidence, improve their

WRITE

Writing About the Focus Question

Now that you have answered the Focus Question using all three texts, develop your ideas into a longer piece of writing.

USE EVIDENCE

- Explain why Jackie Robinson is a role model. Use at least one piece of evidence from each text to support your answer.
- If you need more room, use additional paper.

MONITOR

- Use the Writing Checklist as you work to make sure your writing has all of the important pieces of information.
- Use the rubric on page 126 when you have completed your first draft to help you evaluate, revise, and edit your work.

WRITING CHECKLIST ✔

Does my writing . . .

☐ answer the Focus Question?

☐ provide text evidence to support my ideas?

☐ have a clear beginning, middle, and end?

☐ use correct language, spelling, and conventions?

Writing About the Focus Question

USE EVIDENCE Remind students that they should use their graphic organizers as well as their annotations in the texts to write their responses.

Allow students to revisit the texts as frequently as they need to in order to support comprehension and to respond to the Focus Question.

MONITOR After students have completed their responses, have them review the Writing Checklist and revise their writing responses.

DIFFERENTIATE AND EXTEND

In addition to or instead of the writing response, consider having students complete one of the following assignments:

Write Beyond Have students assume the role of one of Robinson's teammates on the Dodgers. Have them describe in a letter to a friend what it was like playing the first game with Robinson.

Interview an Expert Have students write questions they would ask a professional athlete who had to break through a social or cultural barrier to succeed.

Research Have students identify and research the life and career of another athlete who broke through barriers to find acceptance in his or her sport.

Create a Timeline Have students create a timeline that starts at 1947 and chronicles significant events in the civil rights movement.

communication skills, and encourage other students to take what they say seriously. Using academic language sets a tone to indicate that it is time for a thoughtful discussion.

How Do I Use It? In conversation with students, respond to and rephrase students' ideas using academic language to demonstrate the practice. Move from group to group while students discuss how the texts helped them understand why Jackie Robinson is a role model. If students are not using academic language, point out academic words or phrases they could use in addition to the Scaffolded Support on page 124.

SELF-ASSESS and REFLECT

SELF-ASSESS Have students use the Writing Rubric on page 126 to self-assess their writing response and write a final version. Tell them to assign themselves a score from 1–4 (with "4" being the highest) for each category in the first column.

REFLECT Use the Writing Rubric on Student Worktext page 126 to assess each student's writing. Record points for each category in the first column of the rubric. Have students remove the page from their Student Worktexts and place it in their writing portfolios, along with the drafts and final versions of their responses.

SELF-ASSESS and REFLECT

Focus Question Why is Jackie Robinson a role model?

This is the rubric that your teacher will use to assess your writing. Refer to it as you revise your work. After you have finished your final version, review your writing and record your points for each category on the "Student" line in the first column.

	Accomplished (4 points)	Competent (3 points)	Developing (2 points)	Beginning (1 point)
RESPONSE Score: Student _____ Teacher _____	The response answers the question effectively and with insight.	The response answers the question effectively.	The response partially responds to the question but does not adequately address it.	The response addresses the texts but does not address the question.
ORGANIZATION Score: Student _____ Teacher _____	The main idea is convincingly stated. Ideas are organized in cohesive paragraphs that support the main idea.	The main idea is clearly stated. Ideas are organized in logical paragraphs.	The main idea is weak. Ideas are organized in a somewhat logical and cohesive way.	The main idea is missing. The organization of the paragraphs is not logical.
TEXT EVIDENCE Score: Student _____ Teacher _____	Response includes more than one piece of appropriate text evidence from each text. Evidence supports the main idea in a thorough way.	Response includes one piece of text evidence from each text. Evidence supports the main idea clearly.	Response does not include at least one piece of text evidence from each text. Text evidence does not adequately support the main idea.	Response does not contain relevant evidence.
LANGUAGE Score: Student _____ Teacher _____	Writing includes precise and sophisticated vocabulary related to the topic.	Writing includes appropriate vocabulary related to the topic.	Writing includes imprecise and inaccurate vocabulary.	Writing does not include vocabulary that appropriately reflects the topic of the response.
SPELLING AND CONVENTIONS Score: Student _____ Teacher _____	Response includes correct spelling, grammar, and punctuation consistently.	Response includes mostly correct spelling, grammar, and punctuation.	Response has many errors in spelling, grammar, and punctuation.	Response's errors in spelling, grammar, and punctuation make it extremely difficult to understand the response.

UNIT 8

Focus Question What are the benefits of being a kind person?

Texts for Close Reading

Unit 8 • 127

GENRE STUDY

Discuss with students the genres of "The Hare of Inaba" and "The Helpful Stranger."

Remind students that *genre* refers to the format and features of a text and typically falls into one of two categories—literature or informational text. Literature is creative work that doesn't necessarily rely on facts, while informational text is based on factual information. Fairy tales belong to the former category. Fairy tales are typically set in a legendary past and feature fantasy elements. Short stories like "The Helpful Stranger" are fictional narratives that entertain. Have students identify characteristics fairy tales and short stories might share and common characteristics unique to each subgenre.

Focus Question

Have students read the Focus Question on Worktext page 127. Tell them that the texts and illustrations in this unit will help them answer this question.

Texts for Close Reading

Have students read to themselves the descriptions of the texts in this unit.

There is no need to explain what students should expect to find in their close readings or to do any preteaching about the subject matter.

TEXT COMPLEXITY

Standup4change
- Style: documentary
- Knowledge demands: low
- Levels of meaning: literal/inferential

The Hare of Inaba
Quantitative: 630L
Qualitative
- Structure: narrative
- Language: familiar/archaic
- Knowledge demands: medium
- Levels of meaning: literal/inferential

The Helpful Stranger
Quantitative: 750L
Qualitative
- Structure: narrative
- Language: familiar
- Knowledge demands: medium
- Levels of meaning: literal

Unit 8 • 127

Standup4change

Set a Purpose

Explain to students that they will look at the image on page 128 to begin to gain a deeper understanding of the benefits of being a kind person.

Visual Text Analysis

Remind students that an image can be analyzed as a text by looking at its details and making inferences. Direct students' attention to the image on Student Worktext page 128.

Encourage students to annotate the Visual Text. Suggest they use arrows, labels, circles, margin notes, and other markings to highlight details that will help them gain a better understanding of the meaning of the image.

1. Have students record their first impressions about the image. Lead them to discuss as a whole class, in small groups, or with a partner what they think is happening in the photograph.

2. Encourage students to make note of the details that support their observations in question 1. Ask volunteers to read aloud the words on the posters and lead a discussion about their messages. Have students explain as a whole class, in small groups, or with a partner what details they noted and what those details might tell them about the benefits of being a kind person.

3. Guide students to synthesize all the details they see in the photograph to draw conclusions about the photographer's message.

"Standup4change" national program against bullying.

Look at this Visual Text, and make annotations on the image. Review the image or parts of the image as many times as necessary to answer the following questions.

1. What's your first impression of what's going on in this photograph?

    Sample answer: School students have participated in a group program

    to get people to be kind.

    _____

    _____

    _____

    _____

    _____

    _____

    _____

PROFESSIONAL DEVELOPMENT

Annotations

What Is It? Annotations are used to mark up a text to record thoughts, ideas, and understandings while reading. Annotations include underlining or highlighting text, circling key words and ideas, recording important or surprising information, marking places of confusion, and noting questions.

Why Is It Important? Annotating allows students to record their initial thoughts and questions about a text. Students' annotations provide the teacher with valuable information regarding what students do and do not understand. They pinpoint areas of confusion to be dealt

2. What do you see that makes you think that?

Sample answer: The panels are large and look as though they are displayed in a hallway or gym so that many people can see them. The bright colors and positive messages in the display catch people's attention. The messages are about being kind.

3. What do you conclude is the photographer's message?

Sample answer: The message is that the school children support the idea that everyone should be nice and treat other people with kindness.

Text-Dependent Questions

As necessary, encourage discussion with such prompts as:

1. Where was the photograph taken? (Sample answer: I know from the caption that the setting is a school. I think the room is a gym because there are gym mats hung on the wall.)

2. How would you describe the posters? (Sample answer: They are as tall as the school walls. Each poster has images, words, and cheerful colors. One poster has a magic theme and shows rabbits coming out of hats and magic wands. The middle poster has a rainbow-colored umbrella and lots of big rain drops with writing on them. The orange poster is covered with science beakers. Each poster has a positive saying about kindness.)

3. What are some words that describe how the posters inspire you? (Sample answer: *happy, positive, cheerful, friendly, hopeful, kind*)

with during a scaffolded close reading of the text and any subsequent instruction. Annotations also can be used for informal assessment.

How Do I Use It? Tell students that just as they make annotations while reading a text, they can also make annotations on a Visual Text. Tell them that they can circle any important details that they want to connect. For example, in the Visual Text on page 128, they can circle the signs on each panel. Each one has to do with kindness, but shows a different aspect of it.

The Hare of Inaba

Tell students that they will read a fairy tale about eighty-one brothers and a hare.

1st READ

Set a Purpose

Explain to students that they will read to get a general understanding of what the text is about.

Have students read "The Hare of Inaba" independently, annotating the text as they read. Remind students that suggested annotation symbols appear on page 8 of the Getting Started with Close Reading unit. Circulate and observe students' markings and notes, especially questions and anything they found confusing. The observations and annotations may be used to inform instruction. Based on students' needs, you may want to meet with them in small groups.

Use the Text-Dependent Questions to prompt students to engage with the text.

Text-Dependent Questions

1. What is the text about? (It is about eighty-one brothers who travel to Inaba to try to marry a princess. They meet a hare who has his fur plucked out by a crocodile he had tricked. Eighty brothers are mean to the hare, but one is kind.)

Scaffolded Support Use the following scaffolded sentence frames as necessary to support comprehension.

Eighty-one _____ all want to be _____ and marry _____.
The eighty-first _____ is _____ and helps _____.

✔ **Self-Monitoring Strategies can help you check your understanding and clarify a text. Use them as you read.**

☐ Visualize.   ☐ Ask yourself questions.   ☐ Draw conclusions.   ☐ Reread to clarify.

Read this fairy tale about eighty-one brothers and a hare. Make annotations as you read. You may want to review Annotating a Text on page 8.
Sample annotations appear throughout the text.

The Hare of Inaba

This fairy tale is from the Kojiki, *a collection of myths from early eighth-century Japan. This version was written by Mrs. T. H. James in 1892.*

1   There were once eighty-one brothers who were Princes. They were all jealous of one another. Each one wished to be King and rule over the whole Kingdom. Besides this, each one wanted to marry the Princess of Yakami in Inaba.

2   They made up their minds that they would go together to Inaba. Each one would try to persuade the Princess to marry him. Although eighty of these brothers were jealous of one another, they all agreed to be unkind to

?   the eighty-first. He was good and gentle, and did not like their quarrelsome ways. When they set out upon their journey, they made the eighty-first brother walk behind them, carrying the bag. They treated him as if he were their servant, although he was their own brother, and a Prince like the rest of them.

3   By and by, the eighty Princes came to Cape Keta. There they found a poor hare, with all his fur plucked out. He was lying down, looking very sick and miserable. The eighty Princes told the hare, "Go bathe in the sea water. Then lie down on the slope of a high mountain. Let the wind blow upon you. That will soon make your fur grow, we promise."

4   So the poor hare believed them. He bathed in the sea. Afterward he lay down in the sun and the wind to dry. But, as the salt water dried, his skin cracked. He was in terrible pain, and lay there crying. He was in a much

!   worse state than before.

PROFESSIONAL DEVELOPMENT

Think-Aloud Modeling: Annotating

What Is It? Think-Aloud modeling of annotating requires a personal demonstration of marking up a text to note important or confusing information.

Why Is It Important? Ongoing Think-Aloud modeling helps ensure that students are annotating key ideas and points of confusion in order to focus their rereading.

Make notes here about your annotations from each read. You will refer to these notes later when you return to your annotations. Sample notes appear below.

ANNOTATION NOTES

Key Ideas and Details:

Eighty-one brothers, all Princes, are jealous of one another.

They travel to Inaba to persuade the Princess to marry one of them.

One good, gentle Prince is treated badly by his 80 brothers.

On the way to Inaba, the 80 Princes tell an injured hare to bathe in the sea and lie down on a mountain. The hare is worse than before.

Language and Text Structure:

What does "quarrelsome" mean in paragraph 2?

Paragraph 3 introduces the hare.

Quotation marks in paragraph 3 show the Princes are speaking directly to the hare.

Connections and Inferences:

At the end of paragraph 4, the hare is worse than before. I infer that the mean Princes told him the wrong thing to do.

Unit 8 • 131

2. What happened to the hare before he met the eighty brothers? (Sample answer: The hare tricked some crocodiles to get across the water. In paragraph 7, he says that when the last crocodile realized he'd been tricked, he "seized" the hare and "plucked off all" his fur.)

3. What happens to the eighty-first brother at the end of the story? (Sample answer: The final paragraph says the eighty-first brother "wed the Princess" and "was made King of the country" because the Princess "would have nothing to do with" the eighty bad brothers.)

Think Aloud *I'm confused by what the hare describes in paragraph 6. I'm unsure where he's trying to go and how the crocodiles help. I'll visualize what the text says to clarify things. The hare says that he tricked the crocodiles to line up "in a row," and then he walked on their backs to cross the water. I can see that in my mind: the crocodiles formed a bridge across the water.*

Partner Talk Have students discuss the behavior of the brothers, the hare, and the crocodiles.

How Do I Use It? Use Think Alouds to model annotating sections of "The Hare of Inaba." For example, demonstrate annotating an unfamiliar word. Read paragraph 2 aloud. When you get to the word *quarrelsome,* say, *I'm not sure what* quarrelsome *means, so I'll put a question in the margin next to it. I think I'll circle it, too, so I know what my question mark is about. That will remind me to look up the definition of the word. Once I know what* quarrelsome *means, I'll have a better understanding of the text.*

Unit 8 • **131**

The Hare of Inaba

2nd READ

Set a Purpose

Students will return to "The Hare of Inaba" to understand the text structure and how the author's language reveals meaning.

Text-Dependent Questions

1. What is the structure of this story, and how does it change? (Sample answer: The story of the brothers is given in time order. When the hare tells his story to the eighty-first brother in paragraphs 6 and 7, he's looking back in time.)

2. What language does the author use to describe the eight-first brother, and what impression does it make? (Sample answer: In paragraph 2, she says he is "good and gentle" and that he doesn't like "quarrelsome ways." In the last paragraph, she says he is "kind." I get the idea that the eighty-first brother is a nice and caring person. I can understand why the Princess prefers him.)

3. Vocabulary: Multiple-Meaning Word Discuss contextual meanings of familiar and unfamiliar words and phrases.

Paragraph 3: What does *poor* mean in this context? What words or phrases in the paragraph are clues to its meaning? (Sample answer: *Poor* means "sad, sick, or miserable." The hare is in a lot of pain from having his fur plucked out. The clues are "all his fur plucked out" and "looking very sick and miserable.")

Partner Talk Have partners discuss words and phrases that helped them visualize elements of the story.

5 Now the eighty-first brother was way behind the others because he had the luggage to carry. At last he staggered up to the hare and asked, "Why are you crying?"

6 "Oh dear!" said the hare. "I will tell you my story. I was in the island of Oki, and I wanted to cross over to this land. I didn't know how to get over, but at last I had a plan. I said to the sea crocodiles, 'Let us count how many crocodiles there are in the sea, and how many hares there are in the land. And now to begin with the crocodiles. Come, every one of you, and be down in a row, across from this island to Cape Keta. Then I will step upon each one, and count you as I run across. When I have finished counting you, we shall count the hares. Then we shall know whether there are more hares, or more crocodiles.'

7 "The crocodiles lay down in a row. Then I stepped on them and counted them as I ran across. I was just going to jump on shore, when I laughed and said, 'You silly crocodiles, I don't care how many

! of you there are. I only wanted a bridge to get across by.' Oh! Why didn't I boast only when I was safe on dry land! The last crocodile, the one

? at the very end of the row, seized me, and plucked off all my fur," said the hare.

Japanese Fairy Tale Series. No. 11.

INABA NO SHIROUSAGI.

Told to Children by Mrs. T. H. James.

Published by the KOBUNSHA, 2 Yionai Sarujebo, TOKYO.

8 "And serve you right too, for being so tricky," said the eighty-first brother. "However, continue your story."

9 "As I was lying here crying," continued the hare," the eighty Princes who went before you told me to bathe in salt water, and lie down in the wind. I did as they said, but I am worse than before."

10 Then the eighty-first brother said to the hare, "Go quickly now to the river. Wash yourself with the fresh water. Then take the pollen of the plants by the river bank, spread it on the ground, and roll in it. If you do this, your skin will heal, and your fur grow again." The hare did as he was told. This time he was cured. His fur grew thicker than ever.

11 Then the hare said, "Those eighty Princes, your brothers, shall not marry the Princess of Inaba. Although you carry the bag, your Highness shall wed the Princess." Which came to pass. The Princess would have nothing to do with those eighty bad brothers, but chose the eighty-first who was kind. Then he was made King of the country, and lived happily all his life.

PROFESSIONAL DEVELOPMENT

Productive Conversation: Examples

What Is It? Students provide specific examples to support an idea. A student may give an example from the text to support his or her own generality or inference. You may also ask students to find an example to support another student's idea during group or partner talk.

Why Is It Important? Specific examples can provide support for a student's argument. The lack of a relevant example can also reveal weakness in a student's argument. Examples used in Think-Aloud modeling provide concrete demonstrations of the concept.

Make notes here about your annotations from each read.
You will refer to these notes later when you return to
your annotations. Sample notes appear below.

ANNOTATION NOTES

Key Ideas and Details:

The hare tricked crocodiles to cross the sea but had all his fur plucked off.

The kind Prince tells the hare what to do for his fur to grow back.

The kind Prince marries the Princess of Inaba.

Language and Text Structure:

What does "seized" mean in paragraph 7?

Single quotation marks show quotation within dialogue.

"Oh!" in paragraph 7 shows sadness.

"Serve you right" shows the kind Prince thinks hare deserved what he got.

Connections and Inferences:

The hare's tricky plan shows that he is sneaky.

Other brothers probably upset that the 81st brother was chosen by

the Princess because he was kind.

Lesson is: Kindness is rewarded.

How Do I Use It? When students give a generality or make an inference, ask questions that elicit examples from the text. For instance, after reading "The Hare of Inaba," students might consider that the eighty brothers were cruel and did not deserve to marry the Princess or become King. Encourage them to support this conclusion with details from the text— for example, "they all agreed to be unkind to the eighty-first" brother (paragraph 2) and "the Princess would have nothing to do with those eighty bad brothers" (paragraph 11). If students cannot give any specific examples, use this opportunity to guide their thinking. You might prompt them to make cause-and-effect and if-then statements that link ideas.

The Hare of Inaba

3rd READ

Set a Purpose

Students will read to make inferences about the text.

Text-Dependent Questions

1. What is one message of this story? (Sample answer: The story tells us that it is important to give others second chances. It helps them and it helps you. The kind brother helps the hare even though he says to the hare in paragraph 8 "serve you right" to lose his fur after tricking the crocodiles. His kindness then wins the heart of the Princess.)

2. What inferences can you make about the hare's personality? (Sample answer: Based on the description of the hare's actions in paragraph 7, the hare is clever because he figured out a plan to cross over to the mainland. He is tricky, but he is not cruel. He uses and teases the crocodiles, but he doesn't hurt them.)

3. What opinion does the author express in this story? (Sample answer: The author believes that being kind will be rewarded and being cruel or tricky will be punished. In the last paragraph, the Princess chooses to marry the eighty-first Prince "who was kind." The brothers, who are mean, don't get anything, and the hare, who is tricky, ends up getting hurt.)

Partner Talk Have students discuss the inferences they made about the author's point of view about the hare and the lesson he learned.

Return TO THE TEXT

Respond to Reading

You may want to check students' understanding by having them complete page 134 in the Student Worktext.

1. Remind students that a summary should only include the key ideas and details essential to understanding what the text is about. Point out that they can use the graphic organizer on Student Worktext page 134 to capture and organize those key ideas and details. The graphic organizer should then guide them in writing their summaries.

2. Refer students to pages 12 and 13 in Getting Started to help them write their individual summaries.

Have students work independently to answer the questions on page 134 of their Worktexts.

COLLABORATE Have students exchange their final summaries with their partners and review each other's summaries. Remind pairs that when they review and discuss their partners' summaries, they should consider whether or not the summary has the following elements:

- contains only important information
- answers as many of the following as possible: Who? What? When? Where? and How?

REFLECT Have students share ways they were able to better understand a confusing word or phrase in the text.

Return to the TEXT

Respond to Reading: The Hare of Inaba

Review the annotations and notes you made while reading "The Hare of Inaba." Think about how they can help you understand the text.

1. Use this Story Map to help you summarize the text.

Characters (Who)	Setting (Where and When)
81 Princes (brothers) and a Princess the hare the crocodiles	Cape Keta and Inaba

Conflict (What)	Major Events (How)
A hare without fur needs help. 80 brothers are mean to him. The kind 81st brother helps the hare.	80 Princes meet a hare and trick him when he asks for help. The 81st Prince hears the hare's story and helps the hare. The Princess chooses to marry the kind Prince.

2. Use the completed Story Map from item 1 to help you write a summary of "The Hare of Inaba."

Sample answer: Eighty Princes are mean to their kind 81st brother as they travel to Inaba to marry a Princess. The 80 Princes trick a hare, whose fur has been plucked by a crocodile at Cape Keta. The 81st Prince hears the hare's story and helps the hare. The Princess marries the kind Prince.

REFLECT What word or phrases did you find confusing? What Self-Monitoring Strategy did you use to gain a better understanding of it?

Sample answer: I didn't know what "seized" meant in paragraph 7. So I asked myself, "Why didn't the hare run before the crocodile could pluck off his fur?" If the crocodile seized the hare and plucked off his fur, "seized" means "grabbed."

PROFESSIONAL DEVELOPMENT

Intertextual Analysis: Analyzing vs. Summarizing

What Is It? Analysis includes making inferences and drawing conclusions in order to understand the most important meanings, themes, and messages of a text. Analysis draws from what the text says, but goes beyond what is directly stated.

Why Is It Important? Text analysis represents a higher-order thinking skill that is essential for participation in school, citizenship, and work. Additionally, the ability to be metacognitively aware of one's own inferences and conclusions and the evidence that does or does not support those thoughts is important for developing judgment.

Comprehension Check: The Hare of Inaba

Answer the questions to demonstrate an understanding of what the text means.

1. How do the eighty-first brother's actions help him achieve his goal of marrying the Princess? Give evidence from the text to support your answer.

   Sample answer: Paragraph 2 says the eighty-first brother "was good and

   gentle." When the eighty-first brother meets and helps the hare, the hare

   predicts the kind brother "shall wed the Princess. " The Princess "would have

   nothing to do with those eighty bad brothers." She marries the eighty-first

   brother, "who was kind." His kind actions won the heart of the Princess.

2. What inference can you make about how the hare felt about tricking the crocodiles? Cite evidence from the text to support your answer.

   Sample answer: I infer that the hare regretted his actions because paragraph 7

   says "Oh! Why didn't I boast only when I was safe on dry land!" However, he

   only regrets that he did not wait to boast, not that he tricked the crocodiles.

3. What is the theme of "The Hare of Inaba"? Cite evidence from the text to support your answer.

   Sample answer: The theme of the story is that kindness will be rewarded. The

   Princess chose the kind Prince to marry instead of his brothers. Paragraph 11

   says, "Although you carry the bag, your Highness shall wed the Princess,"

   and "the Princess would have nothing to do with those eighty bad brothers,

   but chose the eighty-first who was kind."

Unit 8 • 135

Stop and Assess

Use the following rubrics to assess your students' understanding of the text.

	Item 1 answers indicate:
2	the eighty-first brother is kind and helpful, while the other brothers are cruel, and provide two pieces of text evidence.
1	the eighty-first brother is kind while the other eighty are cruel, with insufficient text evidence.
0	no understanding of how the eighty-first brother is different from the other brothers, and don't cite any relevant text evidence.

	Item 2 answers indicate:
2	inferences that the hare regrets the timing of his boast, but not his trick, and text evidence are cited to support the claim.
1	only what the text states explicitly and don't include inferences.
0	no understanding that the hare regrets boasting too early but does not regret tricking the crocodiles, and don't cite relevant text evidence.

	Item 3 answers indicate:
2	that kindness is rewarded, with strong text evidence to support the claim.
1	that it is good to be kind, with insufficient text evidence.
0	no understanding that kindness is rewarded, and don't cite any relevant text evidence.

How Do I Use It? Students may experience two common problems with analyzing versus summarizing. Some students may be able to retell or summarize (recall) without being able to make connections or inferences in order to analyze more deeply. Scaffolded questions can lead to greater understanding. Regarding inferences made for "The Hare of Inaba," you may ask: *How is the hare like the eighty brothers? How is the hare different? How is that difference significant?* More sophisticated students may make inferences without realizing it and draw conclusions that are not supported by text evidence. For these students, asking them to cite evidence and explain their thinking is essential. *I understand what you're thinking. Can you show me where it says that in the text?*

The Helpful Stranger

Students will read a short story about being helpful.

1st READ

Set a Purpose

Explain to students that they will read to find out what "The Helpful Stranger" is about.

Have students read "The Helpful Stranger" independently, annotating the text as they read. Remind students that suggested annotation symbols appear on page 8 of the Getting Started with Close Reading unit. Circulate and observe students' markings, especially questions and anything they found confusing. The observations and annotations may be used to inform instruction. Based on students' needs, you may want to meet with them in small groups.

Text-Dependent Questions

1. What is the text about? (This text is about a third grade student named Audra who is bullied on the playground by a fifth grader named Brian. When another girl, named Addie, shows up, she helps Audra.)

Scaffolded Support Use the following scaffolded sentence frame and questions as necessary to support comprehension.

Where does this story take place?

_____ wants to play on the _____ , but _____ gets in her way.

Who helps Audra?

Partner Talk Have students discuss the story's setting and sequence of events.

TEXT 2

Read this short story about being helpful. Make annotations as you read. You may make different annotations with each read.
Sample annotations and notes appear throughout the text.

The Helpful Stranger

1   The double doors that led outside Thornhill School opened wide, and Audra ran onto the emerald-green grass. The play structure with its shiny silver slide and swings called her name in the distance. The breeze sang in her ears as she ran toward her best friend, Harley, who was waiting for her at the swings.

2   Suddenly Audra ran into something that felt like a brick wall. She looked up, right into the face of towering Brian Logan. Brian was a fifth grader with a reputation for being mean to third graders.

3   "Where are you going?" Brian asked.

4   Audra wanted to reply, but her tongue felt like it was glued to the roof of her mouth. She had heard stories about Brian but had never talked to him.

5   "You heard me. Where are you going?"

6   Audra pointed to the slide. Brian looked over his shoulder in the direction of where she was pointing. "That slide is only for fifth graders."

7   Audra knew that wasn't true because she always played on it with other third graders. She took a step, but Brian was still blocking her path.

8   "Let her through."

9   Audra turned and looked over her shoulder. The voice was coming from a tall girl with a ponytail who was the same height as Brian. Audra hadn't seen her before. She definitely wasn't a third grader.

10 ? "The playground is for everyone, Brian," she said. Brian looked sheepish as he stepped to the side.

11   "Go ahead," the stranger said.

12   "What's your name?" Audra's words came back to her without Brian to frighten them away.

13   "I'm Addie. Now go play before recess ends."

14 ? "Thanks, Addie," Audra said. Then she scampered across the carpet of grass. Harley waved Audra over, and they sat on their favorite swings. As Audra soared in the air, she saw Addie helping a group of second graders climb a tree. Suddenly, Audra had an idea for how she could repay Addie's kindness. She would help someone in need next time.

PROFESSIONAL DEVELOPMENT

Productive Conversation: Clear Up Confusions

What Is It? In any classroom conversation, students will inevitably give incorrect or incomplete responses. A productive conversation doesn't punish or simply correct the student, but recognizes that an incorrect or incomplete answer is an opportunity to examine and redirect the students' understanding.

Why Is It Important? To arrive at independent conclusions, students learn best when they are guided to examine direct evidence and their own thinking.

How Do I Use It? The rule of thumb when clearing up confusion is to return to the text. If a student reaches an incorrect

The Helpful Stranger

Make notes here about your annotations from each read. You will refer to these notes later when you return to your annotations. Sample notes appear below.

ANNOTATION NOTES

Key Ideas and Details:

Brian, the school bully, tries to keep a younger student, Audra, off

the playground.

A kind girl named Addie stands up to the bully.

Audra gets to play on the swings and decides she will help someone

in need.

Language and Text Structure:

The play structure "called her name."

The breeze "sang in her ears."

"carpet of grass" = grass isn't really carpet but looks smooth like carpet

Connections and Inferences:

Paragraph 4 says that her tongue felt like it was "glued to the roof of

her mouth"—I know that her tongue isn't actually attached with glue,

but I have felt like this before when I can't speak.

Audra wants to be kind to someone else because Addie was kind to her.

The next person may be kind to someone else because Audra is kind.

Unit 8 • 137

2nd READ

Set a Purpose
Students will examine how the language in the text reveals meaning.

Text-Dependent Questions
1. In paragraph 4, what does "her tongue felt like it was glued to the roof of her mouth" mean? (It means that even though Audra wanted to reply to Brian, she was so scared of him, she couldn't speak.)

2. How do the author's descriptions of Brian help you understand his character? (In paragraph 2, Brian is described as "towering," so he's taller than Audra. Paragraph 2 also says that Brian has "a reputation for being mean." "Sheepish" in paragraph 10 shows that Brian knew bullying Audra was wrong.)

Partner Talk Have partners discuss how the author uses language to reveal information about characters.

3rd READ

Set a Purpose
Students will read to make inferences from the text.

Text-Dependent Questions
1. What will Audra most likely do if she sees someone else being bullied? (The final line of the story makes me think that Audra will step in to stop the bullying.)

Partner Talk Have students discuss inferences they made about the importance of being kind to others.

conclusion, or has a misconception about what the text says, ask for evidence to support the idea. Wait time is critical in this situation. The student must have enough time to do a thorough search of the text. If the student does not find the text evidence, ask, for example, *What does "The Helpful Stranger" say about your idea?* If a student offers text that is irrelevant or misunderstood, ask, *What is that sentence saying, in your own words?* Then, ask again for specific words or phrases within the chosen sentence that support the student's thinking. Give wait time. Allow the student to get a full sense of the evidence. Only then turn to peers or Think Alouds for alternative interpretations.

Unit 8 • 137

Respond to Reading

You may want to check students' understanding by having them complete page 138 in the Student Worktext.

1. Have students reread paragraphs 1–7 to determine the problem Audra faces and record what they find in the left column of the graphic organizer. Then have students reread paragraphs 8–14 to determine the solution to Audra's problem and record information in the right column of the graphic organizer.

2. Have students use the information they recorded on their graphic organizers to describe how Audra feels before and after her problem is solved.

3. Refer students to pages 12 and 13 of Getting Started to help them write their individual summaries.

Have students work independently to answer the questions on page 138 of their Worktexts.

COLLABORATE When finished, have students exchange summaries with their partners and review each other's summaries. Remind pairs that when they review and discuss their partners' summaries, they should consider whether or not the summary has the following elements:

• contains only important information

• answers as many of the following as possible: Who? What? When? Where? and How?

REFLECT Suggest that students review their annotations and Annotation Notes to remember when they drew conclusions to better understand the text.

Respond to Reading: The Helpful Stranger

Review the annotations and notes you made while reading "The Helpful Stranger." Think about how your annotations can help you answer the questions.

1. Use information from the text to complete the graphic organizer.

Problem that Audra Faces	Solution
Brian says third graders can't play on the slide. Brian blocks Audra's path. Audra's tongue is "glued to the roof of her mouth."	Addie tells Brian that the playground is for everyone. Brian moves to let Audra pass. Without Brian to "frighten" her words away, Audra can speak again.

2. Use your graphic organizer to describe how Audra feels before and after her problem is solved.

Sample answer: Before her problem is solved, Audra is scared and speechless because her tongue is "glued to the roof of her mouth." After her problem is solved, Audra can speak again because Brian doesn't "frighten" her words away anymore. She is no longer afraid of Brian.

3. Write a short summary of "The Helpful Stranger."

Sample answer: Audra is a third grader who wants to play on the swings. A bully tells her that third graders aren't allowed to play there. A girl named Addie stands up to the bully, and Audra plays on the swings.

REFLECT What words, phrases, and sections did you have to draw conclusions about to make sure you understood?

Sample answer: I had to draw conclusions about paragraphs 2–6 to figure out why Brian was telling Audra she couldn't play there. I concluded that he is a bully.

PROFESSIONAL DEVELOPMENT

Intertextual Analysis: Making Thematic Connections

What Is It? A theme may be present across texts with either very similar or very different topics and structures. Thematic connections draw lines between the deeper meanings or generalized applications of different texts. The focus questions in this book are designed to elicit thematic connections between the texts in each unit.

Why Is It Important? Making thematic connections across texts is one of the highest order skills in close reading. Students must not only find the meaning of individual texts, but must also connect, compare, and contrast those meanings across multiple texts and genres.

Comprehension Check: The Helpful Stranger

Answer the questions to demonstrate an understanding of what the text means.

1. What information does the author communicate when she says that Audra "ran into something that felt like a brick wall"? What other information from the text supports your answer?

   Sample answer: The author communicates that Brian is bigger than Audra

   because he stops her from moving like a brick wall stops things from moving.

   A quotation from the text that supports that answer is in paragraph 2: "She

   looked up, right into the face of towering Brian Logan."

2. How do the characters of Brian and Addie help you understand the benefits of being a kind person? Provide text evidence to support your answer.

   Sample answer: Brian's behavior gives him "a reputation for being mean to

   third graders" that makes Audra afraid of him. Audra has never spoken to him.

   Addie's personality is kind and helpful. Audra is not afraid to talk to her. Audra

   wants to "repay Addie's kindness." She will repay Addie by acting like Addie

   and helping "someone in need."

3. What is the theme of the story? Provide text evidence to support your answer.

   Sample answer: The theme of the story is that kindness is contagious. In

   paragraph 14, it says: "Suddenly, Audra had an idea for how she could

   repay Addie's kindness: she would help someone in need next time."

Unit 8 • 139

How Do I Use It? Each text will have some information to answer the Focus Question, or part of it, in its own way. In this unit, the common theme is the benefits of being kind. Readers explore the theme through a photograph, a fairy tale, and a short story. After they view or read each text, have students summarize in their own words the central meaning of the text. Encourage them to write down a statement expressing the text's theme. Then ask students to compare their three statements and use them to draw conclusions about the common theme. Remind students that their conclusions should help answer the Focus Question.

Stop and Assess

Use the following rubrics to assess your students' understanding of the text.

	Item 1 answers indicate:
2	that the author wants students to understand that Brian is bigger than Audra, and provide text evidence to support the answer.
1	that Brian is bigger than Audra, but do not provide supporting text evidence.
0	no understanding of what the author is communicating with this detail and no text evidence.

	Item 2 answers indicate:
2	that Brian is unkind and Audra is afraid of him, but Addie is kind and Audra wants to be kind too, and provide text evidence to support the answer.
1	that Brian is mean, and Addie is kind, but provide no text evidence.
0	a lack of understanding of how Brian's and Addie's actions show the benefits of being a kind person, and don't cite any relevant text evidence.

	Item 3 answers indicate:
2	that the theme is that kindness is contagious, and provide text evidence to support the answer.
1	that the theme is that kindness is contagious with insufficient text evidence to support the inference.
0	no understanding of the text's theme, and no text evidence.

Unit 8 • 139

ANALYZE and SYNTHESIZE ACROSS TEXTS

Return to the Focus Question

Explain to students that they will fill out a graphic organizer that will help them answer the Focus Question: What are the benefits of being a kind person?

CONNECT TEXTS Have small groups of students discuss how each text they read helps them answer the Focus Question. Have small groups share and compare their discussion notes with another small group.

Scaffolded Support You may provide the following sentence frames to support students in their use of academic language:

> In the text _____ , the author/photographer makes the point that _____ . He/she does this by _____ .

Remind students to use their annotations and summaries to support their answers. They can also reread portions of the texts, if necessary.

Have students complete their graphic organizers individually and then answer the Focus Question.

REFLECT Remind students that each text provides different information about kindness. Ask, *How did reading all three texts give you a greater understanding of the benefits of being a kind person?*

ANALYZE and SYNTHESIZE ACROSS TEXTS

Return to the Focus Question: What are the benefits of being a kind person?

Review your answers to questions about the texts as well as your annotations and Annotation Notes. Think about the discussions you've had about the texts. How does that information help you answer the Focus Question?

Use this graphic organizer to organize information about the texts.

1. In the boxes, record the details from each text that help you answer the Focus Question.

2. Make connections between those details to help you answer the Focus Question. Write your answer in the box provided.

The Hare of Inaba
Sample answer: A kind act helps a hare in pain. A Princess marries a Prince because he is kind.

Standup4change (Visual Text)
Sample answer: Community project encourages people to be kind.

The Helpful Stranger
Sample answer: A person who is treated kindly treats others kindly.

What are the benefits of being a kind person?
Sample answer: Kindness is rewarding and good for the community. Treating others kindly makes a good impression. When one person is kind, it inspires other people to be kind.

REFLECT How did making connections between the three texts help you to answer the Focus Question?

The Visual Text shows a project against bullying and encourages kindness.

Text 1 is about being kind and the benefits of kindness. Text 2 is about how

kindness can stop bullies and inspire others. Together the texts encourage kindness!

PROFESSIONAL DEVELOPMENT

Differentiation

What Is It? The Differentiate and Extend activities at the end of each unit reinforce and extend what students have already learned through close reading of the texts and provide learning experiences other than classroom discussion. For example, the Create a Visual Text activity might ask students to tell stories in storyboard, comic book, or graphic novel form.

Why Is It Important? Visual learners learn and express their thoughts best when using pictorial images and writing. The Create a Visual Text activity allows visual learners to explore and express their understanding in a way that is most comfortable for them. In addition, this assignment motivates

Writing About the Focus Question

Now that you have answered the Focus Question using all three texts, develop your ideas into a longer piece of writing.

WRITING CHECKLIST ✔

Does my writing . . .

☐ answer the Focus Question?

☐ provide text evidence to support my ideas?

☐ have a clear beginning, middle, and end?

☐ use correct language, spelling, and conventions?

USE EVIDENCE

- Explain what the benefits are of being a kind person. Use at least one piece of evidence from each text to support your answer.
- If you need more room, use additional paper.

MONITOR

- Use the Writing Checklist as you work to make sure your writing has all of the important pieces of information.
- Use the rubric on page 142 when you have completed your first draft to help you evaluate, revise, and edit your work.

Unit 8 • 141

Writing About the Focus Question

USE EVIDENCE Remind students that they should use their graphic organizers as well as their annotations in the texts to write their responses.

Allow students to revisit the texts as frequently as they need to in order to support comprehension and to respond to the Focus Question.

MONITOR After students have completed their responses, have them review the Writing Checklist and revise their writing responses.

DIFFERENTIATE AND EXTEND

In addition to or instead of the writing response, consider having students complete one of the following assignments:

Write Beyond Have students assume the role of one of the eighty "bad brothers" in "The Hare of Inaba" and retell the story and the lesson he learned from his point of view.

Design a Brochure Have students create a brochure or pamphlet designed to educate others on the benefits of being kind.

Make a Plan Have students make a plan on ways they can be kinder in their everyday lives. Plans can include both text and visuals.

Create a Visual Text Using graphic applications on a computer or traditional poster board, have students create a Visual Text or storyboard based on "The Helpful Stranger."

students to do extra research and strengthens their computer literacy and computer design skills if they choose to use a computer to create their assignment.

How Do I Use It? Get students started by suggesting they review the different kinds of visual texts they can use, such as comic books or graphic novels. You may wish to have examples of each on hand for students to review. Once students choose their format, have them sketch panels based on "The Helpful Stranger." Remind students that their purpose is to explain the benefits of being a kind person and that they should carefully follow the story's plot and use clues in the text to inform their depictions of the characters and setting.

Unit 8 • 141

SELF-ASSESS and REFLECT

SELF-ASSESS Have students use the Writing Rubric on page 142 to self-assess their writing response and write a final version. Tell them to assign themselves a score from 1–4 (with "4" being the highest) for each category in the first column.

REFLECT Use the Writing Rubric on Student Worktext page 142 to assess each student's writing. Record points for each category in the first column of the rubric. Have students remove the page from their Student Worktexts and place it in their writing portfolios, along with the drafts and final versions of their responses.

Focus Question What are the benefits of being a kind person?

This is the rubric that your teacher will use to assess your writing. Refer to it as you revise your work. After you have finished your final version, review your writing and record your points for each category on the "Student" line in the first column.

	Accomplished (4 points)	Competent (3 points)	Developing (2 points)	Beginning (1 point)
RESPONSE Score: Student _____ Teacher _____	The response answers the question effectively and with insight.	The response answers the question effectively.	The response partially responds to the question but does not adequately address it.	The response addresses the texts but does not address the question.
ORGANIZATION Score: Student _____ Teacher _____	The main idea is convincingly stated. Ideas are organized in cohesive paragraphs that support the main idea.	The main idea is clearly stated. Ideas are organized in logical paragraphs.	The main idea is weak. Ideas are organized in a somewhat logical and cohesive way.	The main idea is missing. The organization of the paragraphs is not logical.
TEXT EVIDENCE Score: Student _____ Teacher _____	Response includes more than one piece of appropriate text evidence from each text. Evidence supports the main idea in a thorough way.	Response includes one piece of text evidence from each text. Evidence supports the main idea clearly.	Response does not include at least one piece of text evidence from each text. Text evidence does not adequately support the main idea.	Response does not contain relevant evidence.
LANGUAGE Score: Student _____ Teacher _____	Writing includes precise and sophisticated vocabulary related to the topic.	Writing includes appropriate vocabulary related to the topic.	Writing includes imprecise and inaccurate vocabulary.	Writing does not include vocabulary that appropriately reflects the topic of the response.
SPELLING AND CONVENTIONS Score: Student _____ Teacher _____	Response includes correct spelling, grammar, and punctuation consistently.	Response includes mostly correct spelling, grammar, and punctuation.	Response has many errors in spelling, grammar, and punctuation.	Response's errors in spelling, grammar, and punctuation make it extremely difficult to understand the response.